Patriarchy at Work

Feminist Perspectives

Series editor: Michelle Stanworth

Published:

Veronica Beechey & Tessa Perkins, *A Matter of Hours*
Seyla Benhabib & Drucilla Cornell (eds), *Feminism as Critique*
Harriet Bradley, *Men's Work, Women's Work*
Pat Carlen (ed), *Criminal Women*
Christine Delphy & Diana Leonard, *Familiar Exploitation*
Felicia Gordon, *The Integral Feminist: Madeleine Pelletier 1874–1939: Feminism, Socialism and Medicine*
Christine Griffin, *Representations of Youth*
Su Kappeler, *The Pornography of Representation*
Liz Kelly, *Surviving Sexual Violence*
Judy Lown, *Women and Industrialization: Gender and Work in 19th -Century England*
Henrietta L. Moore, *Feminism and Anthropology*
Naomi Pfeffer, *The Stork and the Syringe*
June Purvis, *Hard Lessons: The Lives and Education of Working-Class Women in 19th -Century England*
Yannick Ripa, *Women and Madness*
Barbara Sichtermann, *Femininity: The Politics of the Personal*
Michelle Stanworth (ed), *Reproductive Technologies*
Julia Swindells, *Victorian Writing and Working Women*
Sylvia Walby, *Patriarchy at Work*

Forthcoming:

Susan Himmelweit, *Reproduction*
Joan Scanlon, *Bending the Rule*
Michelle Stanworth, *Feminism and Sociology*
Gill Thomas, *Women and the First World War*

Patriarchy at Work

Patriarchal and Capitalist Relations in Employment

Sylvia Walby

Polity Press

First published 1986 by
Polity Press, Cambridge, in association with Blackwell Publishers, Oxford.
Reprinted 1994

Editorial Office: Polity Press, 65 Bridge Street, Cambridge CB2 1UR, UK.

Marketing and Production: Blackwell Publishers, 108 Cowley Road,
Oxford OX4 1JF, UK.

British Library Cataloguing in Publication Data

Walby, Sylvia
Patriarchy at work: patriarchal and capitalist relations in employment.
1. Women — Employment — History 2. Sex discrimination in employment — History
I. Title.
331.4'133'09 HD6053

ISBN 0-7456-0157-X
ISBN 0-7456-0158-8 (pbk)

Phototypeset by Dobbie Typesetting Service, Plymouth, Devon
Printed in Great Britain by Page Bros Ltd, Norwich

Contents

List of Tables

Acknowledgements

I should like to thank the people who have helped me in the writing of this book: especially, my colleagues, friends and students at the University of Lancaster; in particular, the Lancaster Regionalism Group, especially John Urry, and the Women's Research Group; the EOC for financial assistance with the job loss project and Anne Green for her superb interviewing on that project; the careful editors at Polity Press and Basil Blackwell; and Heather Salt and Mave Connolly for typing the various drafts of the manuscript.

1
Introduction

> As the available pool of unemployed labour is expanded among men by their relative repulsion from industry and trade, it is expanded even more among women by their increasing attraction into industry and trade . . . The logical cumulation of these trends is the equalisation of the labour force participation rates of men and women.
>
> *(Harry Braverman)*

> We, as an organisation are opposed to the introduction of women as a general principle.
>
> *(Jack Tanner, President, Amalgamated Engineering Union, 1940)*

Why has the extent and nature of women's paid employment changed so markedly since industrialization? What are the implications of this for the position of women in society more generally? The theme of this book is the tension between the social forces which shape gender relations. As the quotations above suggest, there is on the one hand a tendency, thought by writers like Braverman to be overwhelming, for women to be drawn into the expanding industries, while on the other, there have been significant social forces, represented by Jack Tanner, the leader of the Amalgamated Engineering Union in 1940, to prevent this from happening. In assessing the practical and theoretical significance of these social forces, I will challenge many orthodoxies in social thought. This book will develop a view of women as significant actors in resisting their exploitation. It will depart from the dominant view of women as acquiescing in their fate. Conventional class theory, which pays little attention to gender relations, will be found wanting, and replaced by a more comprehensive and rigorous approach to the analysis of social inequality. Against the traditional view, that the position of women in the labour market is determined by their position in the family, I will argue for the importance of labour market structures in confining women to a subordinate position in the household.

The book is a challenge to conventional views on stratification in British society. The social division of labour, such a prominent part of most analyses of social stratification, cannot be understood without an understanding of the gender division of labour. It is not merely that an analysis of sexual divisions needs to be added onto the existing literature, but rather that on its own terms stratification theory, and especially narrowly defined class analyses, cannot be adequate without taking gender inequality into account.

I will not stop at merely criticizing orthodox accounts of social inequality but will engage with and revise feminist approaches to the analysis of gender inequality and propose an alternative. I will attempt to develop a theory of gender inequality, to build an adequate model of patriarchy and to demonstrate the significance of patriarchal relations in employment for the explanation of the position of women in contemporary society.

Chapter 2 starts with a review of existing theories of gender inequality. These fall into five types, according to whether gender inequality is viewed as: theoretically insignificant or non-existent; derivative from capitalist relations; an autonomous system of patriarchy, which is the primary form of social inequality; so intertwined with capitalist relations that they form one system of capitalist patriarchy; or the consequence of the interaction of autonomous systems of patriarchy and capitalism. While the last of these is the only one that I consider to be theoretically adequate, the existing formulations of this approach have severe problems. I try to construct my own model of patriarchy and its relations with capitalism, and this is to be found in chapter 3.

One of the major problems of existing models of patriarchy is that they either tend to treat patriarchy as a monolithic unity, and underestimate the significance of the relative autonomy of different sets of patriarchal relations, or they tend to include so many different aspects in an *ad hoc* way that they degenerate into mere description. My model of patriarchy tries to overcome these problems by constructing patriarchy as a set of relatively autonomous patriarchal relations which are interrelated in a definite manner. A further problem in existing models of patriarchy is the inadequacy of the analysis of the relationship between patriarchal and capitalist relations. Most approaches tend to give too much effectivity to either patriarchal or capitalist relations and, further, they characterize this relationship as one of harmony, which the empirical evidence does not support. I have characterized the relationship between patriarchy and captialism as one of tension and conflict and tried to assess the importance of both patriarchal and capitalist relations. Further, I have argued that patriarchal relations in paid work are of crucial importance in the articulation of the two systems.

Thus the first part of the book constructs a new theoretical model of patriarchy and its relations with capital. The remainder is an attempt to demonstrate the model's effectiveness in a particular empirical area which is of central importance in the relation between patriarchy and capitalism; that of gender and employment. The quotations from Braverman and Tanner demonstrate the contradictory nature of the social forces affecting women's employment. Braverman assumes that employers' demands for cheap, deskilled labour will determine the pattern of employment. Here we see the delightful prospect of capitalists enforcing equality between men and women, at least in respect of paid work. Yet this scenario immediately strikes us as unlikely, even absurd. Why should this be so? What are the forces which prevent such a development? Tanner gives voice to patriarchal objections to women's employment. It is patriarchal work-place organizations such as his male-dominated union that have been the immediate obstacle to Braverman's vision of gender equality. Yet the question is only transformed, not answered. Why should these worker organizations be so opposed to women's employment? This opposition is rooted not merely in men's fear of women undercutting their wages and conditions of work, but also in a system of patriarchal relations which women's employment threatens to disrupt. Yet again, this is too simple. The forms of patriarchal organization are varied and they intersect in complicated ways with capitalist relations and the technicalities of specific production processes. All these must be explored before an adequate analysis can be built up.

Women's labour is a central issue in the conflicts and tensions between patriarchal and capitalist interests. Thus chapter 4 turns to an examination of the literature on gender and employment. By means of a historical analysis, the processes which have culminated in the present gender division of labour in employment are laid bare in chapters 5, 6 and 7. The analysis uses archive material of employers and unions as well as a range of secondary sources. It focuses on three contrasting areas of employment: cotton textiles, engineering and clerical work. In these three types of work, not only is patriarchal workplace organization found to be a major force in determining gender patterns of employment, but patriarchal organizations themselves take a variety of forms. The present pattern of gender and unemployment will be seen to be the outcome of overlapping of rounds of restructuring, a process in which these different patriarchal forms of workplace organization play a key role.

2
Theories of Gender Inequality: a Critique

Explanations of gender inequality are often classified either as radical–feminist or socialist–feminist (e.g. Coote and Campbell, 1982). Other writers have developed classifications with many complicated divisions (e.g. Sebastyan, 1979), while others reject any such classifications on the grounds that they are too constraining (e.g. Stanley and Wise, 1983). The dichotomy between socialist–feminist and radical–feminist, while picking up on an important division in writings on gender relations, fails to accommodate significant writings which do not belong on either side of such a divide, and which indeed explicitly attempt to make a synthesis out of the two opposing positions. This dichotomous classification is now surpassed by recent writings which themselves fall into two: some argue that dichotomy in the explanation of gender inequality should be overcome by saying that this inequality results from a single system of capitalist patriarchy; others argue that inequality is the outcome of an interaction of autonomous systems of patriarchy and capital.

This would produce four categories of writings on gender inequality–and a fifth, as well, for the sake of completeness, for those writings based on the theoretical insignificance or non-existence of gender inequality:

- gender inequality as theoretically insignificant or non-existent;
- gender inequality as derivative from capitalist relations;
- gender inequality as a result of an autonomous system of patriarchy, which is the primary form of social inequality;
- gender inequality as resulting from patriarchal relations so intertwined with capitalist relations that they form one system of capitalist patriarchy;
- gender inequality as the consequence of the interaction of autonomous systems of patriarchy and capitalism (dualist writings).

The first category includes the writings of many mainstream sociologists. Gender inequality is theoretically insignificant for these writers because of their emphasis on class relations and their use of the family as the unit in analysis of stratification. Also included in the group are functionalists who characterize gender relations in terms of social roles which are considered different but equal. The second category is that of writings which seriously examine gender relations in their own right but conclude that they are ultimately, if not directly, derivative from capitalist social relations. The so-called 'domestic-labour debate' is an important example of this type of position. Writings of the third category make a decisive break with traditional ways of looking at gender relations and see patriarchy as a system of social inequality in its own right which is not derivative from any other. A wide range of social institutions are taken as the basis of patriarchy, but reproduction and sexuality are given particular importance. The fourth set of writings attempts a compromise between the previous two by arguing that capitalist and patriarchal social relations are so intertwined that they should be properly considered to be part of one social system of capitalist patriarchy. The fifth approach attempts this compromise differently, by arguing that patriarchy and capitalism are two separate social systems which can neither be reduced to each other nor conflated into one system. Here patriarchy and capitalism are seen to interact and affect each other whilst being analytically independent.

It is difficult to allocate some writers to categories, especially those working with similar theoretical frameworks but for whom the relations between gender inequality and capitalism are very different. For instance, Delphy (1977) views patriarchy and capitalism as autonomous systems, but says so little about capitalism that her place in the fifth rather than the third category is not immediately obvious, whilst Harrison, who develops a very similar theoretical concept to Delphy's in the housework mode of production, attributes so much greater effectivity to capitalism, that his place in category five rather than two is again problematic. Yet to have placed Delphy and Harrison in different categories despite their similar usage of the notion of a housework/ domestic mode of production would have been to accord too little significance to similarities of their important theoretical innovations.

Gender Inequality as Theoretically Insignificant or Non-Existent

Much mainstream stratification theory has treated gender inequality as theoretically insignificant, although this is now often recognized as a problem. Some sociologists have ommitted to consider gender inequality altogether, in part or all of their works. For instance Beteille (1977) ignores inequality between men and women. He simply states that

> There are two major manifestations of inequality in contemporary societies . . . property and social class and race. (Beteille, 1977:21)

It has also been common in British sociology for samples to be drawn of only men for a project which purports to be of general significance for British society, as for instance, in studies of social mobility by Glass and Hall (1954), Goldthorpe et al. (1980) and Stewart et al. (1980). Sociologists have differed in the extent to which they have attempted to justify their near total focus on men. Attempts at justification are much more common in the recent works, while some of the earlier studies did not even attempt to defend the policy.

Goldthorpe et al.'s (1969) sample of affluent workers is entirely composed of men, yet despite a detailed explanation of how the sample came to be chosen there is no attempt at justification of the maleness of the sample. The authors do not consider women to be members of classes in their own right, implicitly assuming that a woman's class position is determined by that of her husband. There are constant references to 'workers and their families' (e.g. pp. 7, 13, 19, 25, 26, 34, 44, 50, 51), while the worker is always referred to as male, for example when referring to 'the class situation of the industrial worker in present day society':

> Despite these changes, *he* remains a *man* who gains *his* livelihood at the disposal of an employer. (Goldthorpe et al. 1969: 157; my emphasis.)

They do not attempt to justify this conceptualization.

It would not be correct to say that Goldthorpe et al. ignore gender altogether, since they do make references to the male workers' wives. However, their noting of the evidence they have about the significance of these women is not incorporated into their theoretical understanding and this leads to contradictions. Thus they note that the greater household income of the white collar families than of the blue collar families in their samples was due to the greater tendency of women married to white collar men to be in paid employment.

> It was the wives' contribution that accounted for the slightly higher average family income of the white-collar couples. (Goldthorpe et al. 1969: 129a).

Yet the significance of this empirical evidence is contradicted in the conclusion which suggests that overtime working is the only way manual workers can increase their standard of living.

> And indeed for men in most manual grades the achievement of affluence is likely to require some substantial amount of overtime working. (Goldthorpe et al. 1969: 158.)

Here the authors slipped back from considering the family as the unit to considering individual workers as the unit of the class analysis. If they had consistently taken the family as the unit then they would have been forced to conclude that the level of affluence was crucially determined by women's employment status. It is only by taking individuals as the unit that Goldthorpe et al. can consider overtime and not women's earnings as crucial to the level of affluence. Yet if individuals are the unit then the implicit justification for investigating only male workers (with women introduced only as wives of these men) must fall. It is only by inconsistent selection of the unit of the analysis that Goldthorpe et al. fail to note the significance of women for the shape of the class structure.

More recent work has usually attempted to justify the neglect of gender relations. Resource constraints are sometimes cited as the reason for the omission of women from the sample of workers drawn, but a theoretical justification for this major decision is not given. For instance, Blackburn and Mann (1979) do note the theoretical significance of the relation between male and female workers in determining the conditions of employment for both groups, and their significance for the internal structuring of the working class. However, they still exclude women from their sample of manual workers. They suggest that the reason for this is inadequate resources to study both men and women (Blackburn and Mann, 1979: 39) and that they chose the larger group to study. Given the significance accorded to sex barriers in their theoretical account of the workings of the labour market, their omission of women in the actual sample is inconsistent and inadequately justified.

Lack of resources is also cited by Goldthorpe et al. (1980) as one of their reasons for not looking at women's mobility as well as men's. A further way of justifying the exclusion of women from studies of social stratification is to say that this is done because everyone else has followed the practice. For instance Stewart et al. (1980) simply state that they will consider only male clerks and that the debates that they are concerned with have been about men.

> In this chapter we shall be concerned with male clerks. The debates to which we are addressing ourselves have been primarily concerned with male employment and the data upon which we draw are for men. (Stewart et al., 1980; 93.)

This is quite extraordinary since they go on to state that the mobility of the men which is their primary concern is dependent upon the lack of mobility of women, that gender relations in clerical work are the key to understanding their central concern of male clerks' mobility. Later in the book the authors reveal further their confusion and uncertainty as to how to deal with gender relations:

> Whether women are proletarianised raises complex questions which we hope to examine elsewhere, but the answer seems to be no. They have always been employed in routine positions, mainly in specifically female jobs . . . They come from diverse backgrounds and follow different life-styles, which are largely determined by factors other than their own occupations. (Stewart et al., 1980: 193.)

The authors have not decided how the position of women clerks is to be determined, being unclear as to whether it is to be their own occupations or 'factors other than their own occupations'.

Many social stratification writers of the 1970s and 1980s have attempted an explicit theoretical justification for leaving gender relations on the periphery of their work. This is typically done by arguing that the family rather than the individual is the basic unit in social stratification (for instance, Parkin, 1972; Goldthorpe et al., 1980; Westergaard and Resler, 1975). Parkin (1972) clearly sets out the main components of this argument, (although it should be noted that his later position (1979) is somewhat different and accords greater significance to gender). He argues that women's position in the stratification system is determined primarily by their families and that the position of the family is determined by its male head:

> for the great majority of women the allocation of social and economic rewards is determined primarily by the position of their families–and, in particular, that of the male head. (Parkin, 1972: 14–15.)

He states that the similarities of position that women share with each other are insufficient to override the divisions between women caused by their relationships with their fathers and husbands. He goes on to suggest that this is what the majority of women feel as well.

Likewise Goldthorpe et al. (1980) argue that the family and household is the unit in analyses of stratification and that men largely determine the position of the family (p. 67a). They go on to emphasize that they do not envisage many women occupying different class positions from those of the male heads of households (p. 188).

> It is difficult to envisage any factors which, over the period in question, would be likely to result in any *sizeable* number of women occupying markedly different class positions from those of the male 'heads' of their families, or possessing attributes or engaging in activities which would in themselves materially influence the class position of the family unit. (Goldthorpe et al., 1980: 288.)

There is a conceptual slippage here in that, if the family is the unit of stratification, then by definition women cannot occupy a different position from the other members of the household. The position of these authors is inconsistent.

Glass and Hall also argue that a woman's class position is

determined by that of her husband or father (1954: 83). Westergaard and Resler (1975) also take the family as the unit in stratification theory. They do this by equating social inequality with class inequality and then class inequality as that between different family units. They differ from Parkin (1972) and Goldthorpe et al. (1980) in arguing that women do make some contribution to the overall position of the family; however, they conclude after examining the evidence that men's contribution is the most important.

Britten and Heath (1983) similarly wish to retain the family as the unit in stratification theory and similarly argue that the resources that women bring to it should be seriously taken into account. Unlike Westergaard and Resler, they conclude that women do make a significant contribution to the place of the family in the stratification system. Determination of the class position of the family, they argue, must take into account the possibly differing occupational positions of men and women. They conclude that the cross-class family is a significant although much neglected phenomenon.

An article by Goldthorpe (1983) is the most developed attempt yet to justify the conventional position by arguing that women's paid work is of such limited significance that the class position of married women is determined by that of their husbands. Goldthorpe criticizes both the critics of the use of the household as the unit of stratification, and those who, while retaining this as the unit, try to include women's activities as one of the determinants of the position of the household. He suggests that the derivation of women's class position from that of her husband is not a sign of sexism, but rather claims that it is in recognition of sexual inequality that stratification theory derives a woman's class position from that of her husband.

Goldthorpe argues that sexual inequality means that wives are dependent upon their husbands for the determination of their life chances and that the paid employment of wives has little impact on their situation. He suggests that gender inequality means that a wife's participation in paid employment is so limited that this employment is an inappropriate basis for a woman's class identification.

Goldthorpe attempts an empirical substantiation of these claims using data collected in the Oxford mobility survey. He examines the paid work histories of women for support for his suggestion that the majority of wives are not in continuous employment and that 'a sizeable proportion will withdraw from participation . . . on more than one occasion'. Further, he examines the number of years which elapse between marriage, the first withdrawal from the labour market of the wives, the birth of the first child, and the first re-entry to the labour market after the birth, and argues that, since these timings are to some extent correlated with husband's class, women's employment can be said to be conditioned by the husband's class.

These theoretical justifications for taking the family as the unit of analysis have many problems (Acker, 1973; Allen 1982; Garnsey, 1978; Murgatroyd, 1982; Oakley, 1974; Stanworth, 1984; Walby, 1986a). The most important problem is the way that this ignores social inequality within the family despite ample evidence of substantial inequality between men and women within the household. Women typically spend more hours at work (paid work and housework combined) than men (Gershuny, 1983; Vanek, 1980); women have less access to consumption goods than men within the family (for instance, food, access to the 'family' car, money for spending on leisure pursuits such as drinking (cf. Oren, 1973); women suffer violence from men within the family in a way which is not reciprocated (Pizzey, 1974; Dobash and Dobash, 1980) and provide forms of emotional support and engage in forms of sexuality from which men benefit more than women (see Hite, 1981; Koedt, 1973).

Indeed many writers on gender inequality have focused on the family as the basis of women's oppression. So it is remarkable that theorists of social inequality deliberately treat as a unity that which many regard as the main site of gender inequality. By taking the family as the unit in studies of inequality they conceptually eradicate the inequality that exists between men and women within that unit. I would argue that such conceptual problems can only be overcome by taking the individual rather than the family as the unit of analysis in social stratification theory. The existing problematic conceptualization occurs partly because of the implicit (and sometimes explicit) equation of social inequality with class inequality, and then of class inequality with inequality within the division of paid labour. Inequality between men and women within the family does not fit into these pre-determined categories of unequals. The important issues for these writers is confined to those things which affect class relations. Gender relations are typically considered relevant only in so far as they affect class relations. Gender inequality in itself does not appear in this research programme. Yet for analysts of social inequality to rule out that of gender in this way is a nonsense. It is seriously inadequate even when writers consider the effect gender relations do have on class relations, if they do so without considering gender relations in themselves.

Further problems for the traditional position arise in the practicalities of taking the family as the unit. There is a problem in taking something as a unit into which all people do not fit; a substantial minority of people do not live in family units. It is also particularly problematic to assume that the position of the family as a whole is determined by the male 'head'. Such a person does not exist in a large minority of families, for instance those composed of women only, or of a woman and her children. Again, in a substantial minority of families where there is an adult man, he is not the chief earner because of illness, unemployment, retirement or simply because he does not earn as much as his wife or cohabitee. The standard 'solution' to the problem of the lack of a male 'head' is to treat the woman as the head of that family unit. However, this produces severe anomalies. It means that the source of a woman's class position must change as she marries, separates from a husband, as her husband falls ill or unemployed or dies. This instability in the source of the class position of a woman is very unsatisfactory. Such a situation further means that the occupations of some women are important for the class structure, while those of others are deemed irrelevant. Thus samples of workers being studied for their class position should include husbands, fathers and women 'heads' of households–although this is not in fact done.

While these basic criticisms are now widely accepted, the shape of the alternative approach is much less clear. Some writers have responded to these criticisms by including a small piece on gender relations in work which otherwise ignores it. Poulantzas (1973) notes the significance of the feminization of clerical work in a book which otherwise omits to consider gender relations. Others have accepted the thrust of the critique and state that gender relations are important while doing next to nothing about it in their own work. Parkin (1979) states that a model of class relations which cannot take adequate account of gender divisions is extremely weak, yet his own work does little more than reiterate this point without further development. Townsend (1979) while including gender as a variable in his account of poverty, does so most of the time merely to consider how it affects the relations between men rather than to analyse the inequality of income between men and women.

Numerous critiques of stratification theories focus on the problem of taking the family as the unit in the analysis (see for instance, Acker, 1973; Allen, 1982; Comer, 1978; Delphy, 1981; Garnsey, 1978; Murgatroyd, 1982; Oakley, 1974, 1982; Stanworth, 1984; West, 1978). However, these critiques also have their limitations. While I would not argue with the correctness of their comments, their suggestions for the future conceptualization of gender inequality are rather undeveloped. Thus, while for most of these writers the inequality between men and women in the family is an important part of their critique of the old position, only one of them (Delphy) recommends the building of this insight into a central feature of a new framework for analysing gender inequality. While all assert the importance of gender inequality, the majority assert the centrality of capitalist class relations and this is then held to rule out a concept of the relations between men and women as class relations. This is why Allen concludes her article by asserting that women are not a class:

> The argument is not that women are a separate class: such a proposition necessitates the denial of the centrality of divisions inherent in the relations of production, consumption and exchange which separate men from other men and women from other women. (Allen, 1982: 147.)

Similarly Garnsey asserts that the primary focus is class and that gender is not class.

> It is indisputable that distinctions of race and gender are not class distinctions . . . This is not the question at issue. What needs to be considered is whether the failure to deal systematically with the question of inequalities based on class and gender impairs the usefulness of models of class stratification. (Garnsey, 1980: 231.)

West rejects the notion that women's class position can be derived from that of other family members and similarly holds that the class position of women is determined by the position that they themselves hold in paid work. She also rejects the argument that women constitute a class, because, she argues, women share a class position with men within the capitalist mode of production. So again West is critical of the old approach of subsuming women under their husband's or father's class position, but denies the possibility of women being a class because of the centrality of capitalist class relations.

> The notion that women are a class may be justifiably rejected on the grounds of the shared class position of most men and women. (West, 1978: 228.)

These critics of the mainstream writers have thus stayed very close to the framework which they have been criticizing. In particular, they have assumed the overwhelming dominance of class relations. Their programme for developing a theory of gender relations focuses on the importance of paid employment. This argument has been made on the grounds of the *a priori* significance of capitalist relations, rather than sustained argument about their significance for gender relations. While these critics note the empirical evidence of systematic social inequality between men and women they fail to incorporate this adequately into their conceptual and theoretical schemes. Their criticisms of the traditional subsuming of women under a male head of household remain valid, but most of their suggestions for alternative approaches are seriously limited by this *a priori* acceptance of the centrality of capitalist class relations in an analysis of social inequality. Other critics, e.g. Eichler, admit to uncertainty as to where to go after demolishing existing conceptualizations of women and class:

> We have now seen that class analysis, no matter which viewpoint is taken, is not able adequately to incorporate women. Either we must conceptualise women as a distinct social class, which destroys class analysis since women, who on the basis of their relationship to their husband would belong to one social class, would as workers themselves belong to a second social class and as women to a third social class. Alternatively we have seen that it is equally problematic to subsume the wife under her husband's class membership. (Eichler, 1980: 114.)

She concludes with the suggestion supported by Oakley (1982) that:

> We must start to conceptualise our entire stratification model. (p. 115.)

Eichler is right, but none of the feminist critiques discussed here actually do this.

Gender Inequality as Derivative of Capitalist Social Relations

The domestic-labour debate

The most sophisticated attempt to derive gender inequality from capital may be found in the writings of the 'domestic-labour debate'. This body of writings is an important attempt to conceptualize the material position of housewives and thus the distinctiveness of the material position of women. It does this by attempting to specify the place that housework, or rather domestic labour, has within capitalism. The premise of the debate is that it is possible to locate domestic labour conceptually within capitalism. Its primary focus is not gender inequality, but rather the relationship between domestic labour and capitalism. It is considered that an adequate analysis of this relationship will provide an explanation of the oppression of women. The debate is conducted within Marxist value theory, although a central issue within the debate is whether domestic labour can really be said to produce value and surplus value.

A major contribution of the debate has been to establish that, within Marxist thought, domestic labour should be seen as work, and that the relations under which this work is performed are central to an explanation of the oppression of women. Seccombe (1974), one of the earliest contributors to the debate, argues that domestic labour is unequivocally work and is composed of the work necessary to reproduce labour power on a daily and a generational basis. The products of this labour are the labour power of the husband, the woman herself and the children who are the next generation of labourers.

Most other writers in the domestic labour debate also take this position, in opposition to other tendencies within Marxist thought which see the position of women as determined primarily by ideological structures. These include the notion that it is only cultural lag or ideological backwardness that is the cause of women's subjugation, and a conception of the family as an ideological state apparatus (Althusser, 1971).

However, not all writers in the debate concur on the further issue of what sort of work domestic labour is. They vary as to whether they view it as production, consumption, reproduction or circulation and whether it is productive, unproductive or non-productive of value and of surplus value. James and Dalla Costa (1973) see domestic labour as production. They argue that housework is work, that it is central to the workings of capital, that without it the capitalist system will collapse, and hence that it is production. Further, they argue that domestic labour is productive of both value and surplus value, because the product of women's household labour ultimately becomes incorporated in capital, and they argue that capital derives benefit from this. This analysis has problems in its rather loose use of Marxist terminology, especially in its very broad definition of value.

Other writers have argued that housework is not production but rather consumption, even though it is work. Himmelweit and Mohun (1977) argue that domestic labour is productive only in the sense that it produces use-values for immediate consumption. In its relation to capital, which is the primary focus for Himmelweit and Mohun, domestic labour is seen as consumption. Fee (1976) also argues that domestic labour is to be conceptualized as consumption. The latter makes a distinction between productive consumption and individual consumption on the basis that productive consumption involves the consumption of the means of production in order to convert them into something of higher values (for instance a worker consuming a piece of cloth in order to produce a coat), while the individual consumption involves labourers consuming their means of subsistence (such as buying and eating food). Fee argues that domestic labour is concerned with individual consumption and is not production.

Others have argued that domestic labour is outside the capitalist mode of production, strictly defined. For instance, Smith (1978) argues that while domestic labour is a necessary condition of existence of the capitalist mode of production, it is outside of it.

One of the central issues in the debate has been the relationship between domestic labour and the creation of value and surplus value. Ostensibly, discussion here is about the nature of the process which creates value. At issue is whether all labour creates value, (or rather all labour which is eventually incorporated into capital produces value), or whether the fact that domestic labour is not exchanged with capital on the market is sufficient to disqualify it. James and Dalla Costa (1973) argue that domestic labour does produce value because housework is so important to the workings of capitalism, and because it is labour which is eventually incorporated into capital. Similarly Seccombe argues that domestic labour creates value because it is eventually incorporated into capital via the husband's labour power:

> When the housewife acts directly upon wage-purchased goods and necessarily alters their form, her labour becomes part of the congealed mass of past labour embodied in labour power. The value she creates is realised as one part of the value labour power achieves as a commodity when it is sold. All this is merely a consistent application of the labour theory to the reproduction of labour power itself, namely that all labour produces value when it produces any part of a commodity that achieves equivalence in the market place with other commodities. (Seccombe, 1974: 9.)

In opposition to this it is argued that domestic labour is not directly exchanged on the market with capital and thus that it does not produce value.The argument involves two propositions: that the lack of market exchange means that it is impossible to ascertain the abstract equivalence of domestic labour; and, that because domestic labour is not exchanged directly with capital, it does not produce value for capital (cf. Gardiner et al., 1975; Gardiner, 1975; Smith, 1978).

These debates draw on a simultaneous argument in the Marxist literature as to the nature and usefulness of the distinction between productive and unproductive labour (see for instance, Bullock,973, 1974; Fine and Harris, 1976; Gough, 1972, 1973; Harrison, 1973a). The issues in this debate are whether the distinction between productive and unproductive labour should be made at all, and if so, where the boundary between them should be drawn. The ambiguities of Marx's presentation of the issue in the first three volumes of *Capital* and the fourth volume on *Theories of Surplus Value* have been dissected for internal inconsistency and used as a source of support by these writers. For instance, (Harrison 1973a) denies the validity of the distinction between productive and unproductive labour and claims that Marx's writings on the topic are insufficiently worked through to be taken as an authoritative foundation. He denies the logic of any distinction between socially necessary and unnecessary labour, arguing that to make such a distinction is to illegitimately introduce morality as a criterion in the scientific discourse of Marxism. He argues that whether a worker is a supervisor, or involved in sales or accounting does not preclude that work from being seen as productive from the point of view of capital. Whether or not that work would exist under socialism is not relevant to the issue.

Other writers, such as Fine and Harris (1976), reassert the significance of a distinction between the sphere of production and the sphere of circulation, and the traditional limitation of the generation of surplus value to production, thus excluding the possibility of workers involved in circulation, such as sales workers, from producing surplus value. Within the terms of Marxist theory, as enunciated by both Harrison and Fine and Harris, it is clear that domestic labour does not produce value or surplus value, because it does not meet the criterion that it must be directly exchanged with capital.

There is a second argument against the supposition that domestic labour creates value: that there is no mechanism which could ensure that domestic labour is exchanged at its value, and that thus it cannot create value (Smith, 1978). However, the position that domestic labour does not create value or surplus value is in itself no answer to the question of the place of domestic labour in a social formation. Smith is left trying to argue that domestic labour is a condition of existence of the capitalist mode of production, but that capital extracts no surplus value from it. However, others, such as, Gardiner et al. (1975) argue that capital benefits from the existence of domestic labour, since it enables capital to pay lower wages than would otherwise be the case.

The most serious problem with much of the domestic-labour debate is a failure to confront the issue of the interests of men in the perpetuation of domestic labour. The debate about domestic labour thus occurs in a context which takes as a basic presumption the centrality of capital and is merely concerned with the exact delineation and relation of the elements of this system. This framework seriously limits the types of questions and answers which are possible in the issue of how to understand gender relations. Most writers on the topic have next to nothing to say about gender relations *per se*; they only discuss the relationship of domestic labour to capitalism. Gardiner et al., indeed, when discussing the constitution of their theoretical object, explicitly conclude that this should be the relation of domestic labour to capitalism. This is despite Gardiner's (1975) criticism of Seccombe for paying insufficient attention to the benefits to husbands of their wives' domestic labour. Most of these writings have very little analysis of gender inequality and are based on a mere presumption that capitalism is the problem rather than patriarchy or men. Thus the most important question is settled *a priori*. The interests that men, and in particular husbands, may have in the continuation and shaping of domestic work are almost totally neglected.

Further, these writers face a serious inconsistency between asserting the derivative nature of women's oppression from capitalism, while recognizing the fact that this oppression pre-dates capitalism (cf. Middleton, 1981). It is illogical to suppose that a social system which arose after patriarchy could be deemed to create social inequalities which pre-date it.

Beyond the domestic-labour debate?

The domestic-labour debate has not been the only attempt to analyse gender relations in relation to capitalism. Zaretsky (1976), for instance, suggests that the separation of the family and the economy under capitalism is central to women's oppression today. He argues that this separation developed with capitalism and is the basic cause of the confinement of women to a narrow sphere of life. However, his analysis is crucially flawed by the underestimation of sexual inequality and the sexual segregation of work in pre-capitalist societies (cf. Middleton, 1981). He thus incorrectly attributes these to the development of capitalism, rather than to a system of patriarchal relations which spans this development.

Other attempts have paid more attention to a wider variety of factors affecting women's subordination and tend to be less reductionist in their account of the relationship between women's oppression and capitalism (cf. Molyneux, 1979). Barrett (1980) is a good example of much more complex account of women's oppression from a Marxist–feminist position. Indeed, Barrett almost treats gender relations as possessing sufficient distinction from capitalist relations for her to fall into my category of 'snythesized' capitalist patriarchy. While Barrett argues within an explicit Marxist–feminist framework she is strongly against attempting to explain women's oppression in terms of the supposed needs of capitalism. She argues against tendencies to both reductionism and to economism. Instead she suggests that it is necessary to have a historical account that takes into consideration the struggles between men and women and the complexity of the ideological construction of gender. She argues that while the oppression of women is not a functional necessity for capitalism, the historical development of capitalism has in fact led to a situation in which the oppression of women does have a basis in contemporary capitalist relations. Thus she attempts to meet the objection that capitalism cannot cause something which pre-dates it.

> an oppression of women that is not in any essentialist sense pre-given by the logic of capitalist development has become necessary for the ongoing reproduction of the [capitalist] mode of production in its present form. Hence, the oppression of women, although not a functional pre-requisite of capitalism, has acquired a material basis in the relations of production and reproduction of capitalism today. (Barrett, 1980: 249.)

However, this can logically mean no more than that capitalist relations have significantly affected pre-existing patterns of gender inequality. Barrett's refusal to accept the analytic independence of patriarchal domination together with her rejection of the notion that gender inequality can be derived from capitalist relations, means that there is something of a vacuum in her analysis. This leaves Barrett with an analysis of women's oppression in terms of relatively *ad hoc* explanations based on historical detail. Further, the historical analysis she advocates is not actually carried out in her book, so it remains unclear what this would look like. Her discussion emphasizes the importance of ideology for women's oppression, although she considers many social practices which have a part to play in constructing and reproducing gender relations. Her book is an excellent review of the existing literature and sets out many of the problems in Marxist–feminist analysis. However, rather than resolving the dilemmas that she so astutely sets out, she remains poised within them.

Her analysis, while noting the inadequacy of attributing the oppression of women to the functional necessities of capitalism, fails to capture the importance of men's interests in women's subordination. She does not succeed in providing a framework which can adequately analyse the conflicting interests of patriarchy and capital over, for instance, women's labour. In her analysis of women's paid work she asserts that it is the family and ideology which are crucial for women's subordinate position:

> In assessing the factors which might account for the position of women as wage labourers it is impossible to escape the conclusion that family structure and the ideology of domestic responsibility play an important part. (Barrett, 1980: 157.)

Here Barrett seriously underestimates the significance of patriarchal forces in the workplace and in the state for the poor position women have in comparison to men in paid work. She pays insufficient attention to the role of organized male workers in excluding women from the forms of paid work, especially those with the better pay and conditions (cf. Hartmann, 1979a). Barrett's analysis is more successful than that of many Marxist feminists precisely because she does note the divergence of interests of men and women and does not reduce these to a by-product of capitalism. However, her rejection of a conception of patriarchy as a set of autonomous social relations means that her analysis of gender relations is confined to the level of *ad hoc* explanations of specific occurrences and remains untheorized.

Gender Inequality as a Result of Patriarchy Alone

A radically different approach is taken by writers who argue that gender inequality is not reducible to or derivative from any other social system, but that rather it should be seen as an autonomous system of social inequality. Patriarchy is seen as the primary form of social inequality. Some, but not all, of these writers go on to argue that other forms, such as racism and capitalism, derive from patriarchy. In these analyses, the various forms of oppression suffered by women are seen as sufficiently interrelated to constitute a system in which women as a group are oppressed by men.

There are many variations within the writings in this school. Different bases of patriarchal relations, and, indeed, disagreements as to whether it is appropriate to think of patriarchy as having one base, are a major source of this variation. Further variations are based on differences in the definition of patriarchy, especially as to whether it refers to the domination of men over women, or of fathers over both women and younger men.

Millett (1977) suggests that patriarchal relations are to be found everywhere and are not confined to particular spheres of social life. She argues that every aspect of social life, including the family, economy, force, socialism, religion, sexuality and psychology contributes to the maintenance of patriarchy. Her writing is powerful and subtle, especially in her analysis of sexuality in literature. However, her work does not constitute a theory of gender inequality because of its lack of analysis of the systematic interrelationships between these structures. Ultimately the work is sophisticated, and full of insight, but only descriptive nevertheless.

A similar position can be found in the Redstockings' Manifesto (1970) in which it is asserted that women are a class and that all forms of oppression in society derive from this first, fundamental form of oppression. The Redstockings do not particularly elevate one level to be the basis of this oppression but rather list a series of dimensions along which women are oppressed by men, including political, economic and cultural institutions, force and sexuality. They do not elaborate their explanation of this, in what is only a manifesto and not a long treatise.

Some analyses focus on only one aspect of womens' oppression. For instance, Brownmiller (1976) argues that rape is used by men to intimidate all women and keep them in subjection, and provides many historical illustrations of this. However, she does not provide an analytic framework which relates different aspects of patriarchy to each other, let alone to other social relations. She provides a historical account of men's rape of women, which powerfully communicates the horror of this form of oppression. She is able to undermine conventional approaches to rape, which see it either as the product of a few sick men, or as the result of women's provocation, and to replace them with an account of rape as a form of women's oppression which is firmly rooted in the patriarchal nature of societies. However, she does not establish that rape is the basis of women's subordination. She provides no analysis as to how rape leads, for instance, to women's disadvantaged position in paid work, or women's exclusion from government. Brownmiller establishes rape as one terrible facet of women's oppression but fails to establish it as the basis of that oppression.

Likewise the Leeds Revolutionary Feminists (1981), while arguing that heterosexuality is the basis of patriarchal relations, and graphically pointing to key aspects of that form of sexuality which may trap women into oppression by men, do not relate it to other social relations. They analyse the contradictions which arise when women's most intimate relationships are with those people, men, who belong to the category of oppressors. The Leeds group claim that sexual relationships between men and women inevitably involve the oppression of women. They further argue for the central importance of the institution of heterosexuality in the maintenance of patriarchal relations. They suggest that sexual love obscures the realities of women's oppression and shores up male supremacy. However, the article does not go very far in substantiating the claim, omitting to consider other aspects of patriarchal relations, such as the importance of the sexual division of labour and the significance of a patriarchal state or the relationship of heterosexuality to these. Nor do they consider the significance of capitalist relations in shaping the specific forms of patriarchal relations in sexuality. Thus, again, we have an insightful analysis of one facet of a patriarchal system, but not a theory of patriarchal relations in general.

The writer in the 'patriarchy alone' category who has produced one of the most fully developed theories of patriarchy is Firestone (1974). She does attempt to build a theory of patriarchy in which different sets of patriarchal relations have their place, and even attempts to specify their articulation with class and race relations. Firestone argues that the biology of reproduction is the basis of women's subordination to men. She suggests that child-bearing, breast-feeding, child care, pregnancy, menstruation and all other aspects of the biology of reproduction put women in a vulnerable position *vis-à-vis* men. This weakness through the biology of reproduction enables men to be dominant over women.

Firestone argues that this affects all aspects of the organization of society. She adapts the Marxist notion of base and superstructure to her purpose, suggesting that the real base of social organization is reproduction, and that all else, including the organization of social classes, of government and religion, is the superstructure. She elaborates the connections between these different aspects of patriarchal society in some detail. Thus, for instance, racism is seen to derive from sexism because children brought up in the power-riddled biological family develop a psycho-sexual structure which makes them lust for power. Thus, she argues, in a manner similar to the Frankfurt school, a particular form of psycho-sexual structure leads to power structures in society.

A further example of the elaborate connections that she makes between the biology of reproduction and aspects of social organization is her analysis of love. She argues that the love experience in a patriarchal society is often a bitter one because of the power inequalities which stem from the biological family. Since women are so dependent upon a man when they bear children, it is logical that they must take great care when they come to select a husband, because so much rests on this. This dependence corrupts the love experience because women, who must always be on their guard in order not to be taken advantage of, resort to games and wiles so as not to fall for a man and lose control of the situation. Indeed, women who in the name of sexual liberation do not use these devices are liable to suffer. Men, on the other hand, have their psycho-sexual development so damaged during their upbringing in the biological family that they are incapable of love anyway. Thus most love experiences in a patriarchal society are a bitter disappointment.

Firestone does not believe that these relationships between men and women are immutable. She argues that the technological capacity in contemporary society exists to transcend the problems of the biology of reproduction. She suggests that the primitive methods of reproduction currently in existence may be replaced by the development of human embryos outside of a woman's body, removing the problems that biology has until now posed for women. However, this would only occur if women were able to seize the means of reproduction in a political struggle.

A major problem with Firestone is her tendency to biologism, although this is not as great as some of her critics have argued. Beechey (1979) argues that Fireston is an irredeemable biological reductionist and, indeed, that this is a hallmark of much radical feminist analysis. However, Beechey underestimates the significance and the complexity of the social mediations around biology that

Firestone introduces in her analysis (see also Sayers, 1982). Nevertheless, Firestone does insufficiently consider the amount of historical and cross-cultural variation which has existed in the social organization of reproduction. She makes an error in tending to conflate childbirth with child care, or at least in assuming that the connection between the two is a biological rather than a social fact. Firestone pays insufficient attention to a wide range of aspects of social organization, such as paid work and the state. Her analysis of the relations of patriarchy with class and ethnicity are rather reductionist, ignoring the social structures and institutions which have variously shaped these relationships throughout history. In particular her insufficient analysis of capitalist relations and their interrelationship with patriarchal relations is a serious omission. Further, Firestone places undue faith in technology as a solution to women's reproductive problems (Rose and Hanmer, 1976). While Firestone's theory is one of the most sophisticated and highly developed radical–feminist theories, it is flawed by being too reductionist and by a tendency to biologism.

MacKinnon argues that sexuality is the basis of the differentiation of the sexes and the oppression of women. She considers that this is parallel to the centrality of work for Marxist analyses of capitalism. Indeed, she starts one of her articles thus:

> Sexuality is to feminism what work is to Marxism: that which is most one's own, yet most taken away. (MacKinnon, 1982: 1.)

The forms of power that men have over women are seen to be expressed through sexuality. She uses examples such as sexual harrassment at work (which was the focus of her earlier work (1979), pornography, rape and prostitution. She considers that sexuality constructs gender, rather than gender sexuality. These are all social processes; not biological givens. Women are defined in opposition to men who are the expropriators of women's sexuality. Men sexually objectify women and, through doing so, have power over them. In resisting this patriarchal control over women MacKinnon rejects all forms of objectifying, including 'objective' forms of knowledge. Instead she argues for a raising of consciousness as the feminist method to defeat objectification and oppression.

MacKinnon's work is interesting and important, especially as she powerfully articulates some of the connections which some feminists have made in their political practice. However, I think that it has serious problems. She does not consider the significance of the sexual division of labour as a factor in its own right, merely stating that labour is the province of a Marxist's analysis of class. This separation of class analysis from gender analysis, and then the neglect of the former is problematic. She has not assessed the relative importance of class or labour for gender inequality as compared to sexuality. Further, it is not clear why some of the acts which she considers to be central to women's oppression, such as sexual harrassment, rape and pornography, are not to be considered primarily as acts of violence in which the medium of sexuality is rather incidental. This is related to the problem of defining sexuality. MacKinnon to a considerable extent interdefines sexuality and gender, almost arguing that they are one and the same thing.

> Sexuality is that social process which creates, organises, expresses and directs desire, creating the social beings we know as women and men, as their relations create society. (MacKinnon, 1982: 2.)

In so far as sexuality and gender are interdefined, one cannot be the explanation of the other. MacKinnon's work shares similarities with that of Dworkin, especially Dworkin's analysis of pornography and women (Dworkin, 1981). In her book, Dworkin argues that women *are* pornography to men, and that this is the cause and effect of women's oppression by men. Dworkin provides horrific illustration of her argument of the pernicious nature of pornography for women. Yet again the question remains whether this should be seen as the basis of women's subordination or simply one more facet of it.

Some writers have criticized not only specific texts that use the 'patriarchy alone' approach, but have argued that it is in principle impossible to construct an adequate analysis of gender inequality within it. For instance, several writers have argued against the use of the concept of patriarchy when it involves the notion of a general system of gender inequality.

Barrett argues against using the concept of patriarchy except for very specific types of ideology. She denies the possibility of patriarchy referring to a social system:

> It seems admissable in some contexts to refer to patriarchal ideology, describing specific aspects of male–female relations

> in capitalism but as a noun the term 'patriarchy' presents insuperable difficulties to an analysis that attempts to relate women's oppression to the relations of production of capitalism. (Barrett, 1980: 19.)

She argues that the term 'patriarchy' has several problems, the most general of which is that it is ahistoric and assumes that relations between men and women are unchanging and universalistic. She suggests that this often slides into a biologism which is unacceptable. Indeed, Barrett argues that any attempt to see patriarchy as autonomous is inherently problematic. Use of the term can only be appropriate, she suggests if it is very narrowly defined and refers to specific aspects of ideological relations such as those in the father–daughter relationship described in Virginia Woolf's *Three Guineas* (Barrett, 1980: 15). She further argues that the use of the term often involves confusion between the notion of patriarchy as the rule of the father and that of patriarchy as men's domination of women (p. 16).

However, the problems that Barrett identifies in particular writings on patriarchy are not inherent in the use of the concept. Barrett herself recognizes that a slide towards biologism is not a necessary feature of analyses couched in terms of patriarchy, even if it has been a common problem of several radical feminist writings. She incorrectly assumes that the reason for the tendency towards universalism in analyses using patriarchy is its conceptualization as autonomous from capitalism. She is wrong to suggest that this is a necessary rather than a contingent feature of these analyses. However if a model of patriarchy were to be constructed in a non-reductionist manner then it would be fully possible to account for historical variation. Further, the problem of a slippage between the use of the term 'patriarchy' as referring to the rule of the father or to men's domination of women is again not intrinsic to the concept, merely occurring contingently in certain texts and not in others. Thus, while Barrett has correctly identified some problems with specific writings on patriarchy, she has *not* substantiated her more serious claim that the use of the concept of patriarchy inevitably leads to these problems. The problems of reductionism, biologism, universalism and inconsistent definition should be seen as problems in specific texts which need to be overcome in an adequate analysis of gender inequality, not problems with the concept of patriarchy itself.

Beechey (1979) takes a very ambivalent position on the merits of the concept of patriarchy. She rejects those analyses which see patriarchy as a system of social relations autonomous from capitalism, while retaining the concept as a term to be applied to specific institutions within capitalism (and other modes of production). Thus she is prepared to use it in a limited sense when applied to restricted situations, but rejects any suggestion of patriarchy as a social system. Analyses of women's oppression in terms of patriarchy alone, she suggests, are unable to account for variations in the forms this oppression takes. She argues that such variations cannot be explained without an analysis of capitalism.

Beechey's own position is to see patriarchy in discrete bits, in specific institutions within capitalism:

> I think that a satisfactory theory of patriarchy should be historically specific and should explore the forms of patriarchy which exist within particular modes of production. (Beechey, 1979: 80.)

Thus, on the one hand, Beechey both rejects the notion that patriarchy is an autonomous system and denies that it is reducible to capitalism, with the consequence that her 'historically specific' explanations would be merely *ad hoc*. Yet on the other hand Beechey yearns for an analysis of women's oppression which is integrated into every other analysis:

> How can we utilize a materialist method of analysis in such a way that we can satisfactorily integrate production and reproduction as part of a single process, and which will reveal that gender differentiations are inseparable from the form of organisation of the class structures? (p. 80.)

Here she is seeking an analysis of gender inequality which is part of a system of social inequality and not just a series of historically specific explanations. She is torn between the wish for a systematic explanation of women's oppression and one which is built around specific historical events and specific social institutions. As Beechey herself suggests, this is 'a difficult task'. However, this task is hindered rather than helped by rejecting the notion of patriarchy as an autonomous system of social inequality, and by an incorrect assumption that analyses in terms of patriarchy as a system must be necessarily incapable of accounting for historical variation.

Rowbotham (1981) also sees the concept of patriarchy as entailing insuperable obstacles despite her recognition of the sensitizing function it has played for feminists. She argues that the term necessarily implies a conception of women's oppression that is universalist, ahistoric and essentially biologistic; that it incorrectly leads to a search for a single cause of women's oppression, either in a base–superstructure model or as a quest for the ultimate origins of patriarchy; that it incorrectly separates the oppression of women from capitalist relations; and that it implies a kind of fixity which incorrectly suggests fatalistic acceptance of this state of affairs by women. Rowbotham argues instead for a complex historical analysis which has place for the examination of the reciprocal relations as well as conflicts between men and women.

Rowbotham, like Beechey and Barrett, incorrectly slides from an accurate identification of flaws in particular accounts of gender inequality to an unjustified rejection of the use of the concept of patriarchy in an analysis of women's oppression. These critics move from pointing out very real and important deficiencies in accounts of patriarchy to the false conclusion that all accounts of patriarchy must necessarily suffer from the same problems. This is because they incorrectly locate the cause of these faults. These problems should be seen to stem from features of these accounts in particular, and from the defect that they suffer from having only one main explanatory variable. This common feature of these approaches leads to those accounts being reductionist, static and ahistorical. When there is only one explanatory variable there is little basis for explaining variations in the phenomenon under examination. Thus these accounts are unable to lead to an adequate understanding of either variations in the form of patriarchy, or historical change.

However, the answer to this problem does not lie simply in introducing capitalism as a second or alternative explanatory variable. While the neglect of capitalist relations is a problem, it is not the only one. In addition, the analysis of patriarchy should be made more sophisticated. I will argue below that our concept of patriarchy should provide for several interrelated structures, instead of only one base. This will provide the possibility of explaining the historical variations which do exist in patriarchal relations.

Capitalist Patriarchy

A considerable advance over the 'capitalism alone' and 'patriarchy alone' approaches to explaining gender inequality can be found in the conception of one system of capitalist patriarchy (for instance, McDonagh and Harrison, 1978). Here the impact of capitalist class relations is admitted, but without reducing gender inequality to capitalism, or offering only *ad hoc* explanations.

Eisenstein's work is a particularly interesting and important attempt in this direction. She argues that capitalist and patriarchal relations are so intertwined and interdependent that they form a mutually interdependent system. In her early work (1979) there is greater stress on the extent of the synthesis between capitalism and patriarchy, while in her later work (1984) there is more recognition of conflicts between patriarchal and capitalist interests. However, even in her most recent work she argues against the dualist approach (the view, discussed below, that capitalism and patriarchy are analytically independent), suggesting rather that the relation between capitalism and patriarchy is of a 'semi-autonomous, semi-independent' and semi-dependent nature (1984: 94).

Eisenstein (1979) argues that capitalism needs patriarchal relations in order to survive and vice versa. She suggests not only that the two systems shape each other, but that they should be regarded as fused into one system. She considers her analysis to be a synthesis of Marxism (thesis) and a radical feminism (antithesis). She argues not merely for a notion of a symbiotic relationship between patriarchy and capitalism, but for an integrated relationship in which they have become one system. Their effect on each other and need for each other is seen as too great for them to be conceptualized as separate systems.

However, Eisenstein is sometimes a little ambivalent on this point since she still writes of one system affecting the other. This is especially the case in her more recent work (1984). She suggests (1979) that each system makes specific contributions to the whole. Patriarchy contributes especially a system of order and control, while capitalism provides the economic system driven by the pursuit of profit. These and other aspects of the system combine to form a particular form of political economy.

Eisenstein carries her analysis of gender inequality further in more recent writings which focus upon the state and feminism (1981 and, especially, 1984), developing her account of which elements of patriarchy and capitalism are fused and which are separate. There is a separation between the two systems around the rival demands for women's labour, with capital and patriarchy pulling in opposite directions: household or paid employment. They are fused at the level of the state, where she argues (1984) that patriarchal interests are represented via male capitalists.

The problem with these accounts is that they underestimate the significance of organized patriarchal forces among workers both in the explanation of the changing participation of women in paid work, and in the patriarchal forces which affect the state. This is especially problematic for Eisenstein's analysis of the state, which is her main interest. In her theoretical account she suggests that patriarchal interests are represented via male capitalists (1984: 92). This is despite the fact that she is also at pains in the rest of that book to differentiate the various currents of anti-feminist as well as feminist agitation. She sees variations in patriarchal strategy as arising within the bourgeoisie. The form of the state, in particular its separation from the family, is seen overall as patriarchal. Yet this account is flawed by failing to theoretically integrate patriarchal forces from outside the bourgeoisie. Hence, I would suggest, she underestimates the conflict between patriarchy and capitalism. Thus the way that Eisenstein tries to combine the two sets of relations in her analysis is rather problematic. She is ambiguous on the extent to which it is still possible to write of separate patriarchal and capitalist systems. When she writes of systems needing each other this logically involves a notion of two analytically distinct systems, but that is contrary to her early claims that capitalism and patriarchy are fused into one system. In her discussion of the various elements of the combined system she does attempt to specifcy which part is due to patriarchal forces and which to capitalist. Indeed, her account is most satisfactory when she does specify the elements separately, especially in the parts of her later work (1981, 1984) where she discusses some of the contradictions between the patriarchal and capitalist elements in capitalist patriarchy. In practice Eisenstein reveals the need to clearly distinguish the two systems analytically, although, especially in her early work, she attempts to deny this. Her work is an important advance in that it treats both patriarchal and capitalist forces as important in the determination of gender relations, but important ambiguities remain together with an insufficient specification of the patriarchal forces which are in conflict with capital.

Patriarchy and Capitalism as Analytically Independent

Dualist writings, which treat patriarchy and capitalism as analytically independent, divide into two major groupings: firstly, those which allocate different spheres of society to the determination of either patriarchal or capitalist relations; and, secondly, those which see patriarchal and capitalist relations as articulating at all levels and spheres of society. The first group of dualist writings may be further sub-divided according to which spheres are allocated to capitalism and which to patriarchy. Some writers confine patriarchy to the general area of ideology, culture and sexuality, and capitalism to the economy or production (e.g. Kuhn, 1978; Mitchell, 1975); others confine patriarchy to reproduction and capitalism to production (for instance, O'Brien, 1981). The second group includes such writers as Hartmann (1979a, 1981).

The conceptualization of patriarchy as analytically independent yet coexisting with capitalism is a major advance on the previous formulations considered. It captures the autonomy of patriarchal relations whilst not ignoring the significance of capitalist relations. It leaves the question of the exact nature of the articulation of the two systems as an open, rather than predetermined, question and provides the essential basis of a theoretical framework for analysing gender inequality. Most of these analyses attempt to pinpoint the bases of patriarchal and of capitalist relations. The way in which this has been done in many, however, is rather problematic. The writers tend to make too stark a division between the spheres of influence of capitalism and patriarchy, and they incorrectly isolate the basis of patriarchal relations.

One group of dualist writings insists that the basis of patriarchal relations lies in the broad area of ideology, culture, sexuality and the unconscious. This position is weak in that it merely reproduces the traditional problems of social analysis in which gender relations are relegated to the periphery of social theory, leaving them out of areas traditionally seen as central, such as work and the economic. Gender relations are yet again conceptualized as part of the superstructure, even if they are given slightly greater causal powers in the new overall schema.

A leading example of this approach is Mitchell (1975) who argues that capitalism is located on the economic level and patriarchy on the ideological:

> In analysing contemporary western society we are (as elsewhere) dealing with two autonomous areas: the economic mode of capitalism and the ideological mode of patriarchy. (Mitchell, 1975: 412.)

She is concerned to extract an analysis of the unconscious from Freud's writings while leaving behind his patriarchal bias. An analysis of the workings of the unconscious, she argues, is essential to an understanding of gender relations:

> The patriarchal law speaks to and through each person in his unconscious; the reproduction of the ideology of human society is thus assured in the acquisition of the law by each individual. (p. 413.)

Mitchell argues that the patriarchal law is that of the rule of the father, rather than the domination of men. It operates through the Oedipus complex and kinship system. She suggests that contemporary capitalism does not need this law and therefore that it is potentially redundant. It is, she suggests, the nuclear family which holds these contradictions in check.

Many of the problems in Mitchell's analysis stem from her omissions and from a one-sided focus on the debates around the Freudian analysis of the unconscious. She neglects to consider whether there might be a material basis to patriarchal relations as well as to capitalist relations. Her analysis is predicated on a relatively unexamined assumption that culture and the unconscious are central to an understanding of patriarchal relations and that the economic level is not. In this way Mitchell reproduces the standard problem of much traditional Marxist analysis of gender inequality which fails to consider the significance of the sexual division of labour as an economic phenomenon. She fails to consider the material benefits men derive from women's unpaid domestic labour and the significance of men's organized attempts to limit women's access to paid work. This type of dualist analysis of gender relations in which patriarchy is confined to one level and capitalism to another is thus subject to serious problems.

Another group of dualist writings confines patriarchal and capitalist relations to different spheres: those of reproduction and production respectively. The division of the material level into two parts, in reproduction and production, has a long history. One of the earliest proponents of the conceptual distinction between production and reproduction, if not patriarchy and capitalism, was Engels in *The Origin of the Family, Private Property and the State* (1940). Production was considered to include those tasks involved with the means of existence, of food, clothing, shelter and the tools necessary for survival. Reproduction involved the propagation of the species through the reproduction of human beings. Engels further suggested that men were involved in production, while women were engaged in reproduction, and that this division of labour was 'natural'. Whether or not women were subordinated to men depended upon the relationship between the two spheres of material life in which they were involved. Only when production became more important through its generation of surpluses did men become dominant. These surpluses were simultaneously the basis of private property, classes and the state. With the evolution of private property, men restrained women to monogamous marriages, in order to be sure that they were passing their property on to their biological sons.

Here, Engels constructed a very close link between the form of the oppression of women and private property. However, the closeness of this connection between reproduction and capitalism is not followed by all those who make the distinction between reproduction and production, O'Brien (1981), for instance, does not make such a close link between patriarchal relations and capitalist relations, although she makes a distinction very similar to Engels between reproduction and production. O'Brien argues that most social theorists have seriously underestimated the significance of reproduction for social organization. The variations in the way reproduction is organized, she argues, are crucial to understanding historical variations in gender relations. She treats reproduction as a material base on which there is erected an ideological superstructure, which she then considers to be a reproductive consciousness. Similarly Beneria (1979) argues that reproduction is the root of the different forms of subordination of women and is conceptually distinct from production.

Meillassoux also makes a distinction between reproduction and production in his analysis of 'primitive' societies. He argues that control over reproduction is more important than control over production in such societies. His distinction is between the 'means of material production' and the 'means of human reproduction'. He considers that the latter are made up of 'subsistence and women' (Meillassoux, 1972: 101). O'Laughlin, (1977) in her critique of another piece of Meillassoux's work argues that reproduction should be seen as a subcategory of production. Edholm, Harris and Young (1977) suggest that there is confusion in the use of the term 'reproduction' with one term being used to denote three separate concepts: the reproduction of the entire system of social production, the reproduction of the labour force, and biological or human reproduction. This causes substantial problems in the analysis of gender relations.

The distinction between production and reproduction is arbitrary and unsustainable. Almost every task which these writers might allocate to production could in certain circumstances be allocated to reproduction and vice versa (Delphy, 1977). Child-bearing is the only task which could not be randomly allocated. Most of the writings which attempt to make the distinction make an unwarranted biologistic assumption that child care necessarily follows on from childbirth. There is no task currently performed as domestic labour which could not be bought as a service or good on the market; yet typically, when performed in the home it is considered as reproduction, and if outside, production. For instance, food may be purchased at various stages of preparation, right up to the purchase of an entire meal in a restaurant or canteen; cleaning may be bought in the form of a 'servant', 'daily' or contract cleaners; child care may be bought in as child-minders, nurseries or public schools. It is entirely inconsistent to see a person who is paid a wage to do any of these tasks as being engaged in production and a woman who does them unpaid as being engaged in reproduction. They are all work, socially useful and should be seen as production. A distinction between reproduction and production is unfounded and should be rejected in favour of conceptualizing all these tasks as production. Delphy (1977, 1984) is one of the few writers who does conceptualize all these tasks as production.

The domestic mode of production

Delphy (1977), using certain Marxist notions in order to construct her analysis of patriarchy, argues that the basis of gender relations is the domestic mode of production. She argues that there are two modes of production in contemporary society: a capitalist one and a domestic one. Gender inequality derives from the domestic mode, in which the husband expropriates the wife's labour. The woman does not receive an equitable return for the housework and child care she gives her husband and thus, Delphy argues she should be considered exploited. Delphy bases her argument on the traditional Marxist assumption that the organization of the material level, in particular the relations involved in production, are central to the determination of social organization.

Delphy's innovation is to argue not only that housework is as much a form of production as work in a factory under capitalist ownership, but to follow that analysis through with a conceptualization of a distinctive mode of production in which that work is located. The first step in this line of argument, that housework is work, is relatively uncontroversial today, although when Delphy's work was originally published (in France in 1970) this was not the case. She makes an effective argument that housework is production through the use of analogies, drawing examples from French agriculture. Her argument involves a clear distinction between task content and the nature of the relations of production. The distinction between modes of production is made at the level of relations of production: it is not a task distinction.

The proposition that housework is work is substantiated by demonstrating the essential similarity with tasks which have been unequivocally allocated to the category of production. For instance, she argues that all the processes which go into making a loaf of bread ready for consumption should be considered production. It is absurd to consider only the growing of the grains of wheat as production and to exclude the baking of the loaf. She uses the example of a small peasant farm to point up the absurdity of breaking such processes up and allocating one part to production and not the other. Her point is illustrated by the essential similarity of the goods and services produced by the housewife with those that can be bought on the market. Since all these may be obtained either from the housewife or the market it is illogical to consider that one is production and that the other is not. In each case the essential task remains the same, only the relations under which the work is performed vary.

Delphy then argues that women's relation to production is determined not by the content of the tasks that they perform, but by the nature of the social relations under which they labour:

> I would contend that, on the contrary, far from it being the nature of the work performed by women which explains their relationship to production, it is their relations of production which explain why their work is excluded from the realm of value. (Delphy, 1977: 4.)

She suggests that it is on these distinctive relations of production in which the housewife is involved that we should focus.

Delphy asserts that women share a common class position in which they are exploited by men as a class:

> The appropriation and exploitation of their labour within marriage constitutes the oppression common to all women. Destined as women to become 'the wife of' someone, and thus destined for the same relations of production women constitute but one class. (P. 26.)

She goes on to show that not only is women's position within the domestic mode of production the basis of their class oppression by men, but also that it is their main form of subordination. Thus she argues that forms of oppression outside the family derive from that within it. For instance, the injustice that women suffer more than men when in paid employment is seen by Delphy to be a consequence of their duties within the family (although sometimes these duties are merely used to rationalize prejudices by capitalists).

Delphy argues vehemently against those who say that women's oppression is primarily determined by capitalist relations. She considers such theorizing to be particularly pernicious in its effects on the women's movement. It is wrong to suggest that a woman has the same class position as her husband, as

> it is about as accurate to say that the wife of a bourgeois man is herself bourgeois as it is to say that the slave of a plantation owner is himself a plantation owner. (Ibid.)

Delphy suggests that to do such a thing is inconsistent with the Marxist criteria according to which a person's class position is a consequence of the person's own direct relation to production. Indeed, she argues that much analysis by so-called Marxists on the position of women is in direct contradiction with the key principles of Marxist analysis, and considers her own analysis to be more consistent with the principles of historical materialism.

Accounts of the domestic mode of production similar to that of Delphy may be found in the work of Benston (1970) and Harrison (1973b) who also argues that housework is carried out under different relations of production from capitalist production. However, unlike Delphy, Harrison argues that the housework mode of production is not autonomous from the capitalist one, but rather that it has a dependent relation to it. He argues that, in the social formation of contemporary Britain, capitalism is the dominant mode of production whilst housework is a client and dependent mode. Surplus labour appropriated from the housewife, he suggests, passes to capitalists in the capitalist mode. The mechanism of transfer is through the payment of wages beneath the value of labour power by the capitalist to the proletarian husband.

The central problem with Harrison is his problematic assumption that the husband does not benefit at the wife's expense (Oakley, 1974; Oren, 1973; Vanek, 1980; Gershuny, 1983), although he does grant that it would be possible to modify this assumption so as to see the man as gaining use-values at the wife's expense. So while in some respects Harrison's work is more theoretically rigorous than that of either Delphy or Benston, and might on that account be considered more adequate, it is a serious flaw in his argument to fail to make the exploitation of women a basic feature of his housework mode of production. This flaw underlies his highly dubious conclusion that the housework mode continues to exist not because men benefit, since this is for him purely a contingent feature, but rather because it is of benefit to the capitalist mode of production.

Molyneux (1979) and Barrett and McIntosh (1979) criticize Delphy and Harrison for inadequate application of Marxist concepts to the analysis of gender relations, and in particular for their use of the concept of the mode of production, for economism and for ahistoricism. They suggest that Delphy, in particular, revises Marxist concepts, for instance of 'status' and 'class', in a way which suits her case, suggesting that without these reformulations Delphy would not be able to sustain her argument:

> Here, as often in her work, Delphy extricates herself from a difficult conceptual corner by inserting a sociological term (status) into her argument, thereby evading the theoretical consequences of the marxist vocabulary that she has borrowed. (Barrett and McIntosh, 1979: 98.)

However, they do not go on to establish that this slippage in Delphy's terminology has any serious consequences for her argument. I would suggest that while Delphy's vocabulary is rather loose, this does not affect the main logic or basis of her argument.

Molyneux (1979) argues that neither Delphy nor Harrison adequately specifies the elements of the domestic mode of production. She suggests that a social formation can have only one mode of production unless it is in transition from one mode to another, and this rules out the possibility of a domestic mode of production. However, Molyneux suggests that there can be only one mode of production in a social formation (except in times of transition) on *a priori* grounds citing Balibar's (Althusser and Balibar, 1977) abstract work in support. Yet there is a school of Marxist theories of development which argues that non-capitalist and capitalist modes of production can co-exist, and indeed that their present articulation determines the social formation of many Third World countries (cf. Taylor, 1979). There is considerable controversy in the literature on the question of whether and, if so how, two or more modes of production may coexist in the same social formation. Hindess and Hirst (1977) suggest that the slave mode of production must coexist with other modes of production and cannot exist on its own, while Bradby (1975) has argued that the feudal and capitalist modes of production are in articulation in parts of contemporary Latin America, and Taylor (1979) argues that most contemporary Third World countries are characterized by the articulation of different modes of production. There is a strong basis in the Marxist literature, especially among development theorists, for arguing that two modes of production may coexist in the same social formation, although it has been usual to consider the capitalist mode of production to be the dominant mode. Even Barrett and McIntosh, critics of Delphy's concept of a domestic mode of production, concede that

> a number of modes of production may co-exist within one social formation. (Barrett and McIntosh, 1979: 99.)

and thus disagree with Molyneux, further demonstrating the internal disagreement among Marxists on this point. Thus there is not a Marxist orthodoxy on modes of production to which Molyneux and Barrett and McIntosh can appeal.

Molyneux further criticizes Delphy for placing all women in one class, arguing that the material differences between a woman married to a member of the bourgeoisie and one married to a proletarian are too great for such a classification (Molyneux, 1979: 14). However, this ignores Delphy's argument that the relations of production are the same for each woman, even though the tasks they may do are different. Thus by the orthodox Marxist criteria, these women, having the same relationship to production, could be considered to share a common class position.

Molyneux and Barrett and McIntosh argue that the evidence Delphy uses to support her argument, being limited to the French peasant economy, is of such restricted significance that it cannot provide a basis for her position (Barrett and McIntosh, 1979: 100; Molyneux, 1979: 7). However, this mistakes the role that Delphy's analysis of French peasants plays in her article; Delphy's theoretical argument does not rest on these examples, rather these are only illustrations.

There are further problems with Delphy's analysis which are not considered by Molyneux or Barrett and McIntosh. In her account of the domestic mode of production Delphy does not adequately establish the reasons for its continued existence. That is, she does not explain why women remain in their exploited position in the domestic mode of production. This problem is particularly acute when the domestic mode of production is in articulation with the capitalist mode. The question is how to explain why women do not choose to earn their living by waged labour rather than by marrying and servicing a husband; it is necessary to explain why women remain in the household rather than escaping this patriarchal subordination by becoming wage labourers only. Delphy hints that women's subordinated position in the labour market is important in explaining why women choose marriage rather than paid work alone (1948: 97). However, she is ambiguous on the issue of the direction of the causal relationship between women's position in marriage and in the labour market. On the one hand, she suggests that marriage causes women's position in the labour market (p. 96), and on the other that the link is reversed (p. 20). The reasons for this difficulty are that Delphy neither adequately deals with the interrelationship between the domestic and capitalist modes of production, nor does she adequately examine sets of patriarchal relations outside the household. Thus she omits to consider the role of patriarchal relations in the workplace in pushing women back to the domestic economy for their livelihood. Yet, I would argue that an understanding of patriarchal relations in paid work is essential for understanding why women have not more widely entered the labour market, why conditions and pay are so poor relative to those of men, and thus crucial for the explanation of why women remain in the household.

While I have accepted some of the criticisms of Delphy described here others have been rejected. Delphy's critics incorrectly make a leap from accurately pointing out some problems in Delphy's analysis to assuming that this invalidates any attempt to build a theory of patriarchy as a social system in which men typically dominate women and which is autonomous from the capitalist mode of production. While there are problems in Delphy's work, I would argue that it is nevertheless possible to overcome these without throwing out the concept of the patriarchal mode of production, let alone the concept of patriarchy. Delphy's materialist feminist analysis is an important and creative application of the Marxist method to women's oppression.

The second type of dualist position, that of patriarchal relations coexisting in all spheres and levels of society, is the one I want to argue for here, although existing formulations have some problems. Hartmann presents a powerful analysis of gender inequality in terms of the interrelationship of patriarchy and capitalism. She argues that most Marxist analyses of women's subordination have focused one-sidedly on women's relation to capitalism and have substantially ignored the independent role of male interest in the oppression of women (1979b, 1981). Patriarchy and capitalism, she argues, should be recognized as separate structures which have historically had important effects on each other. Whilst they are analytically independent, they should be seen, in contemporary western society, to operate in partnership. She suggests that patriarchy has its base in men's control over women's labour and builds this into her definition:

> We can usefully define patriarchy as a set of social relations between men, which have a material base, and which, though hierarchical, establish or create interdependence and solidarity among men and enable them to dominate women. (Hartmann, 1979b: 11.)

Job segregation by sex and the family wage, she argues, are important aspect of ways in which patriarchy and capitalism have interacted. She argues (1979a) that men have organized together to exclude women from much paid work primarily, though not exclusively, through the device of job segregation by sex. This serves to lower the wages of women in the jobs that remain open to them and thus to pressurize women into remaining dependents on men within the family. Men demand a family wage which completes this vicious circle, in which women are pushed away from paid work and into unpaid domestic work from which men benefit. Both men and capital are seen to gain from this arrangement. Hartmann argues that, with the family wage, capital and patriarchy find a mutual accommodation.

I am in broad agreement with the main features of Hartmann's analysis, in particular with her view that patriarchy and capitalism are independent yet interacting social structures. However, she is ambiguous about the actual base of patriarchy. The main thrust of her argument is that the base is men's control over women's labour.

> The material base upon which patriarchy rests lies most fundamentally in men's control over women's labour power. (Hartmann, 1979b: 11.)

This is the main concern of Hartmann in most of her analysis. Yet in some places this notion of control is so broad as to be rather vague and she sometimes suggests that other things are more fundamental to, and indeed underlie, this control. For instance, she sees men's control of women's sexuality as important, and suggests that monogamous heterosexual marriage is the basis both of the control of women's labour power and of their sexuality. Other social institutions have their importance, such as 'churches, sports, clubs, unions, armies, factories, offices, health centres, the media etc.' in teaching patriarchal forms of behaviour (1979b: 12). Her position then is that the base of patriarchal relations is very broad, and thus her theory becomes rather loose:

> The material base of patriarchy, then, does not rest solely on childrearing in the family, but on all the social structures that enable men to control women's labour. (Hartmann, 1979b: 13.)

Here we see that the basis of patriarchy identified by Hartmann in this piece of writing could be almost anything.

This looseness is very different from her analysis elsewhere, (1979a), where she emphatically states that job segregation is the basis of men's control over women's labour. Here she argues that male organization, especially in the workplace, which excludes women from much paid work, is the crucial underpinning of patriarchy. Job segregation leads to lower wages for women and hence pressure on them to remain in subordinate positions in the family:

> Job segregation by sex, I will argue, is the primary mechanism in capitalist society that maintains the superiority of men over women, because it enforces lower wages for women in the labour market. (Hartmann, 1979a: 208.)

Thus we see an area of inconsistency and ambiguity within her writings on the question of the basis of patriarchy.

A further problem is to be found in her conceptualization of patriarchy itself. For instance, while she argues that patriarchy is just as important and as materially based as capitalism, she considers only capitalism to be a mode of production. This position is inconsistent, and she does not justify it.

Hartmann's definition of patriarchy poses some problems as well, for she builds into this definition the explanation of patriarchy that she favours. She thus provides no conceptual space to raise issues such as whether patriarchy does have a material base, despite the contentious nature of such an assertion. Further, Hartmann defines patriarchy as a set of social relations primarily between men, not between men and women, and this is misleading.

Hartmann pays insufficient attention to the tension and conflict between capitalism and patriarchy, seeing these primarily as things of the past, with the current situation being characterized by partnership and accommodation. 'In capitalist societies a healthy and strong partnership exists between patriarchy and capitalism' (Hartmann, 1979b: 13). Thus she sees the family wage and job segregation as relatively well-established systems in contemporary society rather than as part of a continuing struggle. However, as I shall argue more fully later, it is incorrect to see patriarchy and capitalism as articulating so harmoniously. While Hartmann does note the difference of interest between men and capitalists over women's labour this is not given the priority it deserves in her analysis.

Hartmann's work is a creative and sophisticated attempt to synthesise the analyses by Marxists and feminists without subsuming one to the other; it is the most successful attempt yet. It is a most important advance in the theory of gender inequality because of its recognition of patriarchy and capitalism as two separate structures with mutual effects. However, she overstates the degree of harmony between the two system, forms an inadequate concept of patriarchy and has an underdeveloped account of the variations in the relations between patriarchy and capitalism.

Young (1981) argues that Hartmann's analysis is flawed by problems common to all dualist analyses. She argues that all such theories fail to establish the nature of the supposed separation between patriarchy and capitalism in a satisfactory manner. That, she suggests, is an inherent and insuperable problem for dualist accounts of gender inequality. The only way that dualists can separate the two systems, argues Young, is the inherently flawed way of the first grouping of dualists (e.g. Mitchell), discussed above: by allocating different spheres of society to each system. Yet women's oppression is not confined to one or two spheres of society in this way. Further, those writers who conceive the sphere of patriarchy as being other than production mistakenly cede the most important sphere of society to capitalism; this makes the analysis of gender inequality ahistorical, and universalizes women's oppression.

Young goes on to suggest that Hartmann only manages to overcome these problems of the allocation of patriarchy and capitalism to separate spheres by locating them both ultimately in the same sphere: that of labour. However, Young claims, this means that Hartmann is then unable to distinguish adequately between the two systems. The problem with this second version, according to Young, is that it is inherently not possible to adequately separate patriarchal from capitalist relations within the material level:

> If, as Hartmann states, patriarchal social relations in contemporary capitalism are not confined to the family, but also exist in the capitalist workplace and other institutions outside the family, it is hard to see by what principle we can separate these patriarchal relations from the social relations of capitalism . . . It seems reasonable, however, to admit that if patriarchy and capitalism are manifest in identical social and economic structures they belong to *one* system, not two. (Young, 1981: 47, her emphasis.)

Dualists then have, at best, a choice of insuperable difficulties: either they allocate capitalism and patriarchy to separate spheres and are unable to deal with aspects of women's oppression which do not fall into the allocated sphere, or, if both systems are seen as rooted in production, then there is no basis for separating them.

I think that Young has identified a real problem in certain texts which have tried to argue that gender inequality is the result of both patriarchy and capitalism. However, I do not believe that this is the insuperable problem she believes it to be, rather that it is a contingent problem in particular texts. Thus she is right to suggest that an analysis of gender relations in terms of a set of patriarchal relations which are confined to one sphere and a set of capitalist relations which are confined to another is problematic, and that those texts which try to overcome this problem by arguing that both capitalist and patriarchal relations coexist in the same institution have a problem in trying to distinguish between the two. However, just because a task is difficult that is no reason for declaring it inherently impossible.

At issue is how to provide the basis of the distinction between patriarchy and capitalism. I would suggest that the search for an institutional basis of the separation is misplaced. Rather it is the distinctiveness of the social relations of patriarchy and capitalism which is the crucial means of separating them. Patriarchy is distinctive in being a system of interrelated structures through which men exploit women, while capitalism is a system in which capital expropriates wage labourers. It is the mode of exploitation which constitutes the central difference between the two systems. The distinctiveness of the patriarchal system is marked by the social relations which enable men to exploit women; in the racist system it is the social relations which enable one ethnic group to dominate another; in capitalism it is the social relations which enable capital to expropriate labour. These social relations exist at all levels of the social formation, whether this is characterized as economic, political and ideological, or as economy, civil society and the state or whatever. These points are developed more fully in chapter 3.

Young's own solution begs the question at stake. She argues for the centrality of the concept of the gender division of labour as a way of transcending the dualism of the patriarchy and capitalism formulation. Yet this is surely one of the phenomena to be explained, not a theoretical concept capable of use as an explanation. It is merely a redescription of the problem in a fairly empiricist way. Further, while she suggests that other elements such as the biology of reproduction and psychological elements of gender identity also contribute, it is unclear why these are not part of the basis of patriarchy rather than extra, albeit essential, aspects. Why should they stand to one side?

Young identifies real problems in many dualist texts. However, she is incorrect to see these problems as inherent in the dualist project, rather than merely contingent problems in existing formulations. I hope in the rest of the book to demonstrate an approach which overcomes the problems Young has identified.

Ethnicity and Gender

A further issue, which is dealt with inadequately by most of the writers so far discussed, is the significance of ethnic inequality for the analysis of gender relations. There are two main points which emerge in writings about this: firstly, that gender inequality takes different forms among different ethnic groups and thus that generalizations about its nature should not be made on the basis of the experience of white western women alone; and, secondly, that racism, and more broadly ethnic inequality, affects the forms of gender inequality itself; that is, it is not merely that forms of inequality are different, but that their intersection creates further issues of relevance.

The first issue is taken up by writers such as Carby (1982), Davis (1981), Hooks (1982), Joseph (1981), Moraga and Anzaldua (1981), Parmar (1982) and Amos and Parmar (1984), who argue strongly that white feminists have not produced an adequate analysis of gender inequality because they have not taken ethnic inequality into account. They argue that the major sites of oppression are not the same for black and white women. The family is seen to have a different place in gender relations among whites than among peoples of Afro-Caribbean origin, since in the latter case the notion of dependent housewife, which has sometimes been considered pivotal in analyses of gender inequality, has little purchase in the face of the high proportion of single-parent households headed by women and the high rate of labour force participation by such women. Further, at certain moments the family has been so important as a site of resistance to racist oppression that it is inappropriate to see it as a major site of oppression of black women.

These writers have argued further that in so far as the specificity of the position of women of colour has been taken into account it has been done inadequately. For instance, the focus of western feminists on clitoridectomy and arranged marriages, when women of colour are being considered, is seen as merely sensationalism, detracting from attention being paid to much more serious issues, and indeed as encouraging of racist attitudes through the representation of such practices as 'barbaric'. These latter problems are sometimes the result of a misplaced and unsubstantiated notion of 'progress' in which western civilization is taken to be the most advanced society in terms of gender relations.

The strongest theoretical claim of some of the writers is that it is not appropriate to take the family as a crucial element in the subordination of women. The issue is whether the extent of variation in the place of the family in gender relations means that the family is not always an important structure in a patriarchal system, or whether this diversity can be incorporated as a variation within the model? There certainly are differences in the form of the household and family by ethnic group (although variations within each group are also important): the most extreme sexual division of labour and regulation of marriage partner is often thought to be found among Asian, especially Pakistani and Bangladeshi families; among people of Afro-Caribbean descent one-parent households headed by women appear more often than in the other major ethnic groups (18 per cent of West Indian and only 4 per cent of Asian and 3 per cent of white households are single-parent families (Brown, 1984: 37)). It should also be noted that the white family and household pattern has varied over time and by class, with the middle-class Victorians having a pattern more like the Asian families of today, and that the one-parent female-headed household more often found among people of Afro-Caribbean descent is becoming increasingly common among the white population today. (Are native whites moving from an Asian to an Afro-Caribbean pattern of household?)

However, I would argue that while these constitute significant differences in the form of the family, it has not been demonstrated that the family is not an important site of the oppression of women. The arrangement of marriages by parents may be no worse a method of selection of a woman's husband than either rating and dating or romantic fantasy, but it is not clear that it is better, or that it tackles the problems inherent in marriage for women. Raising children without a spouse may relieve the mother of certain forms of interpersonal oppression, but the grinding poverty which typically ensues is no liberation into equality either. Further, while a husband and wife may form a mutually supportive alliance against certain features of racism, it has not been shown that that partnership is one of equality.

Writers on ethnic inequality and gender have also discussed the importance of properly analysing the intersection between these two forms of inequality. The relationship between the two is especially important when issues concerning migration of workers are considered (cf. Phizacklea, 1983).

These writers have demonstrated the importance of paying serious consideration to ethnic relations in order adequately to understand the full dynamics of gender inequality. Chapter 3 will develop the issue of how to theorize ethnicity within my approach to gender relations as part of the overall task of specifying the outlines of a satisfactory model of patriarchy which draws on the strengths of existing analyses while overcoming their weaknesses.

3
Towards a New Theory of Patriarchy

The essential skeleton of my analysis of gender relations in contemporary western societies is constituted by a system of patriarchal relations in articulation with a system of capitalist relations–the fifth approach outlined in chapter 2. The actual pattern of gender inequality should be seen as the outcome of the interaction of these two systems together with that of racism. Indeed, I would argue that patriarchy is never the only mode in a society but always exists in articulation with another, such as capitalism.

Whereas the elements of the capitalist system have received much attention from social theorists, those of patriarchy have not. Thus I shall devote most of the space available to developing the model of patriarchal relations, and only a small part to capitalist ones. Existing models of patriarchy have been criticized in chapter 2 for being incapable of analysing variations in the forms of patriarchy, either because they identified only one base to patriarchal relations, or because they suggested that so many things were relevant to the analysis and in such an unstructured way that they became merely descriptive. Hence the model that I shall construct here will be composed of a limited number of relatively autonomous structures, with the relative importance of each specified. The key sets of patriarchal relations are to be found in domestic work, paid work, the state and male violence and sexuality; while other practices in civil society have a limited significance. I shall argue that the social relations in domestic work should be characterized as a patriarchal mode of production and that this is particularly significant in the determination of gender relations. However, when patriarchy is in articulation with the capitalist rather than other modes of production, then patriarchal relations in paid work are of central importance to the maintenance of the system. The patriarchal relations in the state, male violence, sexuality and other aspects of civil society, while having a certain degree of autonomy and significance, have, I shall argue, less importance than the first two sets of patriarchal relations mentioned. However, the relative importance of these sets of patriarchal relations varies. Elements are more or less important according to the nature of the other system of social relations (such as the capitalist mode of production) with which patriarchy is in articulation. The different sets of patriarchal relations should be seen as related to each other; but not in any simple manner. Together they compose a complex system of patriarchy.

I have argued that the sets of patriarchal relations are relatively autonomous, and that the patriarchal divisions of labour in the household and in paid work are the most important in a society characterized by the articulation of patriarchy and capitalism. I shall spell out the relations between each set in more detail below, arguing that some of these sets of patriarchal relations are necessary conditions of patriarchy, while others are not. In addition to the two sets concerned with the organization of work, I would argue that patriarchal relations in sexuality, in particular the institution of heterosexuality, are necessary to the continuance of patriarchy, while the other sets are only contingently so.

I define patriarchy as a system of interrelated social structures through which men exploit women. This formulation is deliberately designed to avoid the problems of building an explanation of what I am trying to explain into my definition of that object (a problem identified earlier in Hartmann's work). The definition has a gender aspect but no generational component for the same reasons, that is, the question of whether men dominate women as men or through their social position as fathers should not be closed off at the point of definition. The definition refers to a system of social relations rather than individuals, since it is presumed that it is at the level of a social system that gender relations may be explained, not that of individual men, nor that of discrete social institutions.

The Patriarchal Division of Labour in the Household

Its significance

The significance of arguing that there is a patriarchal mode of production is that it establishes a basis to patriarchal relations in contemporary Britain which is analytically independent from capitalism. While it is clear that domestic labour is a distinctive form of labour, that, in itself, is insufficient to establish the independence of patriarchal relations from capitalism. Such autonomy can only be established if it can be determined that patriarchal relations form a system, and are not confined to discrete occurrences in specific social institutions at isolated points in time and space.

The concept of the patriarchal mode of production is essential to a theory of the exploitation of women by men independently of the exploitation of proletarians by capitalists. Remedies are needed for the flaws in existing conceptualizations of this mode of production; in particular for the very loose formulation of Delphy's theory (1977) and her omission of several important sets of patriarchal relations, and for the major problem in Harrison's theory (1973b)–that it does not adequately treat the exploitation of women by men within the household. Thus a central part of the task at hand is to establish a rigorous specification of the elements of the patriarchal mode of production and to build the exploitation of women by men into this as a central component. A further issue requiring consideration is that of whether this analysis applies only to native white women, or is of equal or different pertinence to gender relations among people of colour.

I have argued that the most important aspects of gender relations should be understood to result from the articulation of patriarchal and capitalist structures. This should be modified by a recognition of the importance of structures of ethnic inequality. Just as gender inequality is not derivable from capitalist relations, so I also wish to argue that structures of ethnic inequality are not to be reduced to those of capitalism. There is a degree of independence of the dynamics of racist practices from capitalism, and from gender relations. In practice, however the dynamic of ethnic inequality is quite tightly bound up with the development of capitalist relations. In this I follow the approach of Phizacklea and Miles (1980), Rex (1983) and others.

The elements of the patriarchal mode of production

I would suggest that within the patriarchal mode of production the producing class is composed of housewives or domestic labourers, while the non-producing and exploiting class is composed of husbands. The part of the means of production which can be identified as the objects of labour consists of the exhausted people for whom the domestic labourer works to replenish their labour power, that is the exhausted husband, and the children, if any. The part of the means of production which can be identified as the instruments of labour consists of the woman's body, especially in the sense of her reproductive capacity, the house and its contents. It is the relationship between these elements which comprises the patriarchal mode of production.

So we see that the work of appropriation of nature, in which the domestic labourer is engaged, is that of the production of labour power. This is generational production of children, as well as the day to day production of the labour power of her husband.

The exploitation, or expropriation, which is taking place is the expropriation of the surplus labour of the domestic labourer by the husband. As in any other exploitative mode of production this expropriation is made possible because there is a particular way in which the producer does not have complete possession of the means of production. A crucial aspect of the work of the domestic labourer is the labour she performs on the exhausted husband in order to replenish or produce his labour power. The exhausted husband is one of the objects of the domestic labour and therefore part of the means of production. The domestic labourer does not have possession of the husband who enters the labour process as an exhausted person whose labour power she replenishes. She thus has no possession of this part of the means of production and as a consequence does not own this part of the product of her labour. She is separated from the product of her labour and has no control over it while the husband always has possession of this labour power which the wife has produced. She is separated from it on every level: physically; in the ability to use it; legally, ideologically, etc. The husband uses and exchanges that labour power with an employer as if it were his own, even though the wife laboured to produce it. He sells this labour power to an employer and receives a wage which is less than the value of the goods he has produced. He gives a portion of this wage to the wife for the maintenance of the family, and retains some for himself. The portion allocated to the wife's use on herself is typically less than the part of the wage allocated for the use of the husband on himself. In addition the housewife typically works longer hours than the man. Thus she performs more labour and receives less than he does. If the wife's level is taken to be the base, then the extra which he has may be regarded as the wife's surplus labour which he has expropriated. He is able to do this because he has control over the labour power she has produced and hence over the wage he received from the capitalist exchange for it. Therefore the domestic labourer is exploited.

A key characteristic of these relations of production is that they exist as personalized relations between individuals. They are privatized relations involving individual contact with one husband. Thus the forces of production are limited by this situation to a fairly primitive level, relative to productive forces in the other mode of production. Forces of production which would require large scale co-operation, and socialization of the labour process are ruled out. They must remain on this small-scale, privatized level which involves duplication of these tasks many times over. This is technically inefficient and can be seen as a consequence of these relations of production.

The problem of articulation with other modes of production

The patriarchal mode of production necessarily exists in articulation with another mode of production. The husband uses his labour power which has been produced by the domestic labourer within this other mode. Because he has control over his labour power he has possession of the proceeds from putting it into action. Within the patriarchal mode of production, the husband does not use the proceeds of his labour power to compensate the domestic labourer fully for the work she puts into producing it.

It is crucial to be able to explain why the woman does not set up on her own to produce lower power and why she remains in the home to produce the labour power of her husband. I would argue that the reason for this varies according to the mode of production with which the patriarchal mode is in articulation. When the patriarchal mode articulates with the capitalist mode, the primary mechanism which ensures that women will serve their husbands is their exclusion from paid work on the same terms as men. Patriarchal relations within waged work are crucial in preventing women from entering that work as freely as men, and are reinforced by patriarchal state policies. However, other sets of patriarchal relations are also important. When the patriarchal mode of production articulates with other modes, other levels of the social formation become critical for the continuation of the patriarchal one. Under feudalism, for instance, fertility and reproduction are of critical significance (cf. Middleton, 1981). This dynamic articulation with capitalism will be further explored later.

I do not wish to suggest that the patriarchal mode of production has any autonomous laws of development. On the contrary, I would suggest that the other mode of production with which the patriarchal mode is in articulation is particularly important in governing the nature of change. This does not discredit the concept of patriarchal mode of production since the central element in this is not its laws of motion, but rather that of the extraction of surplus. It is the highly distinctive method of extraction of surplus within patriarchy (which plays a key role in the determination of other gender relations) which is the basis of the claim that there is a patriarchal mode of production.

Patriarchal Relations in Paid Work

The patriarchal division of labour in the household does not completely determine the form of patriarchal relations in a particular society; other sets of patriarchal relations also have significance. A most important set of patriarchal relations when the patriarchal mode of production is in articulation with capitalism is that in paid work. As I have already argued, patriarchal relations in paid work are necessary if not sufficient, to the retention of women as unpaid labourers in the household. The control of women's access to paid work is maintained primarily by patriarchal relations in the workplace and in the state, as well as by those in the household.

The form of this control has varied with time and place to a significant extent. The forms of control include: non-admittance of women to forms of training, such as apprenticeships and university degrees which are a condition of practising a particular trade (see for instance, Andrews, 1918; Braybon, 1981; Cockburn, 1981, 1983; Ehrenreich and English, 1979; Oakley, 1976); the non-admittance of women to certain occupations (Home Office, 1929); the restriction of the percentage of women in certain occupations (e.g. the quota on women which has historically been imposed by medical schools); discrimination in hiring practices which reduces or eliminates the number of women in a particular occupation (Bergmann, 1980a; Snell, 1979); the ejection of women from an occupation, or the reduction in their rights to remain in it on marriage (Scharf, 1980); the sacking of women, and in particular married women, before men in situations of redundancy (Mackay et al., 1971); the sacking of part-timers, who are almost exclusively married women, before full-timers in situations of redundancy; practices such as 'last in, first-out', the indirect consequence of which is that women go before men (Connelly, 1978); the ejection of women from certain occupations by legislative action (Andrews, 1918; Braybon, 1981; Humphries, 1981); the restriction on the amount of certain kinds of paid work that women can do, with implications for their entry to those occupations at all, such as the reduction in women's hours in the Factory Acts of the nineteenth century (Smelser, 1959). These exclusionary practices fall into two types: restriction of entry to particular occupations; and ways of ejecting women, rather than men, from certain occupations. They exist in varying forms of directness, from rigid rules which are consistently enforced, such as the ban on women taking degrees at universities in the UK before the late nineteenth century, to more indirect forms which may not always produce the same effect, such as the 'last-in, first-out' practice in redundancy situations.

The agents carrying out these exclusionary practices include: male-dominated trade unions (Hartmann, 1979a, 1981); other male-dominated organizations (Oakley, 1976; Ehrenreich and English, 1979); prejudiced employers (Bergmann, 1980a); and the state (Andrews, 1918; Humphries, 1981). The immediate social and historical context in which these practices have existed is also immensely varied.

Most existing analyses of patriarchy (with the primary exception of Hartmann) have taken patriarchal relations in the workplace insufficiently into account. Yet an adequate analysis of patriarchy must incorporate this as a highly significant element. These forms of exclusionary practice may be seen as a form of social closure (cf. Parkin, 1979; Kreckel, 1980). They are both a product of, and themselves create, highly significant divisions among paid workers. They are to a considerable extent a result of patriarchal divisions elsewhere in society, especially in the household, but cannot be reduced to these. There is an extent to which the struggles around these practices have their own autonomy. However, the resources which are brought to these struggles are related to the resources available to the competing groups in different areas of social life.

Patriarchal relations in the workplace and the state as well as the family, are central to the determination of the position of women in paid work. Capital and patriarchy have rival interests in women's labour, and the position that women hold in paid work cannot be understood without an analysis of the tension between the two. There are theoretical reasons for the importance of paid work for contemporary gender relations: paid work is a crucial site in capitalist relations and this is transmitted to the relations between patriarchal structures when the system of patriarchy is in articulation with capitalism.

The Patriarchal State

The state is a site of patriarchal relations which is necessary to patriarchy as a whole. The state represents patriarchal as well as capitalist interests and furthers them in its actions. This conception of the state as patriarchal as well as capitalist runs counter to most other analyses of it; most accounts do not consider gender relations at all, focusing instead on class relations within capitalism and the relations between these and the state (e.g. Gough, 1975; Jessop, 1982; Müller and Neusüss, 1975; O'Connor, 1973; Poulantzas, 1973). These accounts of the state are inadequate in that they fail to take into account either the impact of gender inequality and women's political struggles on the state, or the significance of state actions on gender relations. These omissions are serious both because these are significant dimensions of state action, and because it leads to a flawed analysis of the issues that these writers purport to address. For instance, an analysis of the development of the welfare state which does not take into account the role of women's political struggles as women (cf. Banks, 1981; Mark-Lawson et al., 1985; Middleton, 1977) would be seriously in error as to the political forces which were operating in that situation. Yet this has been a common practice in many writers on the development of the welfare state (Fraser, 1973; Roberts, 1960).

However, there have been important, if rare, attempts to seriously analyse the relationship between the state and the position of women (Burstyn, 1983; Hanmer, 1978; Wilson, 1977). McIntosh (1978) suggests that the state upholds the oppression of women by supporting a form of household in which women provide unpaid domestic services for a male. She argues that the state should be viewed as capitalist, since it is acting to maintain the capitalist mode of production. Capitalism benefits from a particular form of family which ensures the cheap reproduction of labour power and the availability of women as a reserve army of labour. She suggests, however, that the family is not the ideal form for the reproduction of labour power for two reasons. Firstly, the ratio of earner to dependent is widely variable in actual families and thus some families cannot survive on earned income. The state steps in to shore up the family structure in those instances when it would otherwise fail. Secondly, families by themselves do not necessarily produce the right number of children to meet capitalist requirements for population size, so sometimes explicit population policies are introduced to ensure the maintenance of its members. Thus, for McIntosh, the state's support for the oppression of women is indirect, not direct, since it is through the maintenance of this family form that the state acts to the detriment of women.

While McIntosh does point to various contradictions in capitalism and in state policy her argument nonetheless hinges on the notion that the family is maintained because it is functional for capitalism. This position is problematic in that it does not take sufficient account of the benefits that men derive from the contemporary family structure, and of the divergence between patriarchal and capitalist interests, such as whether women should stay at home or take paid work. Further, the analysis pays insufficient attention to the struggles that take place on the political level which need to be accorded greater autonomy in the analysis.

I would argue that, when patriarchy is in articulation with capitalism, the state should, be seen as both patriarchal and capitalist. Such a dualist conception of the state is only a problem if the state is incorrectly considered to act in a monolithic manner. Much of the recent literature on the capitalist state (see, for instance, Jessop, 1982; Poulantzas, 1973; Urry, 1981a) sees state actions as the result of the political struggle of competing classes and class fractions, so one more set of competing interests is not an insuperable conceptual problem. The state should be considered equally an arena for political struggle and an actor intervening in particular situations. Its actions should be seen as the result of the struggles between different interests. It should not be seen as the instrument of a dominant class, or class fraction.

In a theory like this, it is possible to conceive of the state as both patriarchal and capitalist. Its specific actions in any instance are the outcome of the struggle on the political level of the competing interests involved in both patriarchal and capitalist relations. The state should not be reduced to, or derived from, the economic level, but rather political level should be seen to have considerable autonomy (cf. on the capitalist state Urry, 1981; Jessop, 1982). Any theory of a patriarchal and capitalist state must analyse the struggles of patriarchal and capitalist interests as they are represented on the political level, while also tracing the links to other levels, especially the economic.

The intervention of the state has been, at certain times, of crucial significance in the shaping of patriarchal relations in society. Yet at the same time, it is not the basis of patriarchal power. Rather its actions should be seen as the outcome of the representation of patriarchal interests which are mediated in the political process. While the actions of the state are linked to the economic level of patriarchy, they have a level of autonomy in which the actual outcome of conflicting interests is mediated by conflicts and negotiation at the political level.

Women, who are subordinated within the productive process, have little access to forms of political representation. This is partly because of their lack of power in the sphere of production, and partly because the particular forms of the state and its mode of functioning act to suppress the effective representation of women's interests. In terms of the recent state in a society in which patriarchy articulates with capitalism, these problems of representation have been exacerbated by the late granting of the franchise to women and the formation of the major political parties along lines of division representing the interests of the classes of the capitalist rather than the patriarchal system. Thus there is a limited historic tradition of women's participation in parliamentary politics compounded by the absence of political parties organized around issues of gender relations.

The state acts to support patriarchal relations in a variety of ways. These include: the limiting of women's access to paid work (e.g. the Dilution Acts, cf Andrews, 1918; Braybon, 1981; 'protective' legislation, cf. EOC, 1979); the criminalization of forms of fertility control (e.g. at certain times and places abortion, contraception–cf.

Greenwood and Young, 1976; Gittins, 1982; Gordon, 1977, 1979); support for the institution of marriage through, for example, the co-habitation rule (Fairbairn, 1979), discriminatory income maintenance (Land, 1976), and by regulating marriage and divorce (Barker, 1978; Holcombe, 1983; Smart, 1984); actions against some sexual relations through, for instance, criminalizing male homosexual relations in some periods (Weeks, 1977), and denying custody of children to lesbian mothers; actions against radical dissent, for instance, in the coercive response to the suffrage movement (Morrell, 1981).

One example of the patriarchal actions of the state is that which enabled male workers in the First World War to ensure their re-entry into the relatively highly paid and skilled engineering jobs that they ceded to women for the duration of the hostilities. The economic pressures in this situation would have led the employers to continue to employ the cheaper women workers, if they had been able. However, male workers such as the engineers had sufficient power in conjunction with the government to prevent this from occurring. These men had power in the labour process in that only they could effectively train new workers, and this enabled them to have the power to refuse to train new female employees. The men also had political power in that their interests were represented in the state to a greater extent that that of women, and they were organized in a powerful and effective body in the Amalgamated Society of Engineers. Women, by contrast, had little economic or political power, not even having the right to vote, at this time.

Here we see both the limits and the significance of patriarchal state power. There were limits in that it required other bases of patriarchal power to mobilize the state's resources on behalf of patriarchal interests; and significance in that it prevented the erosion of that form of patriarchal power which was based in the exclusion of women from the skilled engineering trades.

Another example of the patriarchal nature of the state is its response (or rather lack of response) to male violence against women in contemporary Britain. Here women's lack of access to state power ensures that men who rape, batter and otherwise molest women will rarely be punished by the criminal justice system. Women's interests are not sufficiently represented in the state to force any consistency between the rhetoric–that the state attempts to protect everyone against illegal violence–and the reality of widespread male violence against women.

Minor modifications to the state's practices on this issue of men's violence to women have taken place in times of feminist agitation. For instance, in 1976 the Sexual Offenses Amendment Act was passed with the express purpose of giving a raped woman anonymity and of preventing her sexual history being discussed in court. A further example is the introduction, at the end of the nineteenth century, of violence as a sufficient reason for judicial separation. Both these reforms occurred in periods of feminist activity, which led to an increase in the representation of women's interests at the level of the state on the issue of male violence. This is an example of the relative autonomy of the state from the economy and of the significance of events at the political level affecting state actions. But again, there are limits to the significance of the state, in that no serious possibility of effective state action against violent men is possible while the material basis of patriarchy exists.

This lack of prosecution of men who are violent towards women (cf. Toner, 1977; Hanmer and Saunders, 1984) raises important questions as to the traditional definition of the state as a body which has the monopoly of legitimate violence in a given territory (cf. Weber, 1947). I would argue that the state *de facto* accepts male violence against women as legitimate, despite its being carried out by agents who are not usually considered as part of the state apparatus. According to the traditional definition, these violent men must then be seen as agents of the state in carrying out this violence. I would suggest that an alternate approach might be to modify the definition of the state so that it is no longer defined as having the monopoly on legitimate violence. The first position is problematic in that it involves a movement away from the notion of the state as a centralized cohesive body. I would suggest that this is central to the notion of the state. Instead the notion of having the monopoly on legitimate violence should be modified in recognition of men's unpunished violence against women.

Male Violence as a Patriarchal Structure

Male violence should be regarded as a further significant aspect of patriarchal relations; that is, systematic institutionalized, male violence against women should be regarded as a patriarchal structure. The types of violence include: rape, sexual assault, battering and sexual harassment, although this list is not exhaustive and there are real problems in drawing correct boundaries (cf. Hanmer and Saunders, 1983; Law Enforcement Assistance Administration, 1972; MacKinnon, 1982; London Rape Crisis Centre, 1984; Toner, 1977). This institutionalized violence is a relatively autonomous patriarchal structure with some degree of effectivity back on the other structures, but it is not the basis of patriarchy. Conventional conceptions of male violence as the acts of individual sick men are incorrect, as are also those accounts which see this violence as the basis of patriarchy. Instead, male violence against women should be seen as a systematic phenomenon, which is largely an effect of other patriarchal relations, but which has a degree of influence on them in return. While this violence is not necessary for the maintenance of other patriarchal relations it undoubtedly assists them. In addition, the legal violence of the patriarchal state (in the police, prisons, army, etc.) plays a further role in sustaining patriarchy.

The conventional accounts of most male violence against women see it as the individual acts of particular sick men. For instance, West et al. (1978) argue that rape is the result of impaired masculinity in a few men. They suggest that if these men had had normal childhoods and had learnt a normal form of masculinity then these rapes would not have occurred. Similarly, Pizzey (1974) argues that the battering of women by the men that they live with is a consequence of these men having been brought up in homes in which their fathers were violent to their mothers. This, she believes leads to damage to their characters. Pizzey suggests that the battering of women in these domestic situations could be prevented if this cycle of violence was broken for one generation. She does not consider any other sources of this violence.

These accounts are seriously flawed, both methodologically and theoretically. Both studies are flawed by the use of small, unrepresentative samples and the absence of control groups. Gelles (1972) who did use a control group for his study of wife battering was not able to show that all men who battered had come from a violent home, nor that all men who came from a violent home went on to batter.

The more serious problem in these accounts is their astonishing blindness to the multitude of ways in which men in contemporary society learn to be violent. Rather than violence among men being so unusual as to be a sign of mental sickness, there is evidence that it is endemic (Martin, 1976; Dobash and Dobash, 1980; Kirkpatrick and Kanin, 1957; Hanmer and Saunders, 1984). Although it is difficult to obtain an accurate quantification of the amount of male violence against women, nevertheless there are clear indications that it is sufficiently widespread to undermine these 'mental illness' theories. Official criminal statistics on violence against women are widely acknowledged to be a serious underestimate of the number of such incidents (cf. Hanmer and Saunders, 1984; London Rape Crisis Centre, 1984; Walby et al., 1983). For instance, Brownmiller suggests that only between one in five and one in 20 rapes are reported to the police (Brownmiller, 1976: 175) while even the US Department of Justice considers that two to three rapes go unreported for each one reported (Curtis, 1976). A British community study of violence found that 59 per cent of the women interviewed had experienced one or more incidents of behaviour which was violent, threatening or sexually harassing in the previous year (Hanmer and Saunders, 1983: 30). Thus it is incorrect to see violence against women as the occasional product of a sick male mind, rather it is a widespread social institution.

Boys and men are continually exposed to legitimations of violent behaviour by men, both in indirect ways through the media and in more direct ways such as violent sports and in the military training many men receive (cf. Brownmiller, 1975; Fasteau, 1975; Klemmack et al., 1976; Jackson, 1978b; Pleck and Sawyer, 1974; Tolson, 1977). In the face of such a barrage of legitimations it is extraordinary to suggest that violence in men is a product of individual sickness rather than as embedded in their upbringing and systematically related to gender inequality in society.

Some writers have tried to focus on forms of inequality other than gender in order to explain men's violence against women (e.g. Steinmetz and Straus, 1975). Amir (1971) suggests that one pattern which may be discerned in rape is that it is perpetuated by subcultures of violence which are found predominantly among lower-class and black men, rather than middle- or upper-class, or white men. He suggests that this can be related to the frustrations experienced by these groups, which he sees as disadvantaged in society. Thus he suggests that rape may be traced to class and race inequality. However, the evidence used by Amir to support his account is rather dubious since it is based on police records, which are widely acknowledged to be biased against blacks and working-class people. Further there is evidence (Pizzey, 1974; O'Brien, 1975) that men who are violent to women are widely drawn across social division. Amir's argument must be regarded as dubious in the light of a wider review of the evidence.

Some writers have argued that male violence is an integral part of gender relations in contemporary society, and have gone on to argue that it is the underlying basis of this inequality. (Brownmiller, 1975; Hanmer, 1978; Russell, 1975). Similarly, Goode (1971) has argued that force underpins social relations in the family as in other social systems. Thus both Brownmiller and Hanmer believe that male violence against women underpins all other forms of patriarchal relations. Brownmiller argues that rape is the basis of men's control over women (see above), while Hanmer argues that all forms of violence together with the threat of it constitute the basis of men's control over women. Hanmer suggests that this violence acts both to exclude women from access to particular things, such as certain physical spaces, social, economic and political groups, and also to compel the performance of certain tasks, especially domestic services. The threat of violence, she argues, forces women into dependence upon those very people, men, who most threaten them. Hanmer goes on to trace the relationship between this violence and other social institutions. Thus she argues that the state supports the use of violence by men against women both by its economic and welfare policies, in which women are denied alternative economic support to a violent man, and by the non-intervention of the police and courts against this violence, except in exceedingly rare circumstances.

While Hanmer's analysis is one of the most sophisticated discussions of the interrelationships between male violence and other social institutions, there are problems with it. She is correct in drawing attention to male violence as a particularly horrific form of patriarchal control, which has been insufficiently examined in social analysis, but she overstresses its autonomy from other sets of patriarchal relations.

While the results of such violence are horrific, Hanmer has not substantiated her claim that they crucially underpin other aspects of patriarchal relations in contemporary society. She has not been able to demonstrate, for instance, either that women remain in domesticity because of the threat of this violence, or that the threat of this violence is necessary to make women provide domestic services to men. Hanmer herself notes that the incidence of violence against wives bears no direct relationship to the degree to which the wife fulfils traditional expectations. However, the threat of violence does make most women curtail some of their activities, such as walking alone at night.

I would argue instead that violence against women by men in contemporary society is primarily a consequence of other sets of patriarchal relations, rather than the basis for them; that it contingently supports patriarchal relations, but is not necessary for this. Men's violence against women is particularly facilitated by women's weak material position which means that it is difficult to escape a violent relationship, and by the unwillingness of the patriarchal state to enforce the criminal law when men are the aggressors and women the victims. The battering of women by the men that they live with cannot be understood without an understanding of the reasons why it is so difficult for women to escape from these situations. The greatest single obstacle to women leaving violent men is the lack of accommodation to go to (Binney et al., 1981). The lack of an independent wage, or of an adequate one means that many women literally are not able to secure the means necessary to escape–a place to go to, although the overcrowded refuges of the Women's Aid Federation are a newly developed, if necessarily limited, option (National Women's Aid Federation, 1978). However, non-economic factors are also important. In a society where marriage is held in such high esteem, where there is a commonly held notion that romantic love overcomes all problems, where single parenthood is generally stigmatized, and where a woman is encouraged to be emotionally as well as materially dependent on her husband, it is not surprising that it is difficult for women to escape violent relationships. Further the dependent position of women in these relationships makes it difficult for them to negotiate the terms of the relationship in their favour. Thus violence against women by the men they live with is primarily to be explained by the patriarchal structures which lock them into relationships, in which they may have little power, and secondly, by the general culture of aggression among men.

The refusal of the state to adequately prosecute men who rape and batter, in contradiction to the rhetoric of criminal justice, should be seen as a further support to male violence. Such refusals feed the public myths which encourage the perpetuation of such violence (Hanmer and Saunders, 1984; Walby et al. 1983; Hay et al., 1980).

This lack of state support to women who have suffered male violence does not occur either evenly or randomly. Convictions for rape, for instance, are less unlikely when the woman has a conventionally respectable lifestyle (Toner, 1977), where the rapist was unknown, where there was more than one assailant and where substantial violence was used, (Kalven and Zeisel, 1971). Thus in practice women are penalized if they do not conform to conventional sexual mores in that they are less likely to gain a conviction against a man who rapes them than if they did. In this way the selective criminal justice functions as a form of control over women's lives discouraging certain forms of behaviour.

Men's violence against women is not a necessary basis for other patriarchal structures, but it does help to sustain them. Violence does, both directly and indirectly, have effects on women's behaviour, especially in the curtailment of movement. However, this particular set of patriarchal practices is primarily determined by other patriarchal relations rather than determining them.

Sexuality in Patriarchal Relations

Many writers on gender relations have tended either to see sexuality as the basis of women's subordination (e.g. Leeds Revolutionary Feminist Group, 1981; Mitchell, 1975) or have ignored it altogether (e.g. Delphy 1984; Seccombe, 1974). I would suggest that certain forms of sexuality are crucial for patriarchal relations; in particular, that the institutionalization of heterosexuality is necessary for patriarchy since without it the patriarchal mode of production could not exist. The existence of universal, or even widespread, institutionalized homosexuality and lesbianism would preclude the domestic relationship between the man and woman from being at the centre of the patriarchal mode of production.

Freud's (1977) analysis of women and sexuality is ambiguous, moving between statements that anatomy is destiny, to a focus on structures of the unconscious (cf. Burniston et al., 1978). Both positions are unsatisfactory in their neglect of social variations, and are incapable of explaining the historical variations in the forms of sexuality. The symbolic interactionist critique of Freudian analyses of sexuality involves a redefinition of what constitutes sexuality (Gagnon and Simon, 1973; Plummer, 1975; Jackson, 1978a). The symbolic interactionist concept of sexual capacity does not involve notions of biological drives like the Freudian concept of libido and leaves more conceptual space for varying sexual meanings and social determination. A focus on meaning, change, negotiation and reflexivity in analyses of sexuality properly emphasizes its social nature. Jackson's (1978a) analysis of the construction of female sexuality is one of the best applications of symbolic interactionism to the question of gender relations and sexuality. She argues that adolescent females learn forms of sexuality which are perceived as appropriate to their gender roles, rather than this sexuality being a self-evident biological instinct. Thus for this symbolic interactionist, the form of sexuality is determined by the nature of gender relations, rather than vice versa.

However, symbolic interactionism has problems in coping with issues of social structure and historical change. For instance, the concept of patriarchy is really outside the range of concepts admissable in the symbolic interactionist's vocabulary, since it involves notions of social structures that interactionists expressly reject. Thus their analyses are stuck on a micro level and cannot deal adequately with important forms of social structuring and hence with analyses of general changes in sexual meaning. Jackson seeks to analyse the learning of sexual meaning in female adolescents (1978a) and the structuring of sexual scripts which lead to rape (1978b). She leaves the symbolic interactionist perspective behind by introducing notions of structured power relations between men and women.

The Leeds Revolutionary Feminist Group (1981) argue that, on the contrary, the form of sexual relations, and in particular heterosexuality, is the basis of existing gender relations rather than being merely an effect. They forcefully state that heterosexuality is the basis of patriarchal relations and that any woman who engages in heterosexual relations is shoring up the oppression of women. They suggest that the heterosexual couple is the basic unit of patriarchy and that the constructions of sex and love within it conspire to hide the fact that men are women's enemies. They go on to suggest that penetration is in itself a special form of colonization of women's bodies which further aggrandizes men and saps the strength of women. Thus for these writers the institution of heterosexuality is basic to other patriarchal relations. While the Leeds Revolutionary Feminists have correctly identified an important set of patriarchal relations, they have failed to establish the case that these are the basis of patriarchy rather than merely one of the necessary conditions. They underestimate the significance of material factors outside of marriage.

The significance of different sets of patriarchal relations shifts historically (Coveney, 1984; Faderman, 1981; Millett, 1977). Faderman's analysis of the shifting boundary between women's friendships and lesbianism and the societal reaction suggests that when other patriarchal relations are waning in effectivity then patriarchal relations around sexuality will be strengthened. She suggests that when patriarchal relations were secure before the 1920s romantic friendships between women were tolerated and accepted since they did not threaten to undermine patriarchy, but that after the 1920s when the basis of patriarchy was less secure lesbian relationships were more threatening and hence heavily censured. However, she overstates this shift, seeing it too much as a sudden break, rather than a period of change. Nevertheless, she makes a case for the historical variation in the significance of differing forms of control over women's sexuality.

Relations between the Elements of the System

Other practices in civil society (cf. Urry, 1981a) have a less important place in a system of patriarchy. The sites of these relations include education (cf. Byrne, 1978; David, 1980; Deem, 1978, 1980; Sarah and Spender, 1980), the media (cf. Kuhn, 1982; Merck, 1979; Tuchman et al., 1978), language (cf. Spender, 1980; Lakoff, 1975), sport (cf. EOC, 1983b), religion (Ruether, 1974), but together with those already considered, such structures contribute to an interrelated and interdependent system of patriarchy.

In contemporary western society some of the elements are necessary while others are contingent. Patriarchy is in articulation with capitalism and the patriarchal relations in paid work take on special significance. This is because when the two systems are in articulation there is a tension between the interests of capital and patriarchy in the allocation of women's labour time. The appropriation of women's labour by patriarchal forces within the household or capitalists within paid work depends crucially upon the ability of patriarchal forces to mobilize so as to restrict women's participation in paid work: hence the crucial significance of this set of patriarchal relations when those two systems coexist.

I do not want to suggest that the relative significance of these different elements is stable over time and space; rather I would argue that the relative importance of the elements does vary. An example of this already considered is the changing significance over time of heterosexuality as a patriarchal institution. The relations between the elements described in this section are intended to demonstrate the possibility of discussing the relations between the elements in this way, rather than to be an exhaustive study of their interrelationships. The analysis is intended to illustrate my claim that it is possible to construct a model of patriarchy in terms of a set of relatively autonomous elements.

This chapter has examined the system of patriarchy; this is not the same as examining the cause of gender inequality, since to do that requires the investigation of the intersection of patriarchy with capitalism and with racist structures. I have tried to elucidate the main patriarchal structures which together compose the system of patriarchy. (This is further developed in Walby (1987)). Thus patriarchy is used as a theoretical concept and not as a mere descriptive term.

The substantive focus of this book is that of sexual divisions in paid employment. This is selected not merely because it would be impossible to examine the articulation of patriarchal, capitalist and racist structures in all substantive aspects of gender inequality, but also because in contemporary Britain I consider this area to be the most important in determining changes in patterns of gender relations. The tensions between patriarchy and capital over the use of women's labour highlight my theoretical claim that gender relations can only be understood if these two systems are analytically separated. The problems of analysing gender and labour without the conceptual framework developed here will be shown in the next chapter.

4
Theories of Women and Paid Work

Most writers on women and labour suggest that women are peripheral to the labour market because of the family. They typically suggest that women's participation in paid employment increases in times of increased labour demand and decreases when there is a downturn in such demand. This is an approach common to both the orthodox human-capital theorists of mainstream economics, such as Mincer (1962, 1966), and Marxist feminists such as Beechey (1977, 1978) who view this process as the utilization of women as a reserve army of labour. In this approach the family explains women's 'disadvantaged' position in the labour market, and the ups and downs of the market economy are seen as the proximate causes of the increase and decrease in women's participation in paid employment.

I believe this approach to be both empirically and theoretically incorrect. While I agree that there is a connection between women's participation in paid work and in unpaid housework, I believe that the causal direction is primarily the opposite to what these writers have postulated. Women's position in the family is largely determined by their position in paid work rather than vice versa. Further, women have not left paid work in times of depression in the way these theories would predict.

The problems in the conventional explanations stem from their failure to take sufficient account of gender inequality in its own right. In the case of human-capital theorists such as Mincer, the genders are seen primarily as differentiated rather than unequal, while in the case of Marxists, such as Beechey, gender inequality is seen to derive primarily from capitalism. Neither takes sufficient account of patriarchal relations shaping gender inequality. Thus, they are unable to see that women's position in the family is significantly determined by their disadvantaged position in paid work.

The weakness of these positions is also related to their failure to analyse gender relations historically. I would not dispute that for any individual woman today her position in relation to the family significantly affects her view of paid work and her participation in the various forms of work. However, the explanation of an individual's work strategy is not the same as an explanation of the structures which constrain her choices. It is with the explanation of these social structures that I am concerned.

I would contend that the causal connection between the family and gender relations in paid work has, in the last couple of centuries, run primarily from paid work to family, rather than vice versa. It is to the struggles which have kept women out of the better kinds of paid work that I turn for an explanation of women's subordinate position in the family. When denied equality of paid employment with men, women turn to unpaid employment in the household. This is a reasonable work strategy, given the constraints which are imposed on women. It is with these unreasonable constraints that I am concerned in this book.

These constraints have changed over time, but largely as a result of gender struggles in which women have won many improvements and, partly, as a result of changes in the organization of capital and in the relation between capital and labour. The analysis of these struggles and changes is the focus of the last part of the book.

Human Capital Theory and Women's Employment

Mincer's (1962) most important contribution to the debates on the sexual division of labour is his contention that housework is a form of productive labour which is part of the work strategy of a woman. He considers that women choose between paid work, housework and leisure under market conditions, that is, housework is work with a value like any other form of work.

Mincer is a human-capital theorist who explains gender differences as a consequence of women's commitment to the domestic sphere. He sees women's participation in paid employment as 'flexible' due to the alternative forms of work which are open to them in the household. It is the availability of these alternative forms of productive activity which is seen by Mincer to be the explanation of married women spending only part of their time in paid work.

Women, according to Mincer, choose the best time to participate in the economy, according to the ups and downs of the business cycle. Those people who spend only a portion of their working lives in paid work are held to choose these times to coincide with the periods of the business cycle when the most work is available with the best conditions of employment. The import of this is that the periods outside the labour force are seen as voluntary, and not as unemployment.

Mincer considers whether wives are encouraged or discouraged from undertaking paid work by particular wage levels of the husband. The issue here is whether wives work more in times of economic expansion because jobs are available (income effect), or whether they work more in times of economic recession when there is likely to be less income from a husband who might be unemployed (substitution effect). Mincer is able to show that both effects operate and, further, to argue that, in post-war America, the increase in married women's paid employment was primarily due to the increase in the level of women's wages, which outweighed the negative effect of the increase in the husband's income.

Mincer's model assumes that the choice, for women, is not a two-way one between paid work and leisure, but a three-way choice between paid work, leisure and unpaid housework. However, in his early model, Mincer (1962) does not build unemployment into his analysis of women's activities and this is a major source of problems. His model for women's participation in paid employment is different from men's: it defines unemployment out of existence for married women while making it a crucial part of any account of male participation in employment. In his later work, Mincer (1966) does raise the question of unemployment among married women and other secondary workers in relation to the question of whether 'discouraged' workers are 'really' unemployed, and effectively denies the existence, let alone social significance, of disguised unemployment among secondary workers. Although he does explicitly deny that he is rejecting the existence of involuntary employment, this denial is contradicted by his analysis.

A second major problem in Mincer's work is his neglect of patriarchal structures within the labour market. Like most neo-classical economists, Mincer assumes, for his theory, that the labour market works smoothly and perfectly competitively. Inequalities in the wages and participation rates between people in the labour market are conceptualized as merely reflecting the inequalities of human capital they bring to it. This view has been strongly challenged by other economists such as Gordon (1972) and Craig et al. (1982) who argue that there is no such direct correlation between skill and wage level.

A third problem in Mincer's analysis is his assumption that the household rationally decides on its labour market activities so as to maximize its income and leisure as a unit. This ignores the inequality in power within the family which has important effects on the decisions as to the distribution of paid work, unpaid work and leisure *between* the household members. Time budget studies have shown that women do more hours of work (paid and unpaid) than men and have less leisure (cf. Gershuny, 1983). Qualitative studies have shown that husbands sometimes exert considerable influence over their wives' decisions to take paid work (see Scharf, 1980). This, I would suggest, may not be to the advantage of the household as a unit but is done in order that the man retains a position of authority.

Matthaei (1982) retains the human-capital theorists' emphasis upon women's position in the family being a key determinant of their position in the labour market, but combines it with an emphasis on the ideologies of masculinity and feminity. For Matthaei it is ideological notions of appropriate gender behaviour which mediate the relation between the family and women's position in paid work. She argues, for instance, that the sex-typing of occupations is adhered to by both sexes in order to sustain their conceptions of their own masculinity and femininity. These sets of ideas are a necessary part of the differentiation of the sexes so that they may seek each other out for marriage and reproduction. These differences are taken up when new occupations are being created, and each new job is constructed as suitable for either men or women. The sex-typing of occupations is maintained because individuals have a strong interest in maintaining their identity as either masculine or feminine and thus would not only try to stop members of the other sex from entering their area of employment and contaminating it with inappropriate gender values, but also hesitate to enter the terrain of the other sex themselves for the same reason. Matthaei provides an economic history of America in terms of these issues. She concludes by suggesting that there is currently a breakdown in the sexual division of labour.

Matthaei's work provides a much needed historical dimension to the development of sex segregation, and is interesting in its explanation of the links between different aspects of gender relations in society. However, her work is problematic for several reasons. Firstly, her historical accounts omit the struggles which took place over the sex-typing of the various occupations that she describes; these processes were less consensual than she suggests. For instance, male clerks fought the entry of women into this occupation; it was not an issue settled by some smoothly functioning market (see chapter 5). This is related to a second problem: the relation between individual and collective action in the development and maintenance of the sex-typing of occupations. Matthaei treats the issue of boundary maintenance in individual terms; it is an individual who decides not to try to break with the prevailing gender ethos of a job. But this only addresses one small part of the questions around the development and maintenance of sex-typed occupations. It omits the collective social struggles over both the definition of occupations as men's or women's, and over the location of the occupation as a whole in the hierarchy of occupations. This is in turn related to a third problem in Matthaei's work: an overemphasis on the ideological level at the expense of the political. Matthaei's analysis is conducted at the level of the economic, the familial and the ideological; political struggle, and indeed any form of collective action in the workplace and the state, to affect the sex-typing of occupations is almost entirely ignored except for references in passing to the feminists of the turn of the century and their struggle to enter the professions. This lack of analysis of collective struggle is related to a fourth problem in Matthaei's work: the refusal to develop a conception, let alone a theory, of gender inequality. These two omissions are related since Matthaei does not consider that there is a simple conflict of interests between the genders. Indeed at points Matthaei discusses the relation between the sexes as one which is different but equal; (this is especially strong in her discussion of the nineteenth-century household). Yet in failing to discuss these issues Matthaei is unable to get to the root of the issue of why occupations are sex-typed. Rather than some socio-biologistic necessity for biological reproduction, this sex-typing is a matter of struggle between competing social groups, including between the genders.

Capital and Women's Employment

Several writers have turned to Marx's analysis of the reserve army of labour for the basis of an explanation of women's movements in and out of paid employment and applied his non-gendered account to women (Beechey, 1977; Braverman, 1974; Connolly, 1979; McIntosh, 1978). Marx argues that capital calls into being a relative surplus population which serves to support the extraction of profit by capital from the workers. The relative surplus population acts as a reserve army of labour which depresses the level of wages. The existence of a supply of labour which is greater than the demand for it reduces the ability of those in employment to demand higher wages.

> The industrial reserve army, during the periods of stagnation and average prosperity, weighs down the active labour-army; during the periods of over-production and paroxysm, it holds its pretensions in check. (Marx, 1954; 598.)

The existence of a reserve of labour means that in times of expansion there are people upon whose labour capital can draw without the necessity of offering high wages to attract people already employed elsewhere. Marx sees this not merely as advantageous to capital, but as necessary, in that it is essential for it to be possible to employ people rapidly in newly profitable ways, without damaging the existing branches of industry. An industrial reserve army from the relative surplus population is the way that this is achieved.

After showing the function the industrial reserve army fulfils for capital, Marx moves on to an account of the three ways that this is supplied. The first is the 'floating' form of the industrial reserve army. This results from the expansion and contraction of capitalist industry and consequent attraction and expulsion of workers. The second or 'latent' form of the reserve army is composed of workers who have not been employed in capitalist industry, but who are underemployed in their current jobs as a consequence of capitalist expansion. Marx provides the example of agricultural workers affected by the penetration of capitalism into the countryside. Their wages are severely depressed as a result and thus they are ready to move into industrial employment at the first opportunity. The third form is termed the 'stagnant'. This is composed of workers who are in irregular employment for long hours at low wages. Marx gave the examples of workers in decaying branches of employment such as 'domestic industry'. Marx also refers to pauperism, which is the lowest layer of the relative surplus population which, in addition to including some who seek paid work, includes some who are not able to take on such employment, such as the sick and crippled.

Beechey (1977, 1978) suggests that, while Marx did not refer to the gender of the members of the industrial reserve army, capital does, in fact, differentiate workers by gender. She argues that married women are a preferred source of the industrial reserve army for capital and constitute part of the latent reserve (Beechey, 1977). Married women may be paid low wages and may be easily dismissed, according to Beechey, because they are partially supported by their husband's wages. It is married women's financial relationship with their husband that differentiates them from other wage labourers, and gives rise to women's particular and distinctive position in the labour market. Married women are seen not to bear all the costs of the reproduction of their labour power because of their dependence on their husbands' wags. Thus they may be paid lower wages than men and apparently may be dismissed more readily because they can fall back on the financial support of their husband. Beechey suggests that married women are not the only category of potential wage workers whose costs of subsistence are partially borne elsewhere. Semi-proletarianized workers who meet part of the costs of their reproduction from subsistence agriculture are seen by Beechey to have a similar position to married women. She suggests that we need to analyse political factors in order to explain why one category is chosen for the role of reserve army rather than any other.

The 'flexibility' of married women appears to stem from two sources in Beechey's analysis. Firstly, it is partly due to the support of the husband's wage. Beechey states that the advantages for capital of

> those categories of labour which are partially dependent upon sources of income other than the wage to meet some of the costs of the reproduction of labour power . . . are . . .
> (a) they can be paid wages which are below the value of labour power . . .
> (b) they provide a flexible working population which can be brought into production and dispensed with as the conditions of production change. (Beechey, 1977: 56–7.)

The second reason for flexibility seems to be that they have somewhere to go and something to do. Thus writing of why married women are preferable to semi-proletarianized workers as a reserve army Beechey writes:

> One important difference is that married women have a world of their very own, the family, into which they can disappear when discarded from production, without being eligible for state benefits, and without appearing in unemployment statistics (unless they sign on). The existence of the family, and of the fact that the married woman also performs domestic labour within it, differentiates the position of the married woman within the metropolitan society from that of the semi-proletarianised worker who enters into the metropolitan society on a temporary basis. (Beechey, 1977: 57.)

There are both theoretical and empirical problems in this account. The first problem is its inability to explain why, if women are so cheap, capital does not continually employ them in preference to men. Beechey suggests that capital employs women during economic upturns because they are cheaper than men, that is, they can be paid less than the value of their labour power, unlike men. However, if this is the case, there would be no reason, within the logic of capitalism, why they should not be employed all of the time. Beechey suggests that capital wishes to maintain the family and that this puts limits on women's paid employment. However this is inadequate since she makes no suggestion that the use made of women workers during economic booms undermines the family; so Beechey is still in need of an explanation as to why it should be so at other times.

Thus if women are removed from the workforce in times of reduced demand for labour, such as at the end of the First World War, then the social forces involved should not be expected to be capitalist ones. Indeed, as Braybon (1981) has shown, it was the male-dominated unions which were instrumental in removing women from their wartime jobs, not the employers, who would rather have kept them on.

The second problem in the theory of women as a reserve army is the lack of empirical evidence to support it. Women have not been disproportionately removed from paid work as compared with men during periods of economic recession in the manner that Beechey's model of the reserve army would predict. Milkman (1976) shows that women were not pushed out of paid work more than men in the depression of the 1930s in the USA. The OECD (1976) show the same thing for the 1974–5 recession among OECD member countries, and Rubery and Tarling (1982) for post-war Europe. These studies suggest that occupational segregation protected women, in that women were disproportionately concentrated in the service sector which was less hit by job loss than was the manufacturing sector in which men were concentrated. Bruegel (1979) suggests that while women did not constitute a reserve army of labour at the level of the British national economy during the 1970s recession, nevertheless individual women, especially part-timers in manufacturing, were more likely than individual men to lose their jobs. Thus while a minor reserve-army effect remains at the level of specific industries, on the labour market as a whole, women do not constitute a reserve of labour which is drawn in times of economic expansion and thrown out in times of recession. The major pattern which emerges from these empirical tests of the reserve-army hypothesis is the importance of occupational segregation by sex in determining the level of women's employment. This then moves the issue onto why the labour market has such rigid segregation of jobs by sex, an issue which is not dealt with by these studies.

Braverman (1974) suggests that women swell the reserve army of labour, although he argues this in a slightly different way from that of other Marxist writers. He sees women as joining the reserve army when they enter paid employment rather than being engaged solely in housework. It is this increased supply of women workers which swells the ranks of the reserve army for Braverman, rather than their expulsion from paid employment.

Unlike the other writers on the reserve army, Braverman does not see this as merely a fluctuation around an equilibrium point based on the relatively static institution of the family. Rather, he suggests that it is a long-term, irreversible process in which capitalism undermines the family and pushes women into the labour market. The process is seen as parallel to that in which capitalism undermines pre-capitalist formations, releasing workers for employment by capitalists. Braverman writes of the penetration of the market into the family and household as a dual process, in which the goods the household needs are provided more cheaply under capitalist relations of production than they can be in the household, while women are also pulled into paid employment by capitalist employers. His analysis is historically specific in that this process takes place at a particular phase of capitalist development. So for Braverman, capitalism's penetration of the family in the twentieth century has led to the increased participation of women in paid employment and hence to the swelling of the reserve army of labour.

Braverman suggests that men as well as women are joining the reserve army. He notes that the proportion of men in paid work has been declining in post-war America. Although this decline is not reflected in an increase in male unemployment rates in the period examined, Braverman argues that there is a hidden increase in the reserve army.

So Braverman has argued that the reserve army has been increasing in size with both men and women entering it. According to Braverman, men and women enter the reserve army by different routes: men by leaving paid work, and women by entering paid work. This is a little confused. Why should it be held that women enter the reserve army when they *enter* employment while men join the reserve army when they *leave* paid employment? Braverman argues that men who have left the work force are neither students nor voluntary members of a new leisure class, but rather they are people who would take paid employment if they could get some: they are part of the reserve army. While this could be considered reasonable it is entirely unclear why women who have entered the work force and are in paid employment should be regarded as part of the reserve army. They are actively working, not in a reserve waiting to take up employment. While it might be the case that once in paid employment women are quite likely to become unemployed, Braverman does not make this suggestion. Indeed his evidence concerning women's employment is based entirely on figures of women *in* paid employment. Thus I would suggest that it is contradictory for Braverman to argue that women are increasingly becoming part of the reserve army. They are, according to his own data, becoming part of the active work force, not its reserve.

Braverman neglects to consider the role of patriarchal relations in either the labour market or the family. It is now a standard criticism of Braverman that he did not take account of worker organization (Friedman, 1977; Rubery, 1978). His neglect of patriarchal forms of worker organization may be considered a special case of this general neglect. Yet historically a simultaneous resistance to both deskilling and to the entry of women into certain areas of paid work has been a far from uncommon event. The success of skilled male workers in areas such as cotton spinning in resisting both deskilling and the entry of women into an area of work is evidence that Braverman is mistaken to ignore the importance of the organization of male workers in the shaping of the labour process. Braverman's model of the relationship between paid work and housework for women is thus seriously flawed by its neglect of patriarchal relations within the labour market, the state and the family.

Humphries (1983) also argues that there is a long-term process of women being drawn into the labour market. Like Braverman, Humphries sees the construction of the reserve army not as a mere cyclical event, but rather as a permanent trend in which women are increasingly entering paid employment. Her account suffers similar problems to that of Braverman, especially in her lack of consideration of the significance of patriarchal organization in the workplace. In omitting this element Humphries is unable to explain why women were not substituted for male employees long ago.

The problem in most of the analyses of women's employment considered so far have centred around the segregation of employment by sex. This feature has been shown to be of overriding significance in understanding changing sexual division of labour. It is to attempts to explain this feature of the labour market that I shall now turn.

Labour Market Structures and Gender

Having cast serious doubt on the proposition that women's movements out of employment can be explained solely by reference to their position within the family, it is appropriate to move on to look at those writers who focus on labour market structures for such an explanation. Their analyses are usually in two parts: firstly, an explanation of why the labour market is segmented; and secondly, why it is women who tend to fill the lower grade slots.

Four characteristics, according to Barron and Norris, differentiate primary and secondary jobs: secondary sector jobs are unstable, secondary jobs are low paid; there is little mobility across the boundary between the two sectors, and, finally, primary sector jobs are generally tied into long promotional ladders unlike secondary jobs (Barron and Norris, 1976: 49). Barron and Norris suggest that the structure of the labour market is a consequence firstly, of attempts by employers to retain workers whose skills they need, and secondly, of an attempt by employers to buy off the best organized workers.

Barron and Norris suggest that women are primarily secondary workers because of five characteristics which employers believe women to possess: dispensability, clearly visible social differences, little interest in acquiring training, low economism and lack of solidarity. These characteristics are partially the result of the individual's labour market experience and partly the result of aspects of the social structure outside the labour market.

A major problem with Barron and Norris's analysis is ironically, their lack of appreciation of, and analysis of, patriarchal structures in the labour market. Despite their emphasis on the importance of the labour market much of their article is taken up with merely a description of the characteristics that women bring, or are believed by employers to bring, to the labour market. They describe the structuring of the labour market into two sectors in non-gender-specific terms and I would suggest mistakenly ignore the structuring of the market itself by sexual divisions. They treat sexual differentiation as determined largely outside the labour market by the sexual division of labour in the household. This sexual differentiation is then incorrectly treated as a given which is unmodified by the workings of the labour market. There are two ways in which Barron and Norris approach the problem of patriarchal structures but fail to complete their analysis. The most important is the discussion of women's supposed lack of solidarism. This is always seen in terms of women not managing to organize, never in terms of men being organized against women in the labour market. The nearest they get to men being an opposing force is to suggest that male trade unionists do not assist women trade unionists to the point of being obstructive. They never mention men actively organizing against women, although, I would argue this is very important (cf. Hartmann, 1979a; Andrews, 1918; Oakley, 1976; Scharf, 1980). Barron and Norris do refer to general attitudes of hostility to women working, both in general and in relation to particular jobs, but this is seen as relatively diffuse rather than as organized. They are mistaken to see patriarchal intervention in the labour market as so confined to the level of beliefs and to neglect the organization of patriarchal forces. This problem is related to the absence of an historical dimension in their work which might have focused more attention on actual struggles.

Another problem with Barron and Norris's work is to be found in the incorrect assumption that the primary and secondary division in the labour market extends across all jobs in Britain. For instance, clerical work does not fit in this division very well. Rather this division seems more appropriately limited to manual jobs in manufacturing for which it was originally developed.

Other writers have suggested a variety of alternatives such as: the internal labour market (e.g. Doeringer and Piore, 1971); segmentation into several parts (e.g. Edwards et al., 1975; Loveridge and Mok, 1979), and occupational segregation (Hakim, 1978, 1979).

Hakim differentiates between horizontal and vertical segregation of occupations by sex. She suggests that horizontal occupational segregation occurs when men and women work in different types of occupations, and vertical segregation when men are working in higher grade occupations than women. She uses her concept to suggest that in Britain during the twentieth century, horizontal segregation has slightly declined with men entering occupations which were previously exclusively female, though women have not entered male-dominated occupations to the same extent. Vertical segregation, on the other hand, has increased during the twentieth century with women being increasingly concentrated in the least skilled jobs.

Hakim does not consider the division between full-time and part-time jobs to be pertinent to the forms of occupational segregation. She argues that since part-timers are distributed across the majority of occupations it is not a significant factor in occupational segregation. In adopting this position Hakim has seriously limited the import of her analysis by confining herself to looking at very particular forms of occupational segregation and omitting to consider other types of labour market structures which act as barriers to women's advancement in paid work. Hakim discusses in detail the formidable methodological problems entailed in such an analysis, especially the difficulties of consistent occupational classification, rather than attempting an explanation of these changes and lack of changes. We are thus still left with questions as to the nature of the barriers to the movement of women and men into different occupations.

Other writers have also suggested the need to take into account more divisions than one of primary and secondary and have characterized the labour market as 'segmented' rather than 'dualistic' (Edwards et al., 1975; Wilkinson, 1981), or as composed of a 'vertical mosaic' (Kreckel, 1980). One major division between labour market theories is whether the divisions are seen to be based on skill, such as employers attempts to keep workers who have learned valuable firm specific skills (e.g. Doeringer and Piore, 1971) and those who see the segmentation based on power struggles between different groups (Gordon, 1972; Rubery, 1978; Edwards et al., 1975). The latter group of radical labour market theorists can be differentiated again according to whether gender divisions are seen as by-products of struggles between capital and labour (Humphries, 1977a, 1981), or whether they are seen as a central feature of analysis (Hartmann, 1979a), or whether, indeed, they are effectively ignored altogether (Kreckel, 1980). Still others, for instance Edwards, (1979) see sexism as being somewhat independent of capitalism, although Edwards does not follow his analysis through. (For a fuller discussion of Edwards et al. see Walby (1986b).

The Cambridge group of heterodox economists, Craig, Garnsey, Rubery, Tarling and Wilkinson, argue that the labour market is segmented for reasons other than to do with gender relations, and that the location of women in the worst jobs is connected to women's position in the family, in a manner which has some similarities to Barron and Norris (1976). Craig et al. (1982) and Craig et al. (1985) argue that there is an important, but not necessary, connection between the division between primary and secondary firms in relation to their position in the product market, and primary and secondary forms of employment. A primary position in the product market makes it more possible although not inevitable for workers to organize in trade unions and demand primary conditions of work, whereas in the absence of such a position such demands would typically result in either refusal or bankruptcy, since the firm would be unable to pass on the increased costs involved to the purchasers of its products.

Craig et al. (1982, 1985) argue vehemently against the human-capital approach to the explanation of unequal wages. They note that many of the jobs in the secondary firm sector require as much skill as those in the primary sector, despite the fact that wages in this sector are much lower. Further, Craig et al. (1985) find that there is little differentiation among women's wages in the informal payment structures of the secondary sector, despite significant variations in the skill and experience between these workers. This lack of congruence between skill and experience on the one hand, and wages on the other, is used as evidence that the human-capital theory of wages is incorrect. Rather, the level of wages is seen to be the result of the firm's position in the product market, and the result of industrial organization.

Having argued for a distinctive approach to labour market analysis, Craig et al. (1982, 1985) go on to try to explain why it is that women more typically occupy secondary sector jobs than men. They reiterate that this cannot be for human-capital reasons. However, they do suggest that the cause lies within the family rather than within the labour market. They suggest that women's position in the family as the person primarily responsible for the housework leads to reduced expectations of earning a primary wage, and hence that women are more prepared than men to accept a secondary wage. Thus they argue that women's supply price is lower than that of men's because of expectations women hold as a result of their position in the family (Craig et al., 1982: 91).

There are several serious problems with this approach. It is not clear what expectations have to do with whether women will accept higher- or lower-paying jobs. If women were offered jobs which paid the same as men, there is no reason to believe that they would not be accepted. The issue is why women are not offered such jobs to the same extent as men. Here I think their research design is inadequate for the question they are asking. They study only the low-paying jobs in which women are predominantly located, not the higher paying jobs from which they are largely absent. Yet, since the reason for their absence from these jobs is the issue at stake, their lack of investigation of this employment is most unfortunate. They make the error of studying women in low-paying jobs in order to discover why women are disadvantaged, rather than studying the site of the disadvantaging. The location of women primarily in the low-paying sector is the consequence of processes of disadvantage, not the cause of this. I would suggest that it is the patriarchal forces within the labour market which deny women equal access to these jobs which is the explanation of why women are crowded in the low-paying sector. Further, the effect of over-crowding is to lower women's supply price, since the supply of their labour is greater than the available jobs to a greater extent than is the case for men (cf. Bergmann, 1980a,b).

As suggested in chapter 2, major importance must be attached to Hartmann's (1979a) argument that efforts to exclude women from certain occupations represents deliberate attempts by male workers to better their own position at the expense of female workers. She argues that a patriarchal division of labour existed long before the advent of capitalism. This division of labour was, however, perpetuated by male workers in industrial capitalism and exploited by capitalist employers for their own benefit. The most important aspect of this process for Hartmann was the active organization of male workers seeking to exclude women workers from their trades. Hartmann substantiates her argument with a considerable amount of historically detailed information, about both the USA and Britain, during the nineteenth and early twentieth centuries. She describes the movement to restrict the hours that women were able to work in factories, quoting from their proponents' stated views about the place of women being in the home. Her evidence about the USA concentrates upon cigar-making and the Cigarmakers International Union and the case of printing and the National Typographical Union. She argues that the organization of male workers has been instrumental in the exclusion of women from many sectors of skilled work. As suggested in the first chapter Hartmann's analysis has many strengths, yet there are some areas still in need of further development.

Spatial Variations in Women's Employment Rates

The variations in women's employment rate by region are quite striking in Britain, despite the levelling up which has occurred during the post-war period (see Walby (1985b) for a fuller account of this). It is insufficient to have an explanation of women's employment which is unable to encompass such variations. Yet most of the existing literature which does examine the spatial dimension of social processes is unsatisfactory in its approach to gender relations. While some analyses note the differentiation of female and male wage labour and its effects, this is rarely developed and many ignore gender altogether. The focus of these analyses on capital–labour relations has tended to preclude any understanding of the connections between different aspects of gender relations. These tend to be introduced into the analysis in a relatively *ad hoc* manner, rather than being systematically analysed. Some writers have noted the typical differences in wages and job security that women and men workers are able to command (for instance, Massey, 1978, 1979; Massey and Meegan, 1982; Urry, 1981b, 1982; Gregory, 1980; Donnison and Soto, 1980; Marquand, 1980). These differences between men and women are usually treated in isolation from other aspects of gender relations and with little analysis of their causation. So while these analyses note that new forms of employment which are low-waged, insecure and in the service sector are taken primarily by women there is little explanation of why women should take these jobs rather than men, or even why there is such a pool of female labour available. The analyses thus implicitly assume that the determination of these occurrences lies outside their field of study, that is, that women are constituted as workers with few skills and prepared to work for lower wages in a relatively timeless sort of way. Even the varying increase in women's participation in paid work since the war usually calls forth little more than descriptive acknowledgement (cf. Donnison and Soto, 1980, chapter 5). These analyses incorrectly assume unvarying spatial and historical functioning of the family under capitalism. As a consequence, women's disadvantaged labour market position is sited in the family and outside the field of vision of regionalist analyses.

There have been a couple of attempts to explain spatial variations in women's activity rates. Bowers (1970) argues that almost all the regional variation in women's activity rates in 1961 and regional changes in women's activity rates 1954–64 could be accounted for by regional variations in industrial structure. A secondary effect was that a region with an industrial structure conducive to female employment was likely to have an even higher rate of female activity. Bowers attributed this to a demonstration effect and also the increased likelihood of support facilities for women in paid work. Allin (1982) also points to the significance of industrial structure in explaining variations in female activity rates and a similar secondary effect. However, he argues that a 'tradition' of paid work is the most important correlate, even more significant than current industrial structure. While this correlation of regional changes in women's employment and industrial structure is interesting, these studies are limited by their discussion of little other than correlations. These surface phenomena are treated as the causes of variations in women's activity rates in classic positivist manner, with little attempt to identify the structure which generate such correlations. It is the identification of these structures and their interrelationships that are needed for an adequate explanation.

A major issue that is little discussed by these writers is why industries have a particular ratio of female to male employment and why this is relatively fixed over time. Unless this question is answered it explains little to say that regional variations in female activity rates are accounted for by the industrial structure of that region. Allin's use of the notion of tradition begs as many questions as it answers. The fixation of certain patterns of female economic activity at one point in space through time requires explanation, as does the original patterning.

While regional data may be a useful source of comparative material there are problems with this approach. Such an investigation would be based on a presumption that regions were reasonably homogenous units which were clearly differentiated from each other. However, this assumption is untenable because of both the wide variations which exist within regions, and the lack of consistent criteria on which to divide regions from one another (Fothergill and Gudgin, 1982: 22; Massey, 1979). So when regional data is used in this book, they will be used in the clear knowledge that they merely compare averages of widely disparate localities. As has been suggested above, regional differences in women's employment rates are primarily the result of the uneven spatial location of industries with high and low proportions of women workers. Thus regional data may be seen to be a very rough proxy for industrial data as far as women's employment is concerned.

Women's employment *vis à vis* men's cannot be understood without an analysis of patriarchal as well as capitalist relations and a consideration of the articulation of the two. Most existing attempts to analyse women's employment have focused almost entirely upon capitalist relations and the workings of the market. The existence of systematic attempts by men to protect their paid jobs at the expense of women tends to be underplayed if not ignored in these analyses.

Many of the existing debates on changes in women's employment, both within neo-Marxian and neo-classical economics, focus upon the question of whether women constitute a reserve army of labour. Drawing on Marx's analysis of the industrial reserve army some presume that the overriding importance of capital and family structure will lead to women being used in this way. Others have stressed the importance of occupational segregation and other factors which seriously qualify the thesis. The most perceptive argue that women have not functioned as a reserve army of labour but that their patterns of employment are a consequence of employers preferring to employ women who can be paid lower wages and given worse conditions of employment than men because of occupational segregation.

As the next three chapters will show, struggles over female employment have usually resulted in one of two outcomes: the exclusion of women from the area of employment in question: or the segregation of women into jobs which are separate from those of men and which are graded lower. Segregation is often the result of the struggle when patriarchal forces have been insufficiently strong to exclude women altogether. These are not struggles which are resolved at either the national level or for once and for all, but rather are fought over particular issues which are located both spatially and temporally. In practice these have often been fought at the level of a particular occupation or industry, which is necessarily spatially located, at moments when there are changes in production. These changes in production may be due to technical innovations, changes in the product market, or changes in the level of activity in the economy as a whole. That is, changes in the organization of capital often precipitate gender struggles over employment in particular occupations, since they both destabilize the old balance of gender forces and create and destroy particular forms of employment.

Once the sex-ratios in the occupations of particular industries have been set they are usually quite resistant to change. Each round of the restructuring of capital (cf. Massey, 1978, 1984) takes place on the basis of the labour relations and organization of capital fixed in the previous round. The next set of struggles over the gendering of the reformed occupations will then take place on the back of the previous sex-typing, in the context of the new restructuring of capital. The sexual division of labour today is then the result of the accumulation of round upon round of the restructuring of gender relations. The causes of the contemporary pattern then cannot be sought simply in the current balance of power between different social forces, but must include the sedimented forms of the previous rounds.

Many of the few existing writings which do examine the relation between patriarchy (or gender inequality) and the capitalist mode of production assume that there is a harmonious articulation between the two (e.g. Hartmann, 1979a). It is a common presumption that capital benefits from the subordination of women by men and that men utilize capitalist relations in the subordination of women. This model of a neat fit between the interests of capitalists and men underlies many of the discussions on the use of women as a reserve of labour. Here the subordinated position of women on the periphery of the labour market is held to benefit capitalists, while the temporary nature of women's participation in paid work prevents such employment from undermining gender inequality in the family. This position underestimates the conflict between patriarchy and capital and presents an inaccurate picture of historical stasis. Rather, the relations between patriarchy and capital should be seen as historically and spatially variable and riddled with conflict.

5
Restructuring Gender Relations in Employment: 1800–1914

Patterns of women's employment can be adequately explained only if the history of overlapping rounds of restructuring in employment is examined. This restructuring is chiefly influenced by capitalist relations in industry and by patriarchal relations in the household, in workplace organization and in the state. Even though each of these areas has a history which cannot be reduced to the others, and which cannot be divided naturally into the same periods as each of the others, some division of the whole into historical periods is necessary in order to proceed, beginning, in this chapter, with early development from 1800 to 1914. Chapter 6 will examine the period from 1914 to 1945 and chapter 7 the post-war period. While attempting to give some general coverage of each period I shall focus in particular on three major areas of employment: cotton textiles, engineering and clerical work. The cotton textile industry is of particular interest because it was the first major industry in the world to be organized in factories. Its significance as the leading sector during industrialization should not be underestimated: textiles *were* early industrialization. Engineering is of particular interest because it emerged later as a leading sector of the economy, while clerical work has special interest because it is such a large area of employment today, and, despite recent technical changes, is likely to remain so. Cotton textiles, engineering and clerical work have contrasting features which permit attempts to explain their divergent gender patterns of employment. Their workforces have contrasting gender compositions, and these industries have contrasting forms of workplace organization and contrasting histories of state intervention. The gender composition of the workforce in each area is different: mixed in cotton textiles, predominantly male in engineering and predominantly female in clerical. At crucial points of their development they experienced different forms of workplace organizations and state intervention: cotton textiles had non-craft unions and there were legislative attempts to control women's labour; engineering had craft unions with late development of general unions, and occasional legislative attempts were made to control women's labour; clerical work has seen limited forms of workplace organization and little state intervention.

The history of the gender relations in each of these areas of employment is marked by periods of rapid change, usually, but not exclusively, at the points of their expansion and development, together with long periods of relative stability. The analysis of points of change offers particular insights into gender relations in employment. This examination is not intended to be an exhaustive social history of the three areas of employment, still less of gender relations in employment as a while. Rather it is a sociological history of the key points in the comparative development of gender relations in employment in cotton textiles, engineering and clerical work, designed to answer some of the theoretical questions raised in the first part of the book.

Workplace Organization up to 1900

Since workplace organization by men is of considerable significance in explaining the nature of gender relations in employment it is useful to introduce some of the general issues in the analysis of changes in these forms of organization as they affect gender relations. Some histories of trade unions, such as that of the Webbs (1894), emphasize a decisive discontinuity between the emergence of trade unions after the repeal of the Combination Acts in 1824–5 and earlier forms of workplace organization. I would argue on the contrary that there were important continuities in forms of workplace organziation from 1800 until the emergence of the general unions towards the end of the nineteenth century. The most important forms of continuity of relevance to the question here is that these early organizations attempted to control the price at which their members' labour was sold by regulating entry to a particular trade or skill. One of the forms of regulation of entry common to all these organizations was the exclusion of women. This occurred under the guild system of apprenticeship until this was abolished by statute in 1818 (Kramer, 1927). Similarly, it occurred in the trade clubs of journeymen in the early nineteenth century. Although trade unions were illegal under the Combination Acts of 1799, and indeed threatened with legal sanctions from earlier pieces of legislation, workmen did combine, even if ostensibly only in the form of Friendly Societies (see e.g. Thompson, 1968). These early trade unions were able to exercise some control over the entry to their numbers and although the extent of this power in these, and later, organizations and their ability to control skill definitions in the absence of a technical base is subject to controversy (Webb and Webb, 1894; Musson, 1972; More, 1980; Turner, 1962) there is little doubt that they were successful in excluding women. The trade union growth in the period after the repeal of the Combination Acts was initially along similar lines to the existing trade clubs, that is, based primarily on control of the supply of labour through controlling entry to a trade (with the exception, of course, of Owen's short-lived Grand National Consolidated Trades Union). The exclusion of women from skilled trades was facilitated by the strategy used by workplace organizations of this period of attempting to push up the price of their labour by regulating entry to a trade and thus make their labour scarce. Thus as far as the gender implications of workplace organizations are concerned, the traditional distinctions between guilds, trade clubs, craft unions and the new model unions are of little significance.

There is a major division between these workplace organizations and the general unions which accepted semi-skilled and unskilled workers into membership. These workplace organizations generally attempted to raise the price of their labour by collective bargaining in the workplace rather than by control of entry to a trade. However, most of these unions, while in general following this strategy, made an exception as far as women were concerned in the first couple of decades of their existence. Despite their general strategy these unions still refused entry to women in a manner similar to the workplace organizations already considered. Appendix I contrasts the date at which the most important unions of the turn of the century were founded with the date at which they admitted women. In most cases there was a gap of, on average, 20 years. The actions of these unions in this respect can in no way be considered as one of protection of their skills against the attempts of employers to break these down and pay them less, since they did not have skills to protect. Rather these actions must be seen as specifically patriarchal in that they attempted to raise men's wages only, and at the women's expense.

The period of growth of the general unions of the 'new unionism' needs to be divided into two phases in the consideration of gender relations. In the first, women were typically excluded from membership, and only in the second were they admitted. The change in the strategies of these cannot be understood as the outcome of the move to general unions since in the first couple of decades these unions did not admit women. It must be seen at least partly, as the outcome of feminist pressure. There is some important independence of the gender dimension here. During the same period, the last quarter of the nineteenth century and the first 14 years of the twentieth, there was considerable feminist agitation. One branch of this agitation was concerned with the improvement of conditions of women in paid employment and involved such activities as assisting the organization of women workers into trade unions (Drake, 1984; Soldon, 1978). The women's organizations included the Women's Protective and Provident League, later to become the Women's Trade Union League, and the National Federation of Women Workers. They assisted in the setting up of women's trade unions and sought to integrate these into the men's unions (Drake, 1984; Soldon, 1978).

An analysis of the women's trade unions is in itself quite complex. Largely as a result of their relationship with the men's trade unions and ensuing compromises, they were not unequivocal feminist organizations. Most of the women's unions were set up because of the refusal of men's unions to admit women, or because there was no union in that trade, although in later years (from the early part of the twentieth century) some women's unions were founded as breakaways from mixed unions in which women's interests were felt to be subordinated to those of men. The national women leaders of the women's trade unions became thoroughly incorporated in the patriarchal trades union and labour movement, and carried most, if not all, women's trade unions with them. This strategy of co-operation and compromise with the men's trade unions had both costs and benefits: in some instances women did gain access to some trade union resources in the struggle against employers; while in others their ability to struggle against patriarchal practices was seriously weakened.

Women were not passive in the face of these patriarchal practices, despite the general picture most analysts paint of women acquiescing in their subordination. Women struggled in many ways against the problems in their lives, and the notion that they either were passive victims or else found sufficient satisfaction with their lot does not stand up in the face of the evidence.

Organizations of women fighting for women at the turn of the century include the Women's Industrial Council, its predecessor, the Women's Trade Union Association (Mappen, 1985), the Women's Trade Union League and the National Federation of Women Workers. The Women's Industrial Council was an organization composed largely of middle-class women who sought to improve the conditions of working women, especially of the working class. They assisted the organization of working women and sought to expose the appalling conditions to a wider world, hoping to generate enough public concern to force improvement. Working closely with liberal and labour reformers, they were not particularly radical in their vision for working women, often thinking that their interests would be best served by having a husband with a family wage. However, they did recognize that many women did not have a male breadwinner and needed employment for themselves. They assisted in the training of women as well as helping them to organize and seeking wider political support for changes in their position.

However, there are many variations in trade union practices and structures which cut across any division of the history of craft and general unions into periods. For instance, cotton weaving unions were exceptional in that they admitted women from the first, in the early nineteenth century. Cotton weaving in itself is almost unique in its gender relations in that men and women do more or less the same skilled work in the same place for the same piece work rate of pay (although the men do tend to get the better jobs) (Drake, 1984; Liddington and Norris, 1978). This unusual situation derives in part, from the unionization of both men and women at an early stage in the development of power-loom weaving in factories.

The Early Nineteenth-Century Background

During early industrialization there was a significant decline in the tasks typically performed by women, while only a very limited range of new employments were opened up to them (Schreiner, 1918; Pinchbeck, 1981). This situation did not start in the nineteenth century, but rather had been taking place gradually since the seventeenth (Clark, 1982). Some tasks were no longer performed by women in the household largely because they were performed under capitalist relations of production, typically by men. Workshops and factories, using labour-saving machinery, economies of scale and non-human sources of power, were able to produce more cheaply the same goods as the women had made in the household. While this was a quite general shift in gender patterns of employment, there were significant variations in how it took place. The tasks which tended to move out of the household into workshops and factories from the seventeenth century included spinning, brewing, aspects of food preparation and the making of clothing. In addition there was a reduction in the extent to which women participated in the skilled trades alongside their husbands and as widows, while in agriculture there was a decline in the extent to which women carried on semi-independent agricultural production such as dairying and care of a vegetable garden and of livestock (see e.g. Pinchbeck, 1981). While the expansion of industrial capitalism did involve the expansion of employment in the towns, many of the new occupations were monopolized by men, and factory employments available to women, such as cotton weaving, were the exception rather than the rule. The largest single occupation available to women in the nineteenth century was domestic service. The majority of the new forms of employment were not open to women.

Analysis of the changing forms of labour during this period is made more difficult by the failure of many writers to distinguish between types of activity, on the one hand, and relations of production on the other. A term like 'domestic industry' is too often used, confusingly conflating these two aspects of production. As I argued in chapter 2, there is no theoretical basis for a distinction between production and reproduction, and all household labour performed by women should be seen as production. Distinctions based on task have no place in a rigorous theory of gender relations, rather distinctions between forms of work should be made on the basis of differences in the relations of production under which they are performed. Thus the use of the term 'domestic industry' is problematic if, as is often the case, it is applied to certain domestic tasks such as spinning and brewing but not others, such as cooking and washing. It is only appropriate to place such activities in different categories if they are performed under different relations of production and exchange. For instance, spinning, when performed under the putting-out system and organized by small capitalists should be distinguished from spinning done by women for household use. Much spinning had historically been done for household use and, as such, should be considered to be part of the process of the production of labour power, alongside tasks such as cooking and cleaning.

Richards (1982) has put forward an argument that the reduction in women's employment during the early phases of the industrial revolution in Britain was primarily due to the decline in the employments which were open to women and also because the new industrial employments with the exception of textiles were largely closed to women until the middle of the twentieth century. However, I would suggest that this is merely to restate the problem in new terms and not to solve it. He incorrectly takes the sex-typing of occupations for granted, as some sort of natural given, and fails to attempt any explanation of it. I would suggest that the reasons for the sex-typing of the new industrial employment as male is the central question to be asked, and not a phenomenon to be assumed. Richards further suggests that a contributory factor in women's lack of participation in paid work was the large size of Victorian families, the responsibility for which prevented women from entering paid employment outside the household. However, the flexibility of the form of the household shown in the case of the nineteenth-century Lancashire cotton weavers (Anderson, 1971) demonstrates that the family cannot be used as an explanation of women's exclusion from industrial work. The existence of the women weavers of Lancashire demonstrates that such supply-side explanations of patterns of women's employment are inadequate.

An explanation of these changing gender patterns in employment during early industrialization should recognize that while the development of capitalist forces and relations of production are of central importance in explaining the changing types of employment, they are much less important in determining which gender took which form of employment. Thus, for instance, while the movement of spinning from the home to the factory is largely to be explained in terms of the capitalist forces and relations of production, the change in the gender of the people who performed this work from women to men cannot be explained without taking into account patriarchal relations. In many skilled crafts, because they were affected by the industrial revolution, married women were often engaged to some extent in this work through their husband. Indeed on the death of their husbands many, although not all, widows carried on the trade with the full approval of the guild, including, for instance, continuing to train apprentices. Women, however, were rarely admitted to apprenticeships in those trades in their own right, although this was not entirely unknown. With the development of capitalism women lost this form of access to skilled trades. Workshops grew larger and skilled men spent increasing proportions of their lives as employees rather than as masters of their own workshops. The wives of these employees did not then have the opportunity to learn the trade that their husband practised (Clark, 1982).

The exclusion of women should be seen as a result of the intersection of patriarchal relations and capitalist relations. In the original situation the guild restrictions together with the household relations combined to provide women with limited access to the skilled trades, although the women were subordinate to their husband's control. In the later situation the separation of the workshop from the household, a consequence of capitalist development, deprived women of access to the skilled trade in any form at all. A further form of restriction on women's employment arose from the intersection of patriarchal legal controls over women with the growing importance of ownership of capital and access to credit. In the period under consideration married women were legally debarred from owning property or obtaining credit in their own right, since they were legally subsumed under their husband. Despite the rhetoric of individualism and free contract, married women were not even legal persons. This effectively precluded the possibility of female capitalists, the absence of which must thus be explained in terms of patriarchal relations.

There were significant differences in the articulation of patriarchal and capitalist relations in different industries and areas. It is to these variations that I shall now turn.

Cotton Textiles in the 1800s

Cotton textiles were the leading industry of early industrialization. It was this industry which pioneered the new methods of factory organziation and its attendant forms of labour process. It is thus particularly interesting that women and children formed the majority of the early cotton textile factory employees. Women were at the forefront of early industrialization. In 1816, parliamentary returns show that adult men constituted only 17.7 per cent of cotton industry employees (Hutchins, 1915: 72).

Women were encouraged to enter the mills, since the wages, though low by male standards, were higher than women could earn elsewhere (Hutchins, 1915: 72). This situation led to the wider restructuring of gender relations and was eventually met with a strong and organized attempt by patriarchal forces to resist the entry of women to the factories. As the factories became an increasingly important form of employment, the employment of women threatened to undermine patriarchal control in the household and elsewhere. In the pages that follow, I shall describe a range of patriarchal tactics, from strikes against employers who took on women, to attempts at legislative restriction of women's work.

The resistance by men to women's employment in the factories was based both on its disruption to the patriarchal ordering of the family and on its effect on the wages of men.

> The change was resented as a break-up of family life . . . With desparate energy, the unions long opposed the introduction of women workers . . . It means not only his own loss and suffering, but the degradation of his standard of life and the break-up of his home. (Hutchins, 1915: 42–3.)

The male spinners in the early nineteenth century closed ranks against women, barring them from membership, from training and from jobs (see e.g. Hutchins, 1915). With the development of the cotton textile factories the position of mule spinner became the most skilled and best-paid position. Further, mule spinners had considerable authority, especially over their increasingly numerous assistants or 'piecers' (Joyce, 1980; Savage, 1982). The male spinners then began organizing in unions which banned women from joining. In 1829 a conference of spinners from England, Ireland and Scotland in the Isle of Man prohibited women from joining the men's unions. This meeting resolved that the only people who should be taught to spin were certain male kin: sons, brothers and nephews of spinners, or the masters' poor relatives. There were no female spinners in the Manchester union in 1829. The Scottish spinners also resisted women joining them. The Bolton Association of Cotton Spinners only allowed women members in the Piecers Section (the assistants to the spinners–though even this ceased by the 1880s), but not as spinners themselves. Earlier unions in the 1790s had allowed women members, but this ceased by 1829. The 1829 Isle of Man conference did encourage women to set up their own unions, but since the same meeting banned male spinners from training women this was worthless (Hutchins, 1915: 93; Smelser, 1959: 236–7; Liddington and Norris, 1978; 90). In 1838 The Association of Operative Cotton Spinners of Glasgow and Neighbourhood restricted training to sons and brothers of members (Smelser, 1959: 189).

The banning of women from the men's unions was in general an attempt to exlude women from this area of work. The spinners had a considerable degree of authority over the labour process and acted to some extent as internal subcontractors (Littler, 1980). Thus their collective refusal to countenance women taking the skilled job of mule spinner was in many instances an effective veto. Attempts to introduce women spinners on mules by employers met with fierce resistance from men. In 1813 such a movc by employers led to mill-burning, while in Manchester, in 1824, it led to a strike. The local paper, the Manchester Guardian, criticized the men for preventing the women taking these jobs and this produced a lengthy response from a union official. He explicitly defended their actions on the grounds that the women were undercutting the men's wages and that the young women become unnaturally independent:

> 'Are females quietly employed in any department of the cotton mills which the men wish to monopolize? The latter demand their discharge'. In this charge, there is fortunately for you, sir, some shadow of truth. In one instance, where the master declared his determination to fill his mill with women only, the men left their employment. But, sir, this does not apply to the great body of spinners,–there are many instances where women are employed in the same mill, and actually occupy the best departments. We do not stand opposed to women working, but we do enter our protest against the principle on which they are employed. The women, in nine cases out of ten, have only themselves to support,–while the men, generally have families. This the employers known, and of this the unprincipled take advantage. The women can afford their labour for less than the men, and those masters who employ them are enabled to

> come into market on better terms than those employers who do not; thus the fair tradesman is injured and he is ultimately though reluctantly forced to maintain families on the most inadequate means. We wish not to come forward as moralists, but if we could call the inhabitants of Manchester, the parents of children especially, to view the character and conduct of females in a cotton-mill, we think we could present them with an exhibition at once disgusting and appalling. Girls, many of them interesting ones, from 14 to 20 years of age, are thus rendered independent of their natural guardians, who in many cases, indeed, become in consequence of this very employment, dependent upon their children. In this unnatural and unwholesome state of things, the reins of government are broken, and the excited feelings of youth and inexperience let loose upon the world, a prey too often to pride, vice and infamy. (*Manchester Guardian*, November 27 1824.)

This incident occurred in the context of strikes against the introduction of new machinery and against the reduction of wages (Smelser, 1959: 232–5.) In 1842 there was a 'general strike' in all the cotton factories in Lancashire (see e.g. Jenkins, 1980). One of the demands of this strike was that there should be no factories which employed only women.

Legislative Attempts to Restrict Women's Employment

Patriarchal strategies of exclusion took their most organized form in the struggles over passage of the Factory Acts (1844, 1847, 1864, 1867, 1874, 1878, 1891, 1895, 1901). This so-called 'protective' legislation was an important attempt to maintain and reinforce the patriarchal structuring of society, and attempts to construe it as benign and progressive are misplaced. It enforced, rather than diminished gender inequality because of its impact on the position of women in paid work. However, the legislation is viewed by the majority of commentators as protection for exploited groups. An early history of the Factory acts is written as a story of progress against bad working conditions (Hutchins and Harrison, 1911). In a standard text on the development of the welfare state, protective legislation is regarded as a significant reform:

> Althorp's Factory Act was clearly a great turning-point in the history of social policy. It acknowledged the right of the state to intervene where there was an overwhelming need to protect exploited sections of the community. (Fraser, 1973: 21.)

Likewise Thomas, in the conclusion of his detailed account of the Acts, refers again to progress and enlightenment in the development of factory legislation.

> Perhaps the most striking achievement was the establishment of the principle that it is the right, and indeed the duty of the state to intervene between employer and employed, to impose control and regulation, in order to protect those who were unable, in the highly individualistic and competitive industrial system, to protect themselves. When once this basic principle had won general acceptance progress became possible on a wide front, and reform could proceed with increasing momentum. (Thomas, 1970: 32.)

Roberts also sees the factory legislation as a brave new step forward in social policy:

> The significance of the act lay . . . in the insistence that the central government can regulate private enterprise for the public's welfare. (Roberts, 1960: 38.)

This opinion is not confined to liberal reformers. Marx regarded the factory legislation as a useful way to limit the working day. He regarded the passage of this legislation as a victory for the working class in its struggle against capital for a decent existence (Marx, 1954: 2808).

In contradiction to this dominant interpretation I would argue that protective legislation was regressive in its effects on women and is more appropriately described as patriarchal than as reformist. This description is appropriate for those Acts which limited women's paid work more than that of men (which excludes the Acts before 1842 which refer only to children and young persons, and excludes those parts of Acts which refer to women and men equally). The writers considered above and below largely ignore the importance of the gender dimension in this legislation.

Existing attempts to explain the factory legislation tend to fall into four categories: detailed historical accounts, Marxist, Marxist-feminist and functionalist. The first type of account–the historical–gives a detailed catalogue of the events which lead up to each piece of factory legislation (Hutchins and Harrison, 1911; Thomas, 1970; Pinchbeck, 1981; Fraser, 1973). The explanation of the legislation is held to lie in this sequence of events, which is carefully researched and described. These accounts embody a conception of progress and of modernization; the passage of the legislation is seen as evidence of this unfolding process. These accounts are unsatisfactory in that they do not really penetrate beyond surface events; they do not reach to the underlying structural relations and are consequently superficial (cf. Keat and Urry, 1973; Urry, 1981a; Giddens, 1979). In so far as the theme of modernization is held to be an explanatory principle this too is unsatisfactory. It is most unclear whether this is merely a description of processes caused by other events, or whether it is supposed to be an explanation. If it is the latter, then there are serious problems in that it is not adequately specified. Such a vague notion of modernization or progress cannot be held to explain specific historical events (cf. Smith, 1973).

The second type of explanation is that of Marx (1954) and other Marxists, such as Müller and Neusüss (1975). Marx (1954) saw the factory legislation as the outcome of a struggle between capitalists and the working class over the length of the working day. The longer the working day was the more surplus value the capitalists were able to extract from their workers. The lengthening of the working day had, according to Marx, been a trend from the middle of the fourteenth to the end of the seventeenth century. This lengthening was even more savagely extended with the arrival of modern industry. Resistance to this extension involved, according to Marx, a long and drawn-out struggle which led to victory for the working class over the capitalists.

> The creation of the normal working day is, therefore, the product of a protracted civil war, more or less dissembled, between the capitalist class and the working class. (Marx, 1954: 283.)

Marx suggests that the struggle was won largely by the efforts of the working class, but with some assistance from other classes which did not have a direct interest, that is, by the landowners. The explanation of the factory legislation, for Marx, then, resides at the level of political struggle. There is no discussion in this section of *Capital* of the relation of these events to the circulation of capital.

Müller and Neusüss discuss Marx's account of the factory legislation in the context of the development of the theory of the state and in particular of 'state socialism' (or the welfare state). They confront the question of the degree of autonomy, if any, of the state from the circulation of capital, arguing that it is necessary for the capitalist mode of production that workers organize to protect themselves from the ravages of capital. If they did not then capital would reduce their living and working conditions to the point where workers could no longer exist, and hence neither could the capitalist mode of production. Each individual capital would strive to increase the amount of surplus value extracted from each worker and continue to lengthen the working day since it is in the interests of each individual capital to do so. The overall consequence of this, though, would be the premature exhaustion of labour power, thus destroying both the present workers and the reproduction of workers. This would destroy the very basis of the existence of capital (Müller and Neusüss, 1975: 67–9). The long-term 'collective' interest of capital is then, they suggest, the limitation of the working day. While the limitation of the working day is in the interests of capital as a whole, it is not in the interest of individual capitalists to sponsor such a move. While other Marxists have turned to functionalist formulations in order to explain the introduction of 'remedial' state action, (e.g. Poulantzas, 1973), Müller and Neusüss do not. While arguing that the capitalist mode of production 'requires' the working class to organize in its own defence they are keen to stress that it is a political struggle of unsure outcome. They suggest that while it is necessary for the workers to organize, it is not inevitable that their action will succeed. They suggest that the struggles will take a political form with consequent successes and set-backs.

The main problem with these accounts of the factory legislation by Marx and Müller and Neusüss is the total neglect of the gender dimension. They barely note, let alone comment on, the differential impact of the legislation on women and men. They do not discuss the benefits that men may have derived from this legislation and its relation to other patriarchal structures. So while their writing has some interest as an account of the relations between workers, capitalists and state action, it is seriously flawed in its neglect of the question of why the legislation applies to women more than men.

Marxist–feminist explanations of the factory legislation take account of gender while locating it in the context of the capitalist mode of production. The accounts by Humphries (1977a,b), McIntosh (1978) and Barrett and McIntosh (1980) examine such legislation as one part of a more general concern with the maintenance of a form of family where women do not undertake as much paid work as men. These writers argue that the practice of attempting to exclude women from paid work is done primarily in order to protect the family. They have varying emphases as to why capitalism 'needs' the family, but they tend to concentrate on capitalists' interests in the cheap reproduction of male labour power and of the next generation of workers (although a later article by Humphries (1981) stresses instead the importance of bourgeois approaches to female sexuality).

Humphries (1977a,b) argues that the exclusion of women from paid work should be seen as a strategy of the working class in its struggle against capitalism. She does not see this strategy as deriving from the divided interests of men and women, but rather as one from which both male and female members of the working class benefitted. She argues against those writers in the domestic labour debate who suggested that the family was maintained because it was functional for capital. Rather, she suggests, the working class maintained the family in order to protect their collective standard of living and class cohesion. Humphries argues that, in the nineteenth century, capital was strong enough to depress wages to subsistence level whether one family member did waged work or whether they all did. In the former case, one person would receive a family wage, and in the latter the same wage would be fragmented among several family members. In the latter situation, while the family received no greater wage, the capitalist could extract more surplus value and the family would have less time to spend on domestic labour to enhance its living standard. In addition, the family is held to have assisted working-class cohesion and militancy by its financial support to those involved in industrial action, such as strikes and lock-outs, and by maintaining a militant tradition. Humphries suggests that bourgeois ideology was mobilized on behalf of this strategy. She also saw the family as providing a non-degrading form of support for unwaged members of the working class. She supports her argument with reference to the literature on kin ties during the period which, she claims, shows that these were actively sought and maintained by all concerned.

Humphries' analysis does not, however, recognize the division of interests between men and women, in particular, that women deprived of a wage and confined as housewives suffer a lower standard of living than their husbands in the same family (Oren, 1974; Delphy, 1984). She further fails to recognize the interests of men in excluding women from competition for paid jobs.

Barrett and McIntosh (1980) argue that the family wage that Humphries describes never did exist, and that the idea of it had divisive effects on the working class, was detrimental to women in enforcing dependence and low wages and did not increase the wage levels of the working class as a whole. They note that many 'male breadwinners' did not in fact have dependent children to support and that many people did not have a 'breadwinner' to support them. They argue that even if the family wage had existed the beneficial consequences that Humphries suggests would not in fact have occurred. Indeed, they suggest that the idea of the family wage itself had pernicious effects on the working class and on women in particular. Barrett and McIntosh suggest that the family wage and the relative exclusion of women from paid work were demanded by male trade unionists and were simultaneously in the collective interests of capital. They argue that the entry of women into the factories in this period tended to undermine the reproduction of labour power in the family. Conditions were so bad that the physical reproduction of the working class was, apparently, being undermined. This threatened the interests of capital as a whole, as well as the labourers themselves. Thus both bourgeois philanthropists and the working class argued for better conditions for the reproduction of the proletariat. There emerged an alliance between these two groups on these issues which led to, among other things, the Factory Acts. McIntosh and Barrett note that this is not sufficient to explain why these 'better conditions' meant the shoring up of the family rather than alternative commercialized or socialized forms of reproduction and they note the spread of commercialized cleaning, ready-made food and day-care of infants. They suggest that the defence of the family came particularly from the bourgeois philanthropists and their concern with morals relating to sexuality and hard-working husbands. They suggest that the male working class colluded with the bourgeoisie on this issue.

> It appears, however, that the organisations of the working class colluded with pressure from the bourgeoisie to structure the working population along the lines of gender. (Barrett and McIntosh, 1980: 54.)

Barrett and McIntosh also suggest that there was a clear division of interests between men and women in competition for paid work. The notion of women as dependent homemakers coincided with their interest in excluding women from paid work.

While I agree with many of the excellent detailed criticisms of the notion of the family wage made by Barrett and McIntosh, I feel their analysis is limited by the lack of a concept of patriarchy. This absence means that they are unable to develop their very useful account beyond that of historical contingency.

The best example of a functionalist explanation of the factory legislation is that of Smelser (1959, 1967). He sees the factory legislation as part of a process of structural differentiation, suggesting that it was a consequence of pressures on the family which were generated by changes in the organization of the factory. In the early days of the textile mills, he argues, the family tended to be employed as a unit with appropriate jobs for all its members. Early in the nineteenth century, changes in technology meant that this arrangement came under threat, and with it the position of the man as head of the family in work and the household. Smelser suggests that rather than a man employing his own children as assistants, the new spinning technology demanded that he employ more assistants than he could possibly have children. These changes in the relations between members of the family led, Smelser claims, to agitation which eventually brought about a new form of family and a differentiation of the institutions performing those functions previously performed by the family. Thus there emerged the Factory Acts and a new form of family together with the growth of additional institutions such as schools, friendly societies and savings banks.

Interestingly, Smelser recognizes the significance of operatives organizing not only as workers, but also as men. For Smelser, as for Marx, the immediate impetus for the factory legislation came from the operatives, with some assistance from the land owners, while the factory legislation emerged after a protracted political battle. Like Müller and Neusüss, Smelser is concerned to locate the ultimate explanation at a higher level of abstraction than the immediate struggles of the competing groups. While Müller and Neusüss locate this in the capitalist mode of production, Smelser locates it in the functional necessities of society as a whole. Smelser has the conceptual space to discuss gender because of his recognition of the importance of the family, while Müller and Neusüss, with their exclusive attention on the capitalist mode of production, do not.

The problems with Smelser's analysis stem from some errors of historical fact, his use of the functionalist framework and his inadequate conceptualization of gender relations. Smelser states that it was usual for the family to be employed as a unit in the beginning of the nineteenth century, with the father directly supervising his own children. However, historical records show that many of the children were not directly employed and supervised by their own fathers even then. Parents acted as employing agents for less than one third of the working children in textile mills around Preston, while masters and spinners (excluding parents) employed over two-thirds of the working children (Edwards and Lloyd-Jones, 1973). The household composition of the spinners was such that it was, in fact, impossible for the spinners to have enough children of the right ages to act as assistants in the way Smelser argues. They would have too few children and of these some would be too old or too young to be assistants for all the time (Anderson, M., 1971, 1976). So, although the family was used as the unit of employment for some of the time, this could not have been the dominant form of employment relations. Rather, either the master employed directly, or the spinners acted as subcontractors.

There was thus no dominant family pattern of employment in existence in the way Smelser suggests. Hence there could be no breakdown of such a pattern with the consequences that Smelser argues for. However, these critiques of Smelser (Edwards and Lloyd-Jones, 1973; Anderson, M., 1976) focus on the relation of children to the father-spinner and neglect gender relations. They do not consider the implications of the increasing employment of women in the factories or relations between husbands and wives. So while there are problems with Smelser's explanation of changes in generational relations in the family as a consequence of changes in industry, his account of changes in gender relations is not disputed by these critics.

However, there are further problems with Smelser's analysis. The use of functionalism as a mode of explanation (Smith, 1973), creates a tendency to circular argument, whereby something is explained in terms of its effects (although Smelser's historical analysis helps to reduce some of the worst consequences of this type of reasoning). This approach fails to recognize that the new social forms which emerge after periods of strain are not inevitably given, but are a product of social experimentation and struggle. There is also a problem with Smelser's theoretical boxes, which he fills with empirical instances; since these are both so abstract that they could be filled with many other things, and yet over-precise in specifying stages in the process of change which might not occur. Further, there is an inconsistency, in that, while his boxes are described in functionalist terms, which are tilted heavily towards norms and values, his actual historical analysis focuses more on resources and social struggle. I would suggest that his historical account is more iluminating than his theoretical boxes.

Smelser's conceptualization of gender is similarly constrained by his functionalist terminology. It is restricted to the concept of the family, which cannot adequately cope with the strains his historical analysis subjects it to. The concept of the family does not allow proper conceptualization of the power and inequality between men and women, which in practice Smelser describes quite well. Further, while Smelser is concerned to trace the connections between gender relations in the workplace and the domestic sphere, he has a concept which only allows him to conceptualize one–the family–as a social structure. Smelser needs a conceptualization of gender relations in both spheres, as gender inequality is not merely to be found in the home, and also one which embodies notions of power and inequality. In short, Smelser needs a concept of patriarchy in order to do justice to the questions he is asking, and to the rich, historical account he has produced.

An alternative account of the legislation

The passage of the Factory Act cannot be understood without a concept of patriarchy, although a full explanation must involve other social forces as well. My own analysis will examine the position and role of several groupings with distinct interests in this matter including: male workers, female workers, different sets of employers, bourgeois philanthropists and the women's rights lobby. I will examine the positions of the various groupings and their power to mobilize resources in the struggles around these Acts. It will be necessary to consider the situation at various levels of empirical detail and analytic abstraction so as to both be able to explain particular events in terms of proximate causes, while also analysing the structural configuration which made the whole situation possible. I intend to start on a middle level of competing groups, and conclude with a consideration of the overall structural configuration.

Factory employers had an interest in the employment of women since they found it easier to pay them lower wages than men (see e.g. Pinchbeck, 1981). It was a general pattern for women to be paid lower wages than men, although there were great variations in the wages paid, and women weavers did on occasion earn as much as men when they were on piece rates. The view that women were employed because they were cheaper and more docile was summarized by Saunders, one of the Factory Inspectors:

> A vast majority of the persons employed at night, and for long hours during the day are females. Their labour is cheaper, and they are more easily induced to undergo severe bodily fatigue than men. (Parliamentary Papers 1843, vol. xxviii, p. 556.)

The lower wages were explicitly noted by contemporaries as a major incentive for mill-owners to employ women in preference to men (Pinchbeck, 1981: 194; Ure, 1983: 474).

While these low wages were widely accepted there were some overt patriarchal justifications for them. One of the Factory Sub-Commissioners stated in 1833:

> The low price of female labour makes it the most profitable as well as the most agreeable occupation for a female to superintend her own domestic establishment and her low wages do not tempt her to abandon the care of her own children. (Cited in Pinchbeck, 1981: 194.)

The structure of the factory was such that in its early days men were reluctant to enter it, leaving these jobs to parish apprentices and then later to women:

> The domestic tradition and hatred of restraint held men back from the factory in the early days, and although they entered

> later the occupation [weaving] has remained largely in the hands of women. (Pinchbeck, 1981: 180.)

The employers considered women workers more docile and easy to manage. They were considered less likely to join together and protest about their conditions:

> Manufacturers seem to have been anxious to employ women wherever possible. According to Gaskell, men were 'more difficult to manage', and more likely to cause trouble by their combinations. (Pinchbeck, 1981: 187.)

Thus patriarchal relations which made women cheaper, more docile workers in a period of industrialization led to the employment of women more quickly than men in the factories. The lower wages which it was possible to pay women and their lack of militancy and organization ensured that employers derived important benefits from employing female workers. Here we see a clear fit between patriarchal and capitalist interests.

However, this situation also contained some important contradictions. As factory employment expanded, it became the source of a greater proportion of all paid work and this changing pattern threatened men's interests. This employment threatened to become a source of power for women from which men could be relatively excluded. Capitalists' preference for women workers (because their position under patriarchy enabled capital to exploit them more than men) threatened to undermine the basis of patriarchal power in the sexual division of labour. If women were to earn a wage and work long hours away from the home, and men did not, then men would find their control over women significantly reduced. There emerged, then, a contradiction, rather than a fit, between patriarchal and capitalist structures. Access to factory employment became a source of power, while absence from it meant exclusion from this source of power. Some of the contemporary observers, indeed, described the situation in terms very similar to this, (albeit from a position of regret). For instance Lord Ashley, in a speech to the Central Short-Time Committee stated:

> Nor must we omit to press upon the attention of the public the gradual displacement of male by the substitution of female

> labour in a large proportion of the industrial occupation of the country . . . This evil . . . is spreading rapidly and extensively . . . desolating like a torrent, the peace, the economy, and the virtue of the mighty masses of the manufacturing districts. Domestic life and domestic discipline must soon be at an end. Society will consist of individuals no longer grouped into families; so early is the separation of husband and wife, of parents and children. (Cited in Pinchbeck, 1981: 197.)

While some contemporary observers undoubtedly exaggerated the claims of domestic dissolution, the basic thrust of their arguments still remained. There was, for instance, a tendency to exaggerate the proportion of women workers who were married (Pinchbeck, 1981: 197). Nevertheless, married women were employed in the factories and some employers did prefer them over unmarried women on the grounds that they were more attentive and docile because they had dependents to support (Pinchbeck, 1981: 194).

I would argue that the factory legislation should be understood as a consequence of this emerging contradiction between patriarchy and capitalism. It represents a political response from patriarchal interests striving to re-establish patriarchal control which was threatened by the emerging capitalist reorganization of the sexual division of labour.

In this situation state power was the form of power that was used to attempt to re-establish patriarchal control. The state, as argued earlier, should be conceptualized as a patriarchal state as well as a capitalist state. Patriarchal interests were represented at the level of the state, and after a period of political struggle in the nineteenth century, prevailed over the countervailing interests of capital. However, the state should not be seen as a direct instrument of patriarchal interests in a crude unmediated way. Patriarchal interests prevailed, but only after a period of struggle, the outcome of which was not necessarily to be in the interests of patriarchy.

Capitalist relations powerfully influence patriarchal relations and vice versa and the outcome of any concrete interaction cannot be read off logically from the abstract systems. When the patriarchal division of labour was threatened by changes in capitalist organization there was resistance to this by patriarchal interests. The outcome of the ensuing struggle can only be understood by taking into account the specific social forces in that situation. This involves examination of the different social groupings and the resources–economic, political and ideological–that they are able to mobilize. Thus this explanation of the Factory Acts will proceed with an analysis of the specific social forces involved in the passage of this legislation. It will elucidate the strengths and weaknesses of those groups with an interest in the existence or non-existence of these restrictions on women's paid work. I shall start with an examination of the movement to reduce hours in factories. Two groups, the 'bourgeois humanitarians' and the 'male workers', were the most important political actors here, although other groups including the manufacturers, female operatives themselves and the factory inspectorate also played their parts.

The bourgeois humanitarians

These men (for they were largely men) were particularly important in the passage of the Factory Acts. They include Richard Oastler, Michael Sadler, Revd G. S. Bull, Lord Ashley, Robert Owen, Philip Grant, Revd J. R. Stephens, John Doherty, George Candy, John Fielden, Charles Hindley, Lord John Manners and Joseph Brotherton. They were mostly though not entirely Tory and Evangelical (Hutchins and Harrison, 1911; Smelser, 1959). There were three elements in the bourgeois humanitarians' concern for factory conditions which need analysis here: their patriarchal attitudes; their concern with the long-term reproduction of the work-force; and their concern for the distress caused to the factory workers. Most writers have focused on only the last two elements and played down the significance of their patriarchal attitudes (e.g. Fraser, 1973; Roberts, 1960; Thomas, 1970; Hutchins and Harrison, 1911; Webb, 1902; Webb, 1911).

While the elements of their concern with the reproduction of the workforce and their humanitarian concern for people working in bad conditions are important, they cannot explain why the legislative attempts to remedy the situation should have contained such a marked distinction between men and women. Indeed, much of the legislation was not concerned primarily with the general working conditions, but instead was an attempt to remove women and children from these conditions. Much of this legislation had little relevance to men's conditions of work, except in so far as they were obliged to keep women's hours of work if they worked closely together.

Further, the concern of the bourgeois philanthropists was not merely with the general problem of reproduction of the workforce, but rather with the problems being faced by a particular patriarchal way in which the labour force had traditionally been reproduced. Smelser regards the domestic changes as particularly important in the campaign for the Factory Acts.

> These (domestic changes) were among the noisiest and most persistent claims of the factory agitators. (Smelser, 1959: 283.)

These men were concerned that the 'natural' order of the family was being distrubed by women's paid work in the factories.

The concerns of the bourgeois philanthropists for the long-term reproduction of the workforce focused on women because of their perceived importance in the rearing of children. The employment of married women was seen to interfere with the successful bringing up of their children. It was suggested that the children were more likely to die when their mothers took paid work (Hewitt, 1958; Smelser, 1959: 281). The women wre judged to be inadequate housewives, being untrained due to spending their youth in the factory rather than the home. An example of this fear is this statement from W. Cooke Taylor:

> there are, indeed, serious evils connected with the employment of women in factories and, indeed, everywhere, some in their own homes, which must not be passed over without notice. The girl employed all day in the factory has little opportunity of learning domestic economy and of the management of a household. When she marries she is far from being well qualified to fulfil the duties of a wife and mother, and she often neglects both from not knowing how to set about them. (Cited in Smelser, 1959: 282.)

This view that female factory employment was disrupting the patriarchal order of the family was widely held. W. R. Wood, one of the Commissioners appointed to investigate conditions in the mines, reported in like vein:

> the employment of female children and young persons in labour, to the degree which presently prevails, has the effect

> of preventing them from acquiring the most ordinary and necessary knowledge of domestic management and family economy that the young females in general, even when presenting the most tidy and respectable personal appearance before marriage, are nearly ignorant of the arts of baking and cooking, and generally speaking, entirely so of the use of the needle; that when they came to marry, the wife possesses not the knowledge to enable her to give her husband the common comforts of a home; that the husband, even if previously well-disposed, is hence often led to seek at the public-house that cheerfulness and physical comfort which his own fire-side does not afford, whence all the evils of drunkenness in many cases grow up; that the children, quite apart from the evils which the altered conduct of the father may bring upon them, but solely from the bad training of the mother, are brought up in no habits of order and comfort, but are habituated from their youth to all the evils of a disorderly and ill-regulated family, and must give birth a still worse state of things in a succeeding generation; that under these accumulated evils the wife and the mother is perhaps herself the most acute sufferer from the consequences of her own defective education. Such are the evils which the evidence I have taken appears to establish as the result of the temptations offered by the present high rates and wages for the employment of female labour. From this source a fearful deterioration of the moral and physical condition of our working population is rapidly taking place. (Parliamentary Papers 1842, vol. xv, p. 53.)

It is by no means clear that these fears had any real basis in the actual practices in the rearing of children. While the death rate in Lancashire was higher than that in the rest of England and Wales in 1851, it is at least as likely that this was due to other health hazards of the cities such as disease from bad sanitation. The smaller family size of women in paid work may be as likely a result of women with large families ceasing to work as due to the increased death rate of children of mothers so employed.

There is no conclusive evidence or argument that the employment of mothers in factories endangered the lives of their children and the reproduction of the population. Nevertheless, the belief that it did was strongly held (Smelser, 1959: 281). It was seen as appropriate for married women to be at home looking after the children, rather than engaging in paid work in the factory. The family was seen as the appropriate institution to ensure the rearing of children and the feeding, clothing and cleaning of the paid worker, despite the existence of other institutions which did these tasks as well. There was an ideological commitment to the family *qua* family which was not simply for its functionality in the reproduction of labour power. There were ways in which children could be looked after and workers fed and cleansed which did not involve women as unpaid domestic labourers. Ready-cooked food could be bought in pie and other shops. Laundry could be, and was, sent out for others to do on a commercial basis. Cleaning services could similarly be bought on a commercial basis. The reverse side of the paid casual domestic labour that so many women in the nineteenth century performed for others was that the rearing of children and servicing of self and husband did not have to be, and in some quite widespread instances was not, organized on a domestic rather than commercial basis in the nineteenth century. The services existed in a commercialized form and were utilized as such. It is necessary to explain why these commercial forms were not encouraged and developed and why the bourgeois philanthropists preferred to sponsor the patriarchal and domestic way of organizing these tasks. These men (mostly) were operating within a discourse which encouraged the patriarchal family independently of its effectiveness in the reproduction of the workforce.

A further aspect of this discourse was the male bourgeoisie's hypocritical stance on female sexuality. Publicly, these men adhered to the condemnation of non-marital sexuality, particularly for women. In so far as conditions in paid work were held to encourage female sexual activity then they were especially condemned. The factories were believed to encourage sexual contact between the female operatives and the male operatives and masters. The wages enabled women to buy drink and consequent drunkenness was also held to encourage 'immorality' (Smelser, 1959: 283–4). The conditions in the mines particularly horrified the Commissioners who investigated them in 1840–2. The presence of men and women together working in near darkness was held to be an invitation for all sorts of immoral practices. The Commission was obsessed with the sexual conduct of the colliery women (Humphries, 1981). Behaviours such as drunkenness, immodesty and profanity were also held to indicate the likelihood of promiscuity. The Commissioners focused on this aspect of women's work underground to the neglect of other aspects such as physical suffering. There are continual references to the state of undress that the male and female workers are to be found in.

> In great numbers of the coal-pits in this district the men work in a state of perfect nakedness and are in this state assisted in their labour by females of all ages, from girls of six years old to women of twenty-one, these females themselves being quite naked from the waist down. (Parliamentary Papers 1842, vol. xv, p. 24.)

The Commissioners themselves seemed more concerned with the sexual implications of the chains with which women and girls dragged coal carts than with the severity of the labour they implied.

The publication of the Royal Commission's report caused an outcry which focused on these aspects of women's work underground. The report contained emotive pictures of small children pulling coal through narrow seams. These were reprinted in many newspapers alongside written reports of the conditions (Roberts, 1960: 60). MacDonagh (1973) also notes the significance of the sudden exposure to public knowledge of a social evil for subsequent legislative action and suggests that civil servants responded to particular problems rather than planned major initiatives. Indeed I would suggest that public reaction might be considered to be a 'moral panic' in much the same way as the sudden growth of public concern over 'mods' and 'rockers' that Cohen analyses (1973). The legislation on mines was especially important in that it was the first act to ban women from a specific form of paid work.

The moral crusade of the bourgeois humanitarians should be seen as a consequence of three elements: firstly, the humanitarian concern to alleviate suffering; secondly, the concern to protect the long-term reproduction of British workers; thirdly, the patriarchal discourse on women's frailty, their place in the home and their chastity. The position of this group cannot be understood without taking into consideration its patriarchal position.

Male operatives

The male factory operatives were the other major group which sought the restriction of women's paid work in the factories. Their demands may be broken down into three components: firstly, they wished to re-establish the patriarchal form of the family which they saw as being under threat by women's employment in the factories; secondly, they sought to remove women from competition with themselves for the jobs in the factories; thirdly, they wished generally to shorten the hours of all factory operatives.

Most existing analyses of the factory operatives' concern for the factory legislation focuses on the last element, to the neglect of the first two. Indeed it has sometimes been argued that the restriction of the hours of all the factory operatives was the dominant, if not the only real, motive behind the agitation. This is seen as the men merely fighting 'behind the women's petticoats' for the limitation of the hours of all (Hutchins and Harrison, 1911; Webb and Webb, 1894). Hutchins and Harrison suggest that labour militants saw their only hope of success in the reduction of hours in this way since dominant notions of individualism, freedom of contract and laissez-faire precluded the possibility of Parliament voting to legally restrict the conditions under which men sold their labour, while they would do so for women's labour. However, while there might have been a few operatives who held this position this was not the view more generally held among this group. The evidence of the frequency and depth of the patriarchal attitudes of the male operatives is inconsistent with the view that the focus on women's work was merely a smokescreen for a movement genuinely committed to the equal reduction of hours for all workers. Rather, the patriarchal aspect of this movement was a centrally important dimension.

The patriarchal attitudes of the male operatives were related not only to the workplace, and their desire to keep the better forms of employment to themselves, but also to the implications of women's work in the factory for the home. These men opposed women's employment in the mills because it diminished men's authority and comfort in the home. Many of them desired not merely the limitation of the hours of paid work of women, but the ending of this work altogether. There are repeated references to these sentiments in *The Ten Hours Advocate and Journal of Literature and Art*, the journal of the Lancashire Central Short Time Committee

> married women would be much better occupied in performing the domestic duties of their household, than following the never-living motion of machinery. We therefore hope the day

is not far distant, when the husband will be enabled to provide for his wife and family, without sending the former to endure the drudgery of a cotton mill. (*Ten Hours Advocate*, 1846: 34.)

The vice of the system of long hours in factories, in relation to morals, is *its utter incompatibility with domestic life.* (*Ten Hours Advocate*, 1846: 34, original emphasis.)

We learn indeed with pain, that nearly 2,000 married women are taken from their proper sphere in the family, and confined all day in the mill; and we shrink from contemplating the evils thereby inflicted upon their children, and upon society ultimately. We also think, the fact that 8,000 young women are earning an independent livelihood, affords some explanation of another painful feature of society–viz, the early severance of the delicate tie which binds parents and children together. (*Ten Hours Advocate*, 1846: 12–13.)

The *Ten Hours Advocate* reported at length the advantages it saw in the Mines Act passed earlier in the decade which had banned women (and children) from working underground.

Upon the passing of Lord Ashley's act, an almost instantaneous reformation took place. The women, being kept at home, have become tidy and respectable, and the colliers' houses are clean and comfortable. The taste for drinking is gradually giving way . . .

I do not believe any act of parliament ever passed has done so much good in so short a time, to those who were the subjects of the act . . .

I repeat once more that the wages of the colliers, are amply sufficient to enable them to maintain the female members of their families at home to look after his family, cook his victuals, and mend his clothes, and keep everything snug and in good order . . .

. . . A Scotch agricultural labourer, with his wife at home, and with two shillings a day, is infinitely more comfortable than a mill-spinner with double the amount of wages, but whose wife is engaged along with himself all day in the mill. (*Ten Hours Advocate*, 1846: 50–3.)

The male operatives were organized in local short-time committees which were co-ordinated by Central Short-Time Committees for Lancashire and Yorkshire (*Ten Hours Advocate*, 1846: passim;). *The Ten Hours Advocate and Journal of Literature and Art* was the organ of the Lancashire Central Short-Time Committee. This weekly paper carried regular reports of numerous meetings held, resolutions passed, funds collected, petitions drawn up and presented, parliamentary activities and speeches made in order to secure the reduction in hours of work, expecially for women (*Ten Hours Advocate*, 1846, 1847: passim). The journal also carried longer articles on the merits of short-time legislation such as the long piece on the supposed advantages of the Mines Act 1842 which banned women and children from working underground.

The Lancashire Central Short-Time Committee kept in close touch with the bourgeois humanitarians, but was not run by them. Men such as Ashley and Oastler regularly wrote letters to the *Ten Hours Advocate*, a form of communication unnecessary if they had been running the short-time committees and their journal (*Ten Hours Advocate*, 1846, 1847: passim). The short-time committees were financed by the operatives, and their journal is full of references to fund-raising. Most of the money was raised by the cotton spinners (*Ten Hours Advocate*, 1846: 2).

Woman operatives

There is very little surviving evidence of the views of the female operatives themselves. Even those in trade unions exerted little influence over its policy and were absent from the positions of leadership (Foster, 1974: 253). However, there is occasional evidence that the women operatives were opposed to legislation which limited their opportunities for paid work, as in the following letter sent by women workers to a newspaper called *The Examiner*:

> Sir,
>
> Living as we do in the densely populated manufacturing districts of Lancashire, and most of us belonging to that class of females who earn their bread either directly or indirectly by manufactories, we have looked with no little anxiety for your opinion on the Factory Bill . . . You are for doing away with our services in manufactories altogether. So much the

better, if you had pointed out any other more eligible and practical employment for the surplus female labour, that will want other channels for a subsistence. If our competition were withdrawn and short hours substituted, we have no doubt but the effects would be as you have stated, 'not to lower wages, as the male branch of the family would be enabled to earn as much as the whole had done', but for the thousands of females who are employed in manufactories, who have no legitimate claim on any male relative for employment or support and who have, through a variety of circumstances, been early thrown on their own resources for a livelihood, what is to become of them?

In this neighbourhood, hand-loom has been almost totally superseded by power-loom weaving, and no inconsiderable number of females, who must depend on their own exertions, or their parishes for support, have been forced, of necessity, into the manufactories, from their total inability to earn a livelihood at home.

It is a lamentable fact, that, in these parts of the country, there is scarcely any other mode of employment for female industry, if we except servitude and dressmaking. Of the former of these, there is no chance of employment for one-twentieth of the candidates that would rush into the field, to say nothing of lowering the wages of our sisters of the same craft; and of the latter, galling as some of the hardships of manufactories are (of which the indelicacy of mixing with the men is not the least), yet there are few women who have been so employed, that would change conditions with the ill-used genteel little slaves, who have to lose sleep and health, in catering to the whims and frivolities of the butter-flies of fashion.

We see no way of escape from starvation, but to accept the very tempting offers of the newspapers, held out as baits to us, fairly to ship ourselves off to Van Dieman's Land, on the very delicate errand of husband hunting; and, having safely arrived at the 'Land of Goshen', jump ashore, with a 'Who wants me?' Now, then, as we are a class of society who will be materially affected by any alteration of the present laws, we put it seriously to you, whether, as you have deprived us of our means of earning our bread, you are not bound to point out a more eligible and suitable employment for us?

Waiting with all humility, for your answer to our request, we have the honour to subscribe ourselves, the constant readers of the Examiner.

'THE FEMALE OPERATIVES OF TODMORDEN'
(Cited in Pinchbeck, 1981: 199–200.)

A survey of the attitude of cotton textile operatives in 1849 by the Factory Inspectors found more men than women in favour of the reduction of hours of work to ten, which had just been implemented. While a clear majority (70 per cent) of the men were in favour of the legislation only half (nearly 55 per cent) of the women were so (Neff, 1929: 76).

Women's views on work in the mines were collected to some extent by the government commission studying conditions in the mines. Though these views were varied, the general picture is that the women wanted paid work, although they would have preferred less arduous work than that which they had. They would prefer not to work in mines, but would rather have that work than none at all.

Helen Reid, 16, coal-bearer:
The lasses will tell you they all like the work fine, as they think you are going to take them out of the pits.

Ann Harris, 15, putter:
Heartily hates it; could get no other profitable work; it is no women's work, nor is it good for anybody.

Isobel Hogg, 53, was a coal-bearer:
You must just tell the Queen Victoria that we are quiet loyal subjects; *women–people here don't mind work!* but they object to horsework; and that she would have the blessings of all the Scotch coal-women if she would get them out of the pits, *and send them to other labour*. (Parliamentary Papers 1842, vol. xv, p. 30; my emphasis.)

In the early period of 'protective' legislation there was no organized women's voice in the matter, but by the last quarter of the nineteenth century this was no longer the case. While in the early period we can do little more than speculate on the basis of fragmentary evidence as to the opinions of women employees on the legal restriction of their hours of work, by the time of the debates over new legislation in the latter part of the century there were well organized lobbies of women.

In 1873 a Home Office report recommended that there should be a further reduction in the number of hours which could be legally worked for pay by women from 60 to 54. The bill embodying this fell in the House of Commons as a result of feminist arguments articulated by the husband of Millicent Fawcett, although they failed to remove existing legislation (Strachey, 1978: 234–5).

Attempts to extend the 'protective' legislation in 1887 by banning women from working at the pit heads and from working with large hammers in the metal trades were also defeated, largely as a result of the pressure of organized women. In these cases the women workers themselves made deputations to see the relevant ministers and were supported by active middle-class feminists (Strachey, 1978; John, 1984).

There were divisions among organized women, however, on whether 'protective' legislation should be supported. There is a tendency to analyse these as class divisions, with those opposed to the legislation being written off as 'middle class' feminists who did not understand the 'real' needs of working-class women (cf. Webb and Webb, 1894; Jacoby, 1976). However, I think this is better explained as the division between, on the one hand, a patriarchal hegemony in the trade union movement, within which women unionists were likely to be enveloped, and on the other, an independent, cross-class feminism.

Manufacturers

The manufacturing employers were the groups most opposed to the passage of legislation restricting women's hours of work. Many of them saw such attempts to shorten the working day as directly counter to their own interests (Hutchins and Harrison, 1911; Thomas, 1970; Marx, 1954; Smelser, 1959). Most of them believed that the longer the operatives worked the more profitable their enterprise would be. For instance, Nassau Senior argued in 1844 that the profit of a mill derived from the last hour of work and that to limit the hours would mean the destruction of the enterprise in the long run (Hutchins and Harrison, 1911: 88–9). The longer the utilization of the machinery and the longer the operatives could be made to work for a given wage, the bigger the profit undoubtedly was for the manufacturers. There is little doubt that the material interest of the individual manufacturers was in opposition to the limitation of the hours of any of their employees.

The manufacturers were able to mobilize the moral principles of the time in order to support their case. They appealed to the notion of the paramount importance of individual liberty and the non-interference in the actions of individuals. Labour was regarded as free and it was seen as improper for the state to interfere in a contract 'freely' drawn up between employer and employee. State interference was regarded as an evil in itself. The mid-nineteenth century was the heyday of laissez-faire and rampant individualism. Even those in favour of the legislation recognized this, as Charles Hindley noted in a speech reported in the Manchester Guardian:

> . . . it had been anticipated that the passing of the factory act would have the effect of preventing the unwilling toil of a great many adults; but the fact was that very many adult males were being employed 14 hours, and, he understood, even 15 hours per day, and if it were to be proposed in the house of commons to pass an act to protect adult males, in factories, it would be answered that it was an invasion of the rights of an Englishman to prevent him from working as long as he pleased; and the house of commons would not listen to the proposal for a moment. (*Manchester Guardian*, January 10 1849.)

The manufacturers were not united in their opposition to the factory legislation and these divisions have been interpreted by some writers as crucial in the explanation of the passage of the Factory Acts (Foster, 1969; Marvel, 1977). Indeed, Marvel argues that the 1833 Factory Acts can be explained as an attempt by the owners of the more modern mills, which used less child and female labour, to disadvantage their competitors in the older mills, which used more of these categories of workers. Marvel argues that this is the only way it is possible to explain why the Act was passed by a Whig government in which the manufacturers interests were clearly represented. While there may be an element of truth in this, in particular in explaining the timing of this particular Act, Marvel overextends his argument when he claims that this explains the passage of the legislation altogether. There are many more groups and issues involved than just rival manufacturers. Marvel seriously underestimates the importance of patriarchal forces in the passage of the legislation.

The division of opinion among the manufacturers has a further basis. While some manufacturers conformed to the 1833 and 1844 Acts others managed to break the law with impunity. The magistrates who adjudicated on complaints brought under the Factory Acts were often drawn from the same class as the manufacturer brought before them, and indeed may have been related in some manner. Consequently enforcement of the Acts was very patchy (Marx, 1954: 274). This caused concern, among those who conformed, about the competition they suffered from those who were able to work their labourers harder. One consequence of this was to provoke the conforming manufacturers to demand more efficient and uniform enforcement of the Acts (Müller and Neusüss, 1975: 65; Marx, 1954: 274).

Factory Inspectors

The Factory Inspectors themselves developed into an influential body which advocated the extension of the Factory Acts. They adopted the position that the factory legislation was a good thing, and needed further extension. They formed an articulate and authoritative grouping and espoused the patriarchal interests men had in common. The following extract from the report of Horner, a Factory Inspector, in 1844, illustrates this concern to re-establish patriarchal relations within the family which he saw as being undermined by women's factory employment, and demonstrates the patriarchal aspect of the humanitarian concern about overwork in the factories. They wished to bring about a state of affairs whereby employers would find it preferable to employ men instead of women and saw legislation as a way of doing this.

> The substitution of female for male labour, which has increased to so great an extent of late years, is attended with the worst consequences to the social condition of the working classes, by the woman being withdrawn from domestic duties; and diminished comforts at home have the most corrupting influence upon the men. All these evils are much aggravated when the women are worked so excessively that their life must

> be passed between the workshop and bed. The subject has been repeatedly mentioned to me by some considerate and humane mill owners, who know the evil of such a system, and wish to see it put down; and they have urged me to represent to the government the propriety and necessity of preventing, by law, that women of any age work more than twelve hours a day. It would render illegal over-working far more difficult, and, in those mills where the occupier desired to work more than twelve hours, adult men would be employed, who are now either idle or doing the work of full-grown children. There is at present a very sorry state of things in regard to wages in some departments of cotton mills in Lancashire; for there are hundreds of young men, between 20 and 30 years of age, in the full vigour of life, employed as piecers and otherwise, who are recieving not more than eight or nine shillings a week; while, under the same roof, children of 13 years of age are getting five shillings, and young women between 16 and 20 are getting from ten to twelve shillings a week. (Parliamentary Papers 1844, vol. xxviii, p. 540.)

Time and again the Factory Inspectorate saw legislation to reduce the hours women could work as a means of encouraging the employment of men rather than women in the factories. Saunders, a Factory Inspector for Leeds, similarly promoted legislation to prevent women working at night and long hours in this way.

> It is not the least among the advantages of such a regulation, that it would encourage the employment of a greater number of adult males where night work was profitable. (Parliamentary Papers 1844, vol. xxviii, p. 540.)

The Inspectors' recommendations were thus a further element in the pressure to extend the Factory legislation to cover women as well as children. In the Act of 1844 women were included under the same conditions as young persons under 18 (Hutchins and Harrison, 1911: 85–6).

Landed interest

A further group wanted to contain the manufacturing interest. These were the landowners, who were strongly represented in Parliament, particularly by the Tory party. While they might be considered to have had no direct interest on any side of the issues under discussion, they were important because of their rivalry with the manufacturing interest. Their interests were in weakening the manufacturing interest, and hence, indirectly, with the protective legislation (Hutchinson and Harrison, 1911; Smelser, 1959).

Outcome of the struggles over the Factory Acts

The outcome of the struggles over the Factory Acts was affected by the resources each group was able to mobilize, by its skill in doing so and by the interaction of the different groups. Unequal access to state power was of particular importance.

The bourgeois humanitarians had access to considerable political resources to ensure the restrictions on women's work. They were directly represented in Parliament and consequently well placed to help the legislation in its passage, and also in assisting the setting up of Commissions to lend it further support. Their private wealth helped them to spend the time they wanted on the campaign and to distribute such information as they liked. Their position in the social order was also lent authority to the views they espoused (Hutchins, and Harrison, 1911; Smelser, 1959; Thomas, 1970).

The male workers did not have direct access to parliamentary power in the early part of the nineteenth century since at this time they did not have the vote. They were, however, able to place substantial pressure on parliament because they were well organized. They were particularly well organized in arguing for the 1847 Act, the first which limited women's working hours, with co-ordinated short-time committees, their weekly publication the Ten Hours Advocate, mass meetings and travelling spokesmen (Smelser, 1959: 303; Ten Hours Advocate, 1846, 1847, passim). The basis of their organization was in the workplace both in trade unions and in more informal groupings. Some of these organizations were explicitly closed to women, others implicitly. For instance, the unions representing the spinners and the weaver overlookers were closed to women as were these occupations (Parliamentary Papers 1837–8, vol. viii, p. 301) while the Weaver's Union to which women were admitted was controlled by men.

Women were excluded from the bases of the male operatives' power. The women operatives did not have access to the same routes to political influence as the male operatives. They had least access to state power of all the groups considered. Women had neither a vote nor, in the early nineteenth century, organizations to represent their interests. Consequently they exerted little, if any influence, over the introduction of the legislation, although the development of women's organizations later in the century created a different situation then.

The manufacturing employers did have direct access to parliamentary power and many sat directly in Parliament or had their interests well represented by other employers. Their political interests were largely represented by the Whig party, which during the nineteenth century formed the government for part of the time. For part of the nineteenth century they were indeed effective in preventing the passage of protective legislation. Their eventual defeat on this issue is in some ways quite remarkable given the political power they were able to mobilize.

The passage of the Factory Acts should be seen primarily as the outcome of the pressure from the male operatives and the Tory landed interest. The interests of the manufacturers and the women were defeated on this issue. This is not an unsurprising outcome given the different strengths of the groups in the nineteenth century. The male working class was growing in size and organizational power, albeit unevenly. The division of the bourgeoisie into the landed and manufacturing fractions and further divisions within the manufacturing interest were crucial in allowing the modest success of the male working class over this issue. While there are lively debates as to the extent of the interpenetration of these fractions of the bourgeoisie, for instance in their interrelations through marriage, there was nevertheless some division of interest (Thompson, 1965). This split was politically represented to a considerable extent by the division between the Tory and Whig parties. While there are problems as to the extent to which Parliament in the mid-nineteenth century was clearly divided on party lines, it does appear that parties in this period did represent clear divisions on important issues (Aydelotte, 1973). The Corn Laws and the factory legislation were specific issues where they were opposed. The manufacturing interest, under pressure from the urban proletariat, imposed a defeat on the landed interest by the repeal of the Corn Laws which enabled cheaper corn to enter Britain, lowering the profits of the landed classes. While the repeal of the Corn Laws is often seen as a response to the growing political importance of the urban proletariat, the importance of the detailed working of Parliament and the political parties should not be neglected (Moore, 1973). The enactment of the factory hours legislation was, to some extent, an act of retaliation on the manufacturing interest by the landed interest, in that it restricted their exploitation of certain categories of workers and hence reduced their profits. However, the Tory party did not uniformly and whole-heartedly support the factory legislation. Such moves were supported by Ashley and the Tory Radicals such as Ferrand, but not by the majority of the Tories. While the Tories expressed their condemnation of the conditions of the working class, their business interests and their opposition to extending the power of central government meant that they did not fully support such moves through Parliament (Roberts, 1973). The strength of the male workers' demands was crucial to the passage of this legislation and the form of the legislation cannot be understood without an analysis of the patriarchal relations which shaped it. This aspect of the analysis is missing from accounts of the battles between Tories and Whigs and the role of the working class. Yet the shape of the Acts cannot be understood if it is seen as merely Tory versus Whig, or workers versus manufacturers. While all those interests were present, patriarchal forces were crucial to the shape of the legislation as it differentially affected men and women.

The specific manoeuvring of these groups and trade conditions are important for the explanation of the timing of the various pieces of legislation. The repeal of the corn laws in 1846 encouraged retaliation by the landed interest. The male operatives were particularly well organized in the 1840s with their short-time committees, weekly publication, broad-based organization and mass meetings. Further, the depressed trade conditions in 1847 encouraged the belief that the unemployed could be absorbed if hours were shorter (Smelser, 1959: 303). However, these details of the events should not be taken to explain the passage of the legislation. Such events, manoeuvrings and trade conditions merely assist in the explanation of the timing of the specific acts.

This analysis leads to a major reinterpretation of the political turbulence of the first two-thirds of nineteenth-century Britain. This period was marked by the growth and then quiescence of radical dissent and opposition. It is usual to see this in terms of the growth of the political agitation of a rising urban proletariat, followed by some measure of reformist incorporation (e.g. Tholfsen, 1973). A major interpretation of this is in terms of the development of an aristocracy of labour which gained privileges at the expense of other workers, dividing the working class, taking on reformist and even conservative political positions which it transmitted through the rest of the working class (Gray, 1981; Hobsbawm, 1968; Foster, 1974; Moorehouse, 1978; Reid, 1978). While there is a vigorous debate around the various contradictory aspects of this thesis, these features are central to the account.

However, this position is seriously flawed in that it takes into account only the class divisions of capitalism, and neglects those within patriarchy. Rather there was another dynamic running through the agitation of this time, that is, of struggles over patriarchal authority. These were an important part of the dissent of the time, and one important reason for the quiescence of the latter part of the century was, I would suggest, due to the establishment of a compromise between patriarchal and capitalist forces. There are a couple of writers (Smelser, 1959, 1967; Joyce, 1980) who have noticed the importance of the gender dimension of the struggles of the periods. For instance, Joyce (1980) considers that the family was important in re-establishing stability in the Victorian period. He considers that the family was the model, and an important basis of the new acceptance of the new industrial order. He argues that the participation of all family members in the factory work encouraged this acceptance since, according to Joyce, the authority and status structure of the two institutions was very close.

However, Joyce's account (and indeed that of Smelser) fails to grasp the essential character of the struggles over patriarchal authority. They conceptualize gender issues in terms of the 'family' and are unable to cope with the assymmetries of power within the family because the concept of the family has inbuilt notions of unity and accord which they fail to overcome. Joyce, in particular, pays insufficient attentions to men's struggles to re-establish patriarchal control over women.

Effects on cotton textile employment

It is important to recognize that this legislation was only one among several strategies used in the attempt to control women's access to paid work and to re-establish the threatened patriarchal authority. Thus it is not a simple matter to determine the effects of the legislation. In simple numerical terms the proportion of women in the cotton textile mills did not fall after the passage of the Acts. Indeed, the textile industry till very recently remained an important source of female paid employment. Thus the attempts of this period at using legislation to exclude women from paid work were relatively unsuccessful. Patriarchal forces were not able to push through their most radical strategy of excluding women from factory employment. However, it would not be correct to conclude from this that the legislation had no effect on women's access to paid work. The legislation, together with other patriarchal practices, was important in structuring the types of paid work women had access to and the conditions under which it was performed. It produced a situation in which male labour was more attractive to employers in developing areas of the economy. I shall examine this when looking at later periods. Further, male earnings from longer hours and shift premiums remain to this day an important part of the differences in wages obtained by men and women.

Before looking at other forms of patriarchal pressure it is important to elucidate the differences in the gender compositions of the different branches of the cotton textile trade. The two most important processes were those of spinning and weaving, with carding and dyeing and finishing also of some significance. Spinning itself had two major grades of workers: the spinner (or minder) who directed the operation, and the piecers (big and little) who assisted the spinner in such matters as repairing broken ends. Spinners were almost invariably adult males while the piecers were young adults or children, at first of either sex, but later more often male. The assistants would progress from little piecer to big piecer and the men would aspire to the position of spinner. The spinners were the group of cotton textile workers who protected the male composition of their occupation most fiercely and most effectively (see e.g. Lazonick, 1979).

Apologists for the male monopoly of the most lucrative job in cotton textiles refer to the supposed strength and skill necessary to work the large mules (spinning machines). However, there are several reasons why these are not the reasons that women were excluded. Firstly, the fact that men on average were stronger than women does not mean that any individual woman is necessarily less strong than any individual man. If this were the reason we should expect merely a lower proportion of women on the mules than men, yet instead they were almost totally absent. Secondly, heaviness of work was not a bar to women taking such types of employment; at the same time, women were carrying coals out of the mines. Thirdly, the amount of skill involved, as measured by the time it took to learn the job, could not have been much different from that involved in weaving, where there was a majority of women, and women took eight years (between the ages of 12 and 20) to become fully proficient. Since women in neighbouring weaving towns were able and prepared to learn a skilled trade this could not be the reason why women did not learn to spin. Fourthly, women were used as mule spinners in Scotland after a strike which ended in the destruction of the men's union, which demonstrates that there was no absolute reason why women could not do this job (Lazonick, 1979; Savage, 1982; Hutchins, 1915).

Occasionally women did take on the job of mule spinning, but this was fiercely resisted by the organized male spinners. For instance, when three women, who had been piecers, started work on mules at the Lockstock Mill in Bolton in the 1800s the spinners came out on strike, and this was endorsed by the local Spinners Association. After a strike of the 170 men for several weeks the men resolved never to teach any woman to be a piecer again in order to prevent the situation recurring (Liddington and Norris, 1978: 90). Clearly in this instance there was no reason based on lack of skill or strength which prevented the women from being spinners; the hostility of the male spinners, and their ability to control entry to the trade by control over training, was crucial. The three women spinners gained the support of the *Women's Suffrage Journal*, but not the Women's Trade Union League. This division in feminist support was caused by the trade union women being too fearful of losing the support of the men's unions (Liddington and Norris, 1978: 281).

I would argue that the main reason that women did not occupy the position of spinner was because the men had a strong organization which kept them out. The male spinners had strong unions even before the repeal of the Combination Acts (Chapman 1972: 58–9; Lee, 1972: 121–2). They systematically resisted the entry of women into this, the most lucrative job in the cotton textile industry. These men were very well organized, for instance, holding in 1829 a national delegate conference of spinners in the Isle of Man.

This conference resolved to prohibit women from joining the men's unions, and to teach only sons, brothers, nephews and the master's poor male relatives how to spin (Smelser, 1959: 236–7). The Cotton Spinners of Glasgow likewise had a clause in their Articles of Association which forbade the teaching of spinning to other than male kin.

> This association binds and obliges every one of its members to refrain from instructing any individual in the art of spinning, except such as are sons or brothers of a spinner, who may have been, or is at present a member of this association; and it must be remembered, that such persons can only be admissible by having served them as piecers. (Parliamentary Papers 1837–8, vol. viii, p. 301.)

On the rare occasions when there was not a spinners' union, women were used as spinners. For instance, when the mill owners were able to smash the men's organization, women were employed on spinning. In Glasgow a fall in the price of yarn in 1836 after a 16 per cent wage increase in the previous year led the employers to take on the union in an attempt to restore their profits. The bitter strike culminated in the breaking of the union. At this point the employers introduced women onto some of the spinning machines, the common mules and self-actors (Lazonick, 1979: 244).

It was the patriarchal organization of the men's skilled union and their ability to restrict training in their skills to men which was the most important reason that spinning was a male job. The contrast between gender relations in spinning and in weaving, despite the similarities of the labour process, is stark. The majority of weavers were women, although there were also some men weavers working in the same weaving sheds. Like spinning, weaving was a skilled trade which took several years to learn (although this is sometimes underestimated: see Turner, 1962; Phillips and Taylor, 1980). The typical pattern was for a child to assist a weaver (as a tenter) for a couple of years, fetching and carrying weft, starting around the age of 12 or 13. Then she (or he) would start to learn to weave, being taught by one of the weavers. At first they would work on only one or two looms over several years progressively move to four looms, by the age of 20. Both spinning and weaving worked on a sub-contracting basis, in that the spinner or weaver would be paid a piece-rate by the mill-owner, and then employ and pay their assistants themselves out of this money (Hutchins, 1915; Joyce, 1980; Savage, 1982).

Given these similarities between spinning and weaving it is initially remarkable that they had such different gender relations of employment. I would suggest that the crucial difference occurred at the point of transition of these processes from the household to the factory. Spinning was originally a form of employment performed by women. However, the early mechanized spinning introduced in the 1780s, which was at first organized on a putting out basis, came to be performed increasingly by men. The mechanization was a slow process involving first the use of the jenny, used largely by women, and then the mule, used by men (Aspin, 1964: 49; Catlin, 1970: 42; Lee, 1972: 115). This early mule-spinning involved the direction of the labour of others and was also highly productive (Lazonick, 1979: 233; Wadsworth and de Lacymann, 1931: 464). I would argue that it was at that point that the crucial sex-typing of the occupation as male occurred. The men utilized their position of power and authority within the household to take control of this new form of profitable employment and direct the labour of the other members of the household, rather than being either a non-participant or directed by the wife. The transition of spinning to the factory occurred *after* the basic mechanization of the process had occurred, and after the process had become one in which men predominated.

Weaving on the other hand, had a quite different type of move from the household to the factory. The handloom weaving which was performed predominantly by men in the household was not transferred wholesale. Rather the powerloom was first introduced into the factory, not into the home (Pinchbeck, 1981). There was no gradual transition nor slow development of the power-assisted labour process. This discontinuity was important in the transition from weaving as predominantly a male occupation to predominantly a female one.

Once weaving had been established as an occupation suitable for women, they were unassailable in this role. The mill-owners could have skilled weaving at rates of pay substantially less than those for skilled jobs, such as spinning, monopolized by men, although weaving was much better paid than almost any other manual work for women. The legislation restricting women's hours of work failed to dislodge women weavers.

Legislation to restrict women's hours of work was an important attempt by patriarchal forces to re-establish patriarchal control over women in the home and in the workplace, but it was not in fact directly successful in reducing women's employment in the cotton textile mills, which were its first target. Nevertheless, it continued to have a part to play in the restriction of women's access to paid employment (see chapters 6 and 7 below). Further, the Acts did assist the restabilization of patriarchal relations in the family. Women spent more time on housework when their hours of factory work were shortened. Some did cleaning and washing themselves instead of paying for it to be done. This was greeted with considerable satisfaction by the Commissioners (Neff, 1929: 77).

Moreover, the agitation aroused by the entry of women into relatively well-paid work in the factories helped to discourage employers from hiring female labour for newly developing industries. The relative quiescence of the third quarter of the nineteenth century should be seen at least partly as a result of compromise and truce between patriarchal and capitalist forces.

Engineering from 1800 to 1914

Engineering has particular importance as a leading sector in Britain's industrialization, and indeed in the industrialization of the globe. It was the British engineering which made Britain the 'workshop of the world' in the latter part of the nineteenth century. In contrast with cotton weaving this is an area where few women have been employed, and their exclusion continues to resonate in the contemporary western world with the absence of women from employment in technology. Although from the time of the First World War there has been a marked increase in the number of women employed on some engineering processes, they still do not occupy the same proportion of jobs as they do in textiles or clerical work.

Table 5.1 shows the tiny proportion of women engaged in engineering. Between 1851 and 1911 only between 5 and 6 per cent of the engineering workforce were female and most of these were concentrated in a narrow range of trades, mainly in the Black Country. The nature and level of patriarchal organization in the workplace is a very important factor in explaining the exclusion of

Table 5.1 The Proportion of Women in Engineering, 1841-1911

Standard Industrial Classification[1]		1841	1851	1861	1871	1881	1891	1901	1911
VI Metal	T[2]	165,293	289,268	371,878	440,951	475,252	525,743	551,990	590,094
manufacturing	%F[3]	1.2	5.0	4.5	2.3	2.3	3.0	2.7	3.8
VII Mechanical	T	32,400	76,591	117,888	168,631	204,230	265,679	432,087	516,326
engineering	%F	4.8	1.0	0.6	0.8	1.1	0.7	1.5	
VIII Instrument	T	15,844	22,262	27,118	78,878	31,355	34,102	36,159	38,578
engineering	%F	1.6	2.1	3.6	3.7	4.4	6.7	10.0	11.7
IX Electrical	T	–	–	–	–	2,600	13,362	57,104	116,894
engineering	%F	–	–	–	–	1.0	4.1	4.4	8.0
X Shipbuilding and	T	27,219	31,236	52,885	61,421	72,572	94,035	121,293	155,885
marine engineering	%F	0.4	0.1	0.2	0.2	0.2	0.3	0.2	0.3
XI Vehicles	T	38,992	46,754	52,962	58,957	66,954	86,098	125,757	192,738
	%F	0.7	0.4	0.4	0.8	0.7	1.4	2.7	4.1
XII Metal goods not	T	81,091	96,092	135,401	139,956	161,176	174,400	251,120	321,740
elsewhere specified	%F	11.2	15.5	18.6	20.1	20.8	19.6	21.3	21.0
VI–XII All	T	351,761	562,231	758,132	898,794	1,017,139	1,193,419	1,575,510	1,932,285
engineering	%F	1.2	5.5	5.8	4.6	4.7	4.8	5.2	6.2

Source: calculated from census data 1841–1911. Census figures taken from C. H. Lee, 1979, *British Regional Employment Statistics 1841–1971*

Notes: [1]The Standard Industrial Classification has always shown a large number of divisions within engineering. The boundary between engineering is blurred on the one side towards the manufacture of metal and on the other towards fancy metal working such as jewellery. For the purposes of statistical analysis I have included SIC VI metal manufacturing, SIC VII mechanical engineering, SIC VIII instrument engineering, SIC IX electrical engineering, SIC X shipbuilding and marine engineering, SIC XI vehicles and SIC XII metal goods not elsewhere classified. I would have excluded the category of SIC VI metal manufacturing, but for the fact that the census notes warn that there is considerable overlap between this order and SIC XII metal goods not elsewhere classified. This overlap is partly due to the looseness of the descriptions provided by respondents, but partly due to the more basic reason that often both the production of the metal and the manufacture of goods from the raw metal were carried on in the same premises (Lee, 1979: 13). Thus I have included SIC VI in the category of engineering.

[2]T: total

[3]%F: percentage of women

women from the engineering trades. Male workers in engineering were very strongly organized around their own interests during the nineteenth century (and are indeed today). Their organizations were similar to the cotton spinners', and quite different from cotton weavers or clerical workers. Also crucial were the timing of the transfer of engineering to the factory and the timing of the organization of workers. In engineering the male workers were well organized before the work moved into the factory, and they were able to take their organization in with them. This continuity was crucial in their maintaining control over who was employed in this relatively lucrative area of work. In contrast, the male handloom weavers did not follow their trade into the factory, powerloom weaving instead being largely performed by women workers. This discontinuity precluded any basis for men excluding women in weaving, while the early unionization of this area of work assisted the maintenance of levels of wages sufficiently high as to encourage some men to work alongside the women. In the case of clerical work, as we shall see later, the male clerks, by contrast, were able to retain their position at the top of the clerical hierarchy, and although unable to prevent the introduction of women clerks at lower levels they were able to sustain their own privileged position by agreements with employers on segregating the workplace.

The transition to the factory

Before it became concentrated in factories, two important types of engineering work were that of the millwrights who travelled from place to place building and repairing mills and that of the small workshop kept by a master with assistance from his wife and apprentice. These workers were highly skilled and owned their own tools and controlled the labour process. Entry to the trade was by means of an apprenticeship of five or seven years duration (see e.g. Jefferys, 1970; Penn, 1982).

Women were not generally eligible for apprenticeships and hence were not usually able to enter the skilled metal trades in their own right, although there were exceptions to this. However, many married women took up the trade of their husband and assisted in the work. On the death of the husband it was not unusual for the widow to carry on the trade and be admitted to membership of the guild in this way. This work by women was made possible by the close physical proximity of the workshop and the house, the workshop often being attached to the dwelling (see e.g. Pinchbeck, 1981; Clark, 1982).

The movement of this form of production from the workshop attached to the home to the factory had a catastrophic effect upon women's ability to participate. The move occurred as a result of the increasing size and expense of the machinery used and its concentration in fewer workshops owned by the richer masters. More journeymen were unable to set up as masters in their own right and run their own workshops and women lost their major route of access to work in the skilled metal trades (Clark, 1982; Pinchbeck, 1981).

Control over entry

The guild system of apprenticeship was in decay over a long period and in the early nineteenth century was finally abolished in that form. However, skilled artisans retained control over access to their trade and were organized in a variety of trade societies. There was not a clear break in this type of worker organization (Thompson, 1968; Musson, 1972). The skilled metal workers were one of the groups which managed to retain their organization particularly effectively. Their control over their trade was effected by strong controls over entry. They were able to have considerable control over who became apprenticed and over the numbers of the apprentices, despite the repeal of the Elizabethan apprenticeship statute (*The Engineer*, 1892, vol. 73: 199–200; Jefferys, 1970: 16, 58–9). This strategy was widespread among nineteenth century trade unions:

> All unions, almost without exception, limit the number of apprentices, with the avowed object of diminishing the number of workers, and so preventing what might be termed internal competition in any particular trade. (*The Engineer*, 1892: 199.)

The main efforts of the trade societies and craft unions were not focused directly on wages, but rather on enforcing their rules of entry which had consequences for wage levels. Control over entry was the main issue in three strikes by engineering societies between 1831 and 1838, even before the creation of the Amalgamated Society of Engineers (Jefferys, 1970: 79). One of the main aims of the 1851–2 strike and lockout was again the restriction of engineering work to time-served men (Jefferys, 1970: 35–42).

Unlike later types of workplace organization, these craft-based forms sought to control the conditions on which they sold their labour power primarily by restricting entry to their trade, rather than by negotiating a rate for the job at hand. This exclusion of others from entering a trade facilitates a particularly strong form of patriarchal control. However, there is no reason inherent in this strategy why gender should be chosen as one of the criteria of exclusion. The principle of this form of closure is that a restricted number undergo an apprenticeship which is then held to be a necessary requirement of practising that trade. There is no necessary reason why women should be excluded from undergoing the apprenticeship. This choice is part of an independent patriarchal dimension, not part of the necessary logic of craft control.

While the strategy of controlling entry has no necessary implications for gender relations in employment, it does facilitate the adoption of specifically patriarchal forms of closure to a greater extent than other workplace organizational strategies. It is precisely because this strategy is based on exclusion, rather than bargaining for the rate for the job regardless of occupant, that it is peculiarly open to combination with strongly patriarchal strategies. A combination like this only occurs in a context in which there is an independent basis to that patriarchal strategy. Such a context existed during the development of engineering.

The reason for the almost total exclusion of women from engineering up until the First World War is the outcome of the combination of a strategy of controlling working conditions by controlling entry, which was sustained in engineering to a greater extent than most other forms of employment, together with the patriarchal interests of the male workers.

The vast majority of the skilled metal workers' societies and unions explicitly banned women from membership (Drake, 1984: 115–17). The Amalgamated Society of Engineers, the largest and most influential of the engineering unions did not admit women until 1943. The Society was formed out of local societies representing the interests of the male engineers in 1851, but local trade societies had exerted considerable influence over the employment of engineers since well before 1800. Indeed the power of the combinations of engineers was one of the reasons behind the passage of the Combination Act of 1799 which attempted to forbid all trade unions (Jefferys, 1870: 11, 29). The refusal of engineering unions such as the Amalgamated Society of

Engineers to admit women was instrumental in the almost total exclusion of women from this type of work. The fact that this exclusion was not simply directed against a group of workers on the grounds of their lack of skill but rather on the grounds of their gender can be seen by the contrast between the dates when the ASE admitted semi- and unskilled men and the time when they admitted women. The semi- and unskilled men were admitted to membership of this union (then the Amalgamated Engineering Union) in 1926, while the 1943 date for women represents a further wait of 17 years. This cannot be explained in any other terms than the patriarchal nature of the union.

There were one or two engineering trades which were minor exceptions to the almost total exclusion of women. The unions in these trades made repeated efforts to expel women, although they were not successful (Drake, 1984: 17–18). The exceptions were mainly concentrated in the metal trades of the Black Country: in particular chain-making, blacksmithing and the brass trade. In 1882 the Black Country metal unions tried to introduce a Bill into Parliament restricting women's entry to the trade of blacksmith. This was vigorously opposed by the Women's Trade Union League and the employers. An attempt at 'compromise' was made by the Secretary of the Lodswinford Nailers who recommended segregating the women to a restricted part of the trade. The metal unions carried their fight to ban women to the Trades Union Congress where in 1887 all the male delegates voted for the exclusion of women from these trades and only the two women delegates voted against it. The male dominated Trades Union Congress voted

> to introduce such amendments to the Factory and Workshops Act as shall prevent the employment of females in the making of chains, nails, rivets, bolts etc., such work not being adapted to their constitution. (Drake, 1984: 20.)

Thus even in those few places where women did find employment in the metal trades they met with determined opposition from male workers (Drake, 1984: 17–18).

Weakness in the exclusionary strategy

It is sometimes argued that the exclusion of women from skilled manual trades by craft unions was simply due to the men's attempts to retain their position in relation to employers, and that this followed on logically, and somewhat inevitably, from their position as skilled workers. That is, that the exclusion of women was a given in a strategy of control over entry, which was itself almost inevitable given their position *vis à vis* their employers. This view is contradicted by the evidence of instability, from the turn of the century, in the strategy of exclusion as a means to secure high wage levels and by the internal divisions within the engineers' union as to whether this was indeed the best strategy for them to follow after this time. During the twentieth century the growing employment on new labour processes of workers who had not served apprenticeships undermined the effectiveness of the engineers' exclusionary strategy. The slowness with which the union moved to a grading and 'rate for the job' strategy demonstrates that a union strategy cannot be simply read off from the workplace situation of its members, and shows the importance of considering the relative independence of political and organizational factors.

The strategy of exclusion as the main means of controlling the rate of remuneration and the conditions of employment is dependent upon there being some skill or other power that the workers possess in order to sustain it. During most of the nineteenth century and before, the basis of the engineers' power lay in their control of the labour process, through their skill and control over training, combined with the organizational strength to turn these potential powers to full advantage. The employers repeatedly tried to undermine the basis of this power through the introduction of new machinery which they hoped would obviate the need for highly skilled workers. They introduced machine after machine, but during most of the nineteenth century their hope was not fulfilled. This was partly because, while these new machines could be used to turn out the old type of product with less skilled workers, they opened up the possibility of new advances in the quality and speed of work, if they were used by skilled workers, and it was also partly because of the strength of the engineers' organization, which backed their claims that the new machines should be worked by skilled, time-served men. Struggles over these issues were endemic in the nineteenth-century engineering trades (Jefferys, 1970: 24, 35–42, 125).

In 1897 there was a series of disputes culminating in strikes and a national lock-out. A central issue was whether certain new machines should be worked by other than skilled men. Two of these disputes were at the Sunderland Forge and Engineering Company and at the Armaments Company of Barrow, where the masters had introduced new machines and put unskilled labourers to work on them. The engineers' union wanted these machines to be worked by skilled men (*The Engineer* 5 March 1897: 253, 19 March 1897: 307, 26 March 1897: 323, 2 April 1897: 355; Jefferys, 1970: 143–8). The machines which were in dispute included boring machines and hand saws. The employers refused to countenance the Union's demands and the Engineering Employers Federation wrote to one of the local branches of the Amalgamated Societies of Engineers (ASE) on 24 December 1896 to this effect:

> The Federation distinctly decline to admit the right of your Society to claim for your members exclusive right to work any particular class of machines.
>
> The machines are the property of the employers and they are solely responsible for the work turned out by them. They, therefore, will continue to exercise the discretion they have hitherto possessed of appointing the men they consider suitable to work them. (EFEA, 1897: 3.)

The employers claim to appoint whom they pleased, whether skilled or not, was apparently upheld with the defeat of the ASE in the lock-out. Although the ostensible cause of the lock-out was a dispute over the shortening of the working day to eight hours, the 'machine question' was the real basis of the dispute. In this dispute the development of a strong organization of employers played an important part in the defeat of the union (ASE, 1886–98).

However, despite the apparent defeat of the ASE, the local societies continued to push the issue of the 'machine question' in those areas where they were strong (Weekes, 1970: 301). *The Engineer* refers to some firms settling this issue according to the 'general custom of the trade', while in other cases employers hoped for change (*The Engineer*, 22 November 1901: 541). Tactics used by the men to resist the introduction of 'handymen' and other non-apprenticed labour included refusing to teach them, and refusing to rectify any problems in a handyman's job (Jefferys, 1970: 157).

Weaknesses in the strategy of exclusion were recognized by the union's leaders: on occasion they tried to shift the strategy of the union from one of exclusion to one of demanding the rate for the job at different levels and grades. There were also attempts to broaden the membership of the union at various times (e.g. 1892, 1901). However, until the 1920s the leaders' attempts to do this were largely unsuccessful and a gulf opened up between the union officials at the centre and the rank and file members in local societies (*The Engineer*, 1892: 538, 28 June 1901: 677, 12 July 1901: 37; Jefferys, 1970: 166; Weekes, 1970: 87, 315).

The Engineer describes the struggle of the union leaders at the quinquennial delegate conference in 1901 to extend the membership by including semi-skilled operatives. It suggests that Mr G. N. Barne, the General Secretary of the Amalgamated Society of Engineers,

> has had a somewhat tough struggle with not a few of the more conservative delegates (*The Engineer*, 12 July 1901: 37.)

The union leaders were unable to introduce the alternative strategy of the rate for the job because of resistance from the rank and file members and the employers. This was despite the unions' inability, after the turn of the century, to sustain effectively the policies implied in a craft union stance. Although the introduction of new machinery meant that by this period the old strategy was being repeatedly undermined by the employers, the union leaders were unable to effect a change in union policy (Weekes, 1970: 82, 315, 360).

The exclusionary strategy adopted by the engineering unions was not automatically given, but was one chosen from at least two major possibilities. The maintenance of the exclusionary policy of the ASE despite its no longer being appropriate for the industrial relations situation, calls for explanation. This is usually given, as in *The Engineer*'s report, in terms of the rank and file being 'conservative'. This 'conservativeness' contains a significant patriarchal element that commentators usually underestimate or ignore.

Engineering from 1900 to 1914

The years immediately prior to the First World War saw the beginning of the introduction of women into engineering. This occurred particularly on new types of semi-skilled work, and in the Midlands (Hutchins, 1915: 66; Lewenhak, 1977: 141) and was greeted with considerable opposition by the men already working in engineering. On these new types of work there was no consensus between men and employers on who should do them. Women's access to them was bitterly resisted by the men. The work included machine tending, press-work, stamp-work, metal-cutting, printing, brass work, pen-making, machine ironing in laundries, tin pot- and bucket-making:

> It is in these kinds of work that difficulties occur in imperfectly organised trades; it is here that the employer is constantly pushing the women workers a little further on and the male workers a little further off; it is here that controversies rage as to what is 'suitable to women', and that recriminations pass between trade unions and enterprising employers. (Hutchins, 1915: 66.)

From around the turn of the century there appeared the beginnings of a shift towards a strategy of the rate for the job rather than that of exclusion. In part this was due to the emergence of new general unions which did not have a technical basis for their policies of exclusion. In part it was due to feminist pressure from bodies such as the Women's Trade Union League, which continually brought the advantages of the latter policy, and the dangers of under-cutting inherent in the former, to the attention of trade union leaders.

An example of such a change is in the radically different response of the Trades Union Congress to the demands of the Black Country metal unions that the TUC should support its demand for the exclusion of women workers from these trades. In 1887 the TUC overwhelmingly supported this demand, while in 1908 the Congress called for equal pay for women and the organization of women workers as an alternative policy to prevent under-cutting (Drake, 1984: 20, 66–7). However, while the stance of the TUC changed over this period, that of the bulk of members of the Amalgamated Society of Engineers did not.

Both the strength and the strategy of the engineering unions, in particular the Amalgamated Society of Engineers, were crucial in explaining the absence of women from engineering in its formative period in the nineteenth century. Further the strength and strategy are to be explained primarily by the slow entry into the factory of an already organized craft.

Clerical Work from 1870 to 1914

Clerical work, which employs such a large number of women today, was a small, largely male occupation until the end of the nineteenth century. The very significant expansion of clerical occupations between 1870 and 1974 is largely accounted for by the changing structure of capital. This period saw a significant increase in the size of employment units as a consequence of mergers between firms and increases in state bureaucracies. It also saw the development of a more refined division of labour. The increase in the amount of clerical work stems from these changes in several ways. Firstly there was increased need by capital and the state for methods of accounting and co-ordination commensurate with the forms of control used in large hierarchically organized bodies. Secondly, there was an increasing division of labour in that certain functions of monitoring and co-ordination in such organizations were being separated out as a special set of jobs rather than being integrated with manual labour itself. Thirdly, there was the growth of new service industries whose specialized products required a higher proportion of mental to manual labour than traditional manufacturing. These changes started during the period 1870–1914, and accelerated in the inter-war period (See Braverman, 1974; Holcombe, 1973; Abercrombie and Urry, 1983; Anderson, G. L., 1976; Lockwood, 1958).

Increase in the proportion of women clerks

There was an enormous increase in the proportion of clerks who were women during the years 1870–1914, especially in the years after 1890. Between 1901 and 1911 the number of women clerks increased by 110 per cent, whilst that of male clerks increased by only 17 per cent. The proportion of female clerks in 1901 was 18 per cent, and by 1911 this had increased to 33 per cent (Anderson, G. L., 1976: 2). The education system at the end of the nineteenth century made possible the acquisition of basic skills of literacy and numeracy by girls as well as boys (Deem, 1978; Holcombe, 1973). However, while educated boys had a range of occupations open to them, this was not the case for young women. At this time the professions were largely closed to women, and most of the professions which today employ women, such as nursing and social work, only existed then in embryonic form. Thus the potential supply of sufficiently literate workers at this time might be considered to be composed of a higher proportion of women than men (Davies, 1979).

Employers were keen to employ women for their more lowly clerical jobs. They preferred women partly because they were cheaper to employ than men and partly because they were easier to manage. Women clerical workers earned less than men and employers appeared to be well aware of the advantages of this to themselves (Holcombe, 1973; Anderson, G. L., 1976: 59). Women clerks were also preferred because they were seen to be more punctual and efficient than men clerks (Anderson G. L., 1976: 59), and 'better adapted' and reconciled to lack of promotion (Holcombe, 1973). In short, employers preferred female clerks because they worked better and at lower wages than male clerks.

Women were first admitted to the Civil Service as clerks as a result of the takeover of the Electric and International Telegraph Company (which employed a few women clerks) by the newly formed Post Office in 1869. From 1871 there was a rapid expansion of women clerks in the Post Office. The employers' reasons for this expansion were stated as being the cheapness and skill of these women; for a given level of wages they considered that they got more highly skilled women than they could men. Further they left promotion for men because they usually retired from the work on marriage. Mr Scudamore, a senior Post Office official expressed his preference for women thus:

> In the first place, they have in an eminent degree the quickness of the eye and ear, and the delicacy of touch, which are essential qualifications of a good operator.
>
> In the second place, they take more kindly than men or boys do to sedentary employment, and are more patient during long confinement to one place.
>
> In the third place, the wages, which will draw male operators from but an inferior class of the community, will draw female operators from a superior class.
>
> Female operators thus drawn from a superior class will, as a rule, write better than the male clerks, and spell more correctly; and where the staff is mixed, the female clerks will raise the tone of the whole staff.
>
> They are also less disposed than men to combine for the

> purpose of extorting higher wages, and this is by no means an unimportant matter.
>
> On one other ground it is especially desirable that we should extend the employment of women. Permanently established civil servants invariably expect their remuneration to increase with their years of service, and they look for this increased remuneration even in the cases, necessarily very numerous, in which from the very nature of their employment they can be of no more use or value in the twentieth than in the fifth year of their service . . . Women, however, will solve these difficulties for the department by retiring for the purpose of getting married as soon as they get the chance . . .
>
> On the whole, it may be stated without fear of contradiction that, if we place an equal number of females and males on the same ascending scale of pay, the aggregate pay to the females will always be less than the aggregate pay to the males; that, within a certain range of duty, the work will be better done by the females than by the males, because the females will be drawn from a somewhat superior class; and further, that there will always be fewer females than males on the pension list. (Quoted in Martindale, 1938: 17–18.)

Contemporary observers noted the attractiveness to employers of the relative cheapness of women's labour and considered that it was responsible for lowering the level of renumeration of clerical work as a whole. Choizza Morey MP, writing in 1908 on the front page of the first issue of *The Clerk*, the journal of the National Union of Clerks, expressed this concern.

> The rapid multiplication of clerks in the last twenty years and the invasion of the field of employment by an enormous number of women and girls, many of whom, unhappily, are content to accept exceedingly low wages, has continuously lowered rates of renumeration for clerical labour, and in their unorganized condition clerks have been unable to resist the economic pressure. (*The Clerk*, 1908: 1.)

Some employers directly substituted women for men clerks, although the dominant pattern was rather one in which women took the majority of the newly created jobs. A few employers did proceed with more or less direct substitution of women for men. The story of a 'well-known limited liability company' which 'dispensed with fifty male clerks and substituted girls' (*The Clerk*, 1908: 48) made headlines in the daily newspapers and raised considerable discussion in the journal of the National Union of Clerks (*The Clerk*, 1908: 48, 54). The 50 per cent turnover of jobs from male to female in the Post Office Savings Bank in one decade (Price, 1977: 104) is very likely to have been produced by more or less direct substitution. It was certainly widely believed among clerks that women were being substituted for men, as *The Clerk* repeatedly reported.

> Over and over again women are substituted for men because of cheapness. (*The Clerk*, 1908: 9.)

> Others had been discharged wholesale so that their places might be filled by female clerks at half the wages. (*The Clerk*, 1908: 3.)

However, not all schemes to substitute women for men came to fruition. For instance, one plan to substitute young women for male clerks in some transport offices fell through (*The Clerk*, 1908: 7). Further, the substitution of women for men, however greatly feared, did not lead to any absolute drop in the number of male clerks. During this period while the numbers and proportion of female clerks increased dramatically the numbers of male clerks did not drop, only their proportion did. This supports the picture of men retaining their established positions in general, if not in every instance, while women took the bulk of the jobs in the new clerical occupations.

While most commentators note the advantages to employers of the cheapness of women's labour as a reason for the expansion of women's clerical employment, the resistance of existing male clerks to this expansion is given little attention. The process is viewed as a smooth one shaped by the interests of employers. For instance, Braverman (1974) sees the expansion of women's employment as a consequence of demand for women's labour within particular occupations.

> The growing participation of women in employment has thus far been facilitated by the stronger demand for clerical employees and the relatively stagnating demand for operatives. (Braverman, 1974: 353.)

Indeed, Braverman can see no reason why these trends may not end up with equal rates of labour force participation for men and women (p. 392). He is not unaware of the sex segregation of employment, but is unable to incorporate an understanding of this into his account. He considers it as merely an outcome of 'custom and living practice' (p. 353). Braverman's lack of attention to the significance of workplace organization for sex segregation is in keeping with his (much criticized) omission of worker organization and resistance (see Elger, 1979; Wood, 1982).

Lockwood's (1958) analysis of clerical work is similarly flawed by his inadequate treatment of gender relations. Lockwood's account of the reactions of male clerks to the entry of women to clerical work is ambiguous and inconsistent. On the one hand, he suggests that there was little concern on the part of the men, and that there was no direct competition.

> They were the cause of a certain mild amusement on the part of their male colleagues, but of no real concern. Their work was peripheral to the main activity of the office and they were not competing directly with men. (Lockwood, 1958: 122.)

On the other hand, he suggests that there was some 'strong resistance' to women's entry and uses metaphors of barriers being broken and indeed military references to 'invasion' and 'entrenchment'.

> But as early as 1870 this exclusiveness was being broken down by women . . . [By the turn of the century, in] commerce [women] were still a small minority, and in banking, insurance and law there was strong resistance to their employment. (Lockwood 1958: 122.)

He goes on to consider how the entry of women contributed to the lowering of the status of the clerical occupation.

Men's opposition to female clerks

There is, in fact, evidence of considerable hostility to the introduction of women clerks among existing male clerks, although those researchers who have noted this have not realized its significance. These male clerks were convinced that the entry of women to clerical work was responsible for depressing the pay and status of their positions. There are widespread reports of this hostility (*The Woman Clerk*, 1919: 6; Martindale, 1938: 22, 24, 25, 26, 28; Humphreys, 1958: 43, 55, 56; Anderson, G. L., 1976: 39, 119; Price, 1977: 104; Holcombe, 1973: 168, 174; Lewenhak, 1977: 116).

A flurry of correspondence appeared in the *Manchester Guardian* in November 1886 on the problematic effects of the entry of women to clerical work. These male writers argued that women 'naturally' accept lower wages than men with which they could not compete. One suggested the establishment of a clerk's union to control the entry of women so as to enable male clerks to earn a family wage and keep women at home out of paid work altogether. Another suggested that women became unfitted for the role of housewife as a consequence of working in an office, since they would not learn how to perform household tasks adequately. Yet another male correspondent suggested that the office was dangerous for women because they were sexually vulnerable while in a man's world (Anderson, G. L., 1976: 39). An editorial in *The Office* on 9th August 1880 asserted that women were entering a field of labour that should be men's and that they should rather be at home (Price, 1977: 104).

Male postal employees made frequent objections to the introduction of female clerks which were published in their journal *The Civilian*. There was especial difficulty in introducing women into branches of the Civil Service other than the post office. Complaints included the one that women undercut men's salaries (Holcombe, 1973: 168, 174). Another facet of the problems faced by women was the introduction of the marriage bar in this period, which prevented all married women working in the Civil Service.

Opposition by men to women clerks in the Post Office Savings Bank had a long history. The first 40 women introduced there in 1875 met with vigorous opposition. *The Civilian*, the Post Office journal (later the journal of the Civil Service), reported these protests from the entire staff, including a proposed meeting (Martindale, 1938: 25). These protests gained renewed vigour in 1890–1 when a further increase in women clerks was proposed (Price, 1977: 104–5; Humphreys, 1958: 43–5).

The General Secretary of the National Union of Clerks, Mr Elvin, held as his ultimate goal the exclusion of women, not merely from offices, but from all paid work. In an article in the union's journal he considered that certain problems in the office would remain

> until that ideal time arrives when female labour will not be known in factory workshop or office. (*The Clerk*, 1908: 131.)

These various contemporary correspondents raised the same objections to women clerical workers as did the male objectors to women workers in the textile mills and underground in the mines. They complained about competition for jobs, the depression of levels of income for men, that women would not be adequate housewives, that women were sexually vulnerable in paid work, and argued that men should be paid well enough to keep 'their' women at home and out of men's sphere of paid work. It should be noted that the men's hostility was not directed merely at any workers who threatened to undercut their pay and work conditions, but rather that it took a specifically anti-woman form. The men referred to their desire that women should not be in paid work at all, and that they should rather be at home in the role of housewife. Their protests were thus concerned not merely with rival workers who were undercutting them, but were part of an attempt to establish a sexual division of labour with men monopolizing paid work and women confined to housework. This was not a case of skilled workers merely trying to maintain their position *vis à vis* capitalist employers, but rather had a specifically patriarchal dimension.

On some occasions these men's hostilities to women clerks broke out into industrial action. One such incident occurred at the Post Office Savings Bank in 1890–91. Rumours that the management was intending to substitute women for male clerks, fuelled by the management stating that it intended to increase the number of women clerks, led to a protest meeting of clerks in October 1890 outside the bank, which was reported by several papers. The official reaction was a minute which censured the men's action. In response the male clerks held another meeting and drew up a memorial, the Civil Service version of a petition. This appeared in the *Evening News* before being received by the Postmaster General who then issued a warning to the men. After this warning was also published in the *Evening News* together with the men's reactions to it the officials had two of the leaders of the agitation transferred to other departments. The focus of the men's struggle then shifted to overtime and pay, leading to an overtime ban, suspensions and finally sackings (Price, 1977: 104–5; Humphreys, 1958: 43–5).

In a strike organized by the National Union of Clerks in the spring of 1914 the issue of women clerks was one of three grievances. The other two were constantly recurring overtime and low salaries. The women were particularly badly paid and the men saw this being used against them. The firm was practising a policy of female for male substitution in that male clerks were being dispensed with while young women were being taken on. This was believed to be lowering the status of the entire staff. The strike lasted until August 1914 but petered out at the onset of war with a consequent management victory (Anderson, G. L., 1976: 119).

The men's struggles varied in extent and effect, by industry and region. This was at least partly responsible for the very uneven proportion of women in clerical work across industry and region. The ratio of male to female employment in white collar work showed variations which may be considered indicative of variable outcomes of the struggle between employers and male clerks (although other causes must be considered relevant as well). While in 1911 women constituted 40 per cent of clerks in the civil service, and nearly a third among commercial clerks, they constituted less than 2 per cent in railways and banking (calculated from Anderson, G. L., 1976: 56). The local variations were likewise very great with the proportion of female commercial clerks in 1891 ranging from 6 per cent in Bristol, Manchester and Leeds and 9 per cent in London, to 20 per cent in Birmingham and 25 per cent in Edinburgh (Crossick, 1977: 55a).

While some of the national bodies of the unions representing clerical workers did have some policies for equal treatment for men and women, others did not. The National Union of Clerks, founded in 1898 from an amalgamation of the Clerks Union and National Association of Clerks did have an official policy of equal treatment of men and women (*The Clerk*, 1908: 5; 1918: 80; 1919: 50). Indeed the organ of the NUC *The Clerk*, was highly critical of an earlier clerk's union which did not admit women to membership. It attacks this position with gusto:

> You, fellow clerks–and short-sighted churls, have yourselves forged the weapon which has been and still is, slaying you. You have refused equality to women; the result is she is economically of less value to the community. She can do the same work as you do, and do it as well as you can, but because you refuse to admit her individual value she is swamping you, as she must

> do when she is brought into competition with you. (*The Clerk*, 1908: 9.)

Here we see very different strategies being followed by organized clerks as to how to counter the undercutting of existing wages by women. Some unions, such as the insurance clerks' unions (Drake, 1984: 171), practised exclusion, while others (such as the National Union of Clerks (NUC)) attempted to organize women. However, the decision of the NUC to organize women and attempt to raise their wage levels rather than exclude them was hardly based on sympathy for the feminist cause. Rather the union addressed a male interest:

> Gentlemen, in the hope that you will grant to women full equality with you–not entirely for her sake, but for yours, and your sons', and your sons' sons'. (*The Clerk*, 1908: 9.)

Indeed, women were seriously underrepresented on the national council of the NUC, and, in the period before 1918, no women were appointed to official positions (Drake, 1984: 172). In 1914 this union supported a strike in which one of the grievances was the increasing pressure of women clerks (Anderson, G. L., 1976: 56), and one of its General Secretaries believed that ultimately women should be removed from paid employment (*The Clerk*, 1908: 131).

This ambiguous view of female clerks was not unnoticed by women workers themselves. In 1903, after failing to obtain special representation on the executive, some women broke away from the National Union of Clerks to form the Association of Women Clerks and Secretaries. Similar breakaways occurred in several Civil Service departments, leading to the foundation of the Association of Women Clerks in the Post Office in 1901, the Civil Service Typists Association in 1908 and a separate organization of women clerks at the Board of Trade in 1911 (Lewenhak, 1977: 116). *The Woman Clerk*, organ of the Association of Women Clerks and Secretaries, was concerned about the dangers to women of being in mixed unions 'having regard to the feeling against women amongst a certain element in the rank and file' (*The Woman Clerk*, 1919: 6).

Both the union strategy of excluding women and that of organizing women were based on the pursuit of the interests of the male clerk. This pursuit of male interest did not take a single direction, but rather a variety of strategies were open to and tried by the male workers, of which these were the main two.

Sex segregation

It has been argued that the high degree of sex segregation within the clerical occupations precluded competition between women and men (Anderson, 1977). Women tended to be employed in the lower-level occupations such as typing and shorthand writing, while men were employed in the higher-level occupations such as book-keeping and correspondence clerk (Anderson, G. L., 1976). I would agree that this segregation may indeed be seen as severe, since it involved not merely elements of vertical segregation (in that men tended to be in higher level occupations), but elements of horizontal segregation also, in the fact that there were no promotional ladders connecting the occupations filled by women to those filled by men. A typist could not expect to be promoted to positions of authority in the office however well she typed. In so far as this segregation was upheld, and, in so far as the structure of occupations was static, there would be little direct competition between male clerks and female clerks. Anderson (1977) argues that these conditions were met and that there was indeed little direct competition between clerks of different sexes. He suggests that the effect of women's entry to clerical work on male clerks has been much exaggerated, and that any effects were limited because of this sex segregation of employment within clerical occupations. Women were not seen as undercutting men's wages, because they were not in direct competition with them; neither did they have a serious displacement effect, for the same reason.

However, there are three problems with Anderson's argument. Firstly, while direct competition and substitution may not have been the rule there is evidence that it did occur on some occasions (*The Clerk*, 1908: 5, 9, 48, 54; Price, 1977: 104). Secondly, Anderson ignores the dynamic aspect of changes in the division of labour in which new occupations are constantly being created and old ones being destroyed. Thus, while direct competition may not have been a common situation, indirect competition between men and women for the possession of the new occupational slots was not ruled out by sex segregation, and was indeed a highly likely occurrence. Thirdly, Anderson fails to provide an explanation of the rigidity of the sex-typing of the clerical occupations. Such an explanation is crucial to understanding the basis of the supposed lack of competition between men and women clerical workers.

I want to suggest an alternative interpretation of job segregation and the relations between male and female clerical workers in this period. I shall argue that job segregation was a negotiated outcome of a three-way struggle between male clerks, employers and women. Rather than being the reason for a lack of competition between male and female clerks, it should be seen as the outcome of such competition.

There is substantial evidence, as already reported, that the male clerks agitated against the possibility of female substitution. These men feared such an occurrence because of their employers' preference for cheap, relatively docile labour. They spoke, wrote, argued and struck against such an eventuality. My argument is that in the face of this unrest the employers used job segregation as a strategy to overcome the men's resistance. Through the use of job segregation, employers were able to side-step entrenched male interests in established occupations, while simultaneously significantly increasing their employment of women in new occupational sub-groups. In this way the men's most immediate fears of displacement were placated, while the employment of cheap female labour proceeded apace. Further, segregation cut across the strategy of the clerical unions which wanted to organize women and demand the same pay and conditions for them as for men. Segregation helped avoid questions of the comparability of wages and terms of employment of male and female clerks since their work was not exactly the same. This left the way open for inequalities of pay to be justified on grounds of inequality in production and to incorporate the men into a hierarchy from which they benefited.

Holcombe's account of the expansion of women's employment in the Post Office may certainly be interpreted in this manner. The introduction of strictly segregated employment for women appears a calculated attempt to prevent the men's complaints about the entry of women workers. Holcombe describes the men's complaints and then continues

> Certainly there was no grounds for such comments, for Miss Smith and the department officials always insisted that the women be employed in strict segregation from men and that they perform different kinds of work from men under the supervision of women officers. (Holcombe, 1973: 168.)

The introduction of women clerical workers into the civil service was accomplished through the creation of new grades for these women beneath those of the established men. Time after time the expansion in the use of women clerks involved the creation of even lower grades with lower wages, fewer opportunities for promotion, less job security and lower status. This was particularly evident in the creation of the lowest grade, the all-female grade of Writing Assistant (Humphreys, 1958: 54, 59–60, 181–2).

Women's entry to clerical employment provided a new, large and growing field of job opportunities. In this respect it somewhat eased the pressure on women of the limited range of occupations available to them. However, this entry was limited by the job segregation within clerical employment itself through which women were denied access to the better jobs and crowded into the lower level jobs. This crowding in the lower level jobs depressed their rates of pay. To some extent then, women who took particularly low wages could be seen as undercutting the wages of other women rather than men (cf. Anderson, 1977: 127). The civil service effectively reduced rates of pay by introducing new grades of female clerical work at lower levels (Holcombe, 1973).

The gender composition of the clerical workforce must be seen as the outcome of the articulation of specific patriarchal and capitalist structures. Employer preference for women clerks for lower level work was confronted by male clerks' hostility to the entry of women to their established positions.

The outcome was the entry of women to the new occupational slots not already monopolized by men and the rigid sex segregation of the workforce. These new slots were created at lower levels of pay and status than the old. Thus while men won their struggle not to have women in direct competition with themselves, employers won theirs to employ women at cheap rates of pay. The result should be seen as the negotiated outcome of a struggle between these patriarchal and capitalist forces.

6 The Two Wars and Between: 1914–45

Two main interpretations are given of the effect of the First World War on women's employment. The first, and perhaps the most popular image of the war, is it made a dramatic change to the way that women were perceived by employers and the public and that it was instrumental in opening up employment for women. The second view is that the war made little difference, since post-war practices reverted to the pre-war ones as men struggled to get patriarchal relations back to normal. This interpretation might be considered the new feminist pessimism. Instead, I shall argue that the impact of the war on women's employment varied by area of employment, primarily according to the strength of patriarchal organization in each particular industry.

The war was a source of major disruption to existing patterns of employment. At the height of activity in July 1917, 1,362,000 women were substituting in some way for men (Andrews, 1918, Appendix D, 184). In engineering, a large proportion, although not all, of the wartime influx of women was expelled at the end of the war, and the pre-war patriarchal relations at the point of production were re-established to a considerable extent. In clerical work in the government service, the wartime women entrants were only partially expelled at the end of the war, and the particularly rigid segregation of men and women workers was not completely re-established in peace-time. In cotton spinning the men were able to resist the entry of women during the war, while in weaving where women had always been employed the numbers of women workers increased for the duration of the war.

The main reason for widely different patterns in women's employment is the nature and strength of patriarchal organization in each area of employment, combined with, to a lesser extent, the significance of that area of employment for the war effort.

State policy towards gender relations at the end of the war was the outcome of conflicting pressures and did not unequivocally support the exclusion of women from paid work. On the one hand, organized feminists were a powerful force in the early twentieth century, while on the other, the men's unions were pushing hard to ensure that women did not permanently remain in skilled jobs. These contrary forces are reflected in a contradictory state policy towards women with the passage both of an Act granting limited female suffrage and of legislation to remove women from some of the industrial jobs men wanted. Further, the Sex Disqualification (Removal) Act passed in 1919 provided for the removal of bans on the employment of women, while government policy on unemployment acted to discourage women from developing an attachment to paid work (Rathbone, 1936; Lewis, 1980: 208). There were, in fact, widely varying patterns of changes to women's paid work in this period according to the area of employment.

The Sex Disqualification (Removal) Act (1919), passed shortly after older women won the vote, ostensibly removed the civil disabilities on women which prevented them from entering public life. The Act opened with a declaration that no person should be disqualified by sex or marriage from exercising any public function. Its four clauses described the areas to which this was to be applied: the admission of women to jury service, to the Civil Service and to universities. However, there were substantial qualifications to each of these. Despite the apparently wide ranging changes in the Act the discrimination against women in these public arenas was not removed. The sub-clauses were partially responsible for this, though the refusal of the central authorities to implement the act was probably more important. Thus the reform of the Civil Service was to be dealt with by the enemy of women's emancipation: the Treasury; women jurors could still be excluded in certain circumstances; Cambridge chose not to make use of the permission to admit women; women peers were still refused entry to the House of Lords; medical women and teachers were sacked on marriage (see Spender, 1984: 127–32).

Unemployment policies during and after the war discriminated against women in such a way as to help push them out of the better forms of work they had entered during the war. Most women did not have access to the unemployment benefits which had long been paid by various friendly societies and the craft unions (Drake, 1984:

Jefferys, 1970). Thus the development of the national insurance schemes was potentially very important for women. The first national unemployment benefit scheme, introduced in 1911, applied to a limited number of industries and most women were not covered. By July 1914 only 10,000 women were employed in the trades covered by the Act although this rose to 500,000 during the course of the war. The coverage of the Act was extended in 1916, and by July 1918 790,000 women and 620,000 men were insured against unemployment. (These figures reflect the temporary percentages of men and women employed in key industries during wartime.) In July 1917 there was an attempt to extend the Act still further to cover all women war substitutes as a result of pressure from the Women's Employment Sub-Committee of the Reconstruction Committee. In November 1918 a non-contributory unemployment benefit scheme was introduced to cope with the problems of the dislocation of employment at the end of the war while an Act of 1920 further extended the scheme. However, there were many exclusions and regulations which affected women particularly adversely (Deacon, 1979: 50–2). The end of the war led to the widespread unemployment of women who had been working in the war industries, yet in early 1919 of about 650,000 women who were unemployed, only 500,000 were receiving benefit (Soldon, 1978: 104; Braybon, 1981: 181–8). The rules around the payment of unemployment benefit were tightly drawn so as to push women either back onto support of husbands or other relatives, or into forms of low paid employment such as domestic service.

Cotton Textiles in the First World War

The substitution of women for men was a highly contentious issue in many areas of employment, especially skilled employment, during the First World War. It rekindled the struggles over the gender composition of the cotton textile industry. In spinning, in particular, the issue of the substitution of women for the men departing to war was the subject of controversy, while in weaving it did not arise in the same form, since many weavers were already women. The degree of militancy and acquiescence on the issue of substitution of women for men as piecers (spinners' assistants) varied according to the district since there were differing local practices on the employment of women as piecers, with women being allowed in some towns but not in others (*Cotton Factory Times*, 12 February 1915: 1, 16 April 1915: 1).

Male spinners had struggled long and successfully to hold onto their privileged position and to exclude women (see chapter 5). During the war the remaining male spinners fought to prevent the entry of women to this occupation (Braybon, 1981: 69, 73; Soldon, 1978: 92). The spinning unions renewed their arguments that women were not able to perform such a job, since it was supposed to be beyond their skill and strength. The Secretary of the Cotton Spinners Amalgamation went as far as to suggest that it was better for the spinning not to be done till the end of the war rather than have it done by women (*Cotton Factory Times*, 12 February, 1915: 1; Drake, 1921: 84–5). Although the number of women involved in some aspects of the spinning process increased a little during the war, the spinners were remarkably successful. Indeed they were successful to the point of factories being unable to work full time, because of a shortage of male spinners (*Cotton Factory Times*, 18 February 1916: 1, 17 April 1916: 1). In this instance the interests of the men were clearly at odds with those of the employers. Another reason why women did not move into cotton spinning during the war was the lack of expansion of cotton textiles as compared with engineering and clerical work.

Engineering in the First World War

In contrast to spinning, women were drawn into engineering in large numbers. In 1914 there were 170,000 women in engineering with less than 20,000 of these in the machine shops, while by 1918 there were 594,000 of which 170,000 were in machine shops (Soldon, 1978: 81). The engineering unions, in particular, the Amalgamated Society of Engineers, were fearful lest this influx should undermine the conditions of work and rates of pay that they had built up over the years. They were anxious to preserve the work both as a skilled and as a male domain. They were concerned that skilled tasks would be broken down, or diluted, and less skilled workers' rates of pay be permanently given for this work. The introduction of 'dilutees' was considered a threat to the skilled man. The union's concern was in the context of a long struggle by the skilled men's unions against employers' attempts to introduce new machines and employ labourers or semi-skilled workers on them (Drake, 1984; Braybon, 1981), but their concern especially to keep the work as a male preserve is underlined by the willingness of the ASE to admit men who learned skilled trades during the war to the union, but not women (Braybon, 1981: 72).

At the beginning of the war the men refused to drop the restrictions on employment practices which they had previously established, despite pressure to do so. In 1915, however, the 33 principal unions met with government and employers and drew up an agreement which allowed for dropping the union's restrictions for the duration of the war only. No women's unions were invited to the meeting which drew up this agreement (Anthony, 1932: 88). The Treasury Agreement which resulted permitted the employment of women on the skilled men's rates on war work on the condition that the women would be paid the men's rates if they were actually doing the same work as the men had done. This agreement was later given the force of law in the Munitions Act. There were many disputes as to whether the women were doing only part of the men's work and not the whole of it, thus rendering them ineligible for the men's rates of pay (Andrews, 1918; Drake, 1984; Braybon, 1981; History of the Ministry of Munitions, 1976). There were further disputes in some areas about the entry of women at all despite the agreements reached by employers and unions. Indeed the biggest strike led by the Shop Stewards' Movement during the war was over precisely such an issue. In 1917 a Rochdale firm substituted women for men on commercial work which was not directly for the war effort and which was thus not directly covered by the Treasury Agreement. This led to strikes by the skilled men which were first of all local, but which then spread to all Lancashire involving 60,000 workers, and then wider still to 48 towns throughout the country involving 250,000 workers (Frow and Frow, 1982: 49–51).

The Amalgamated Society of Engineers maintained its refusal to allow women to join the union, seeing the women as only temporary interlopers. Such organization of the women as occurred was done by the newly emerging general unions such as the Workers' Union, or by the National Federation of Women Workers, an all-female union set up by the Women's Trade Union League to organize women workers where the men's unions refused to accept women or where there was no relevant union (see e.g. Braybon, 1981).

After the end of the war the government passed the Restoration of Pre-War Practices Act (1919), which reinforced the Treasury Agreement and further legalized and legitimated the expulsion of women from engineering work. This Act was passed after some considerable pressure from both the Labour party and trade unions, in particular, the Amalgamated Society of Engineers. Through the summer of 1918 district committees of the ASE passed resolutions urging the restoration of pre-war practices which were forwarded to the Ministry of Munitions. There was considerable industrial unrest which could be attributed to the government's reluctance to pass this measure, including a strike at Coventry in which this was one of the main grievances (History of the Ministry of Munitions, vol. VI Part II pp. 89–90). The Engineering Employers National Federation wanted the Bill to be more limited, but backed down in the face of the strength of the Society's demands (Engineering Employers' Federation Minutes, Principal Series, vol. 17, 30 May 1919, p. 108).

At the end of the war women workers largely left engineering. Jefferys, in what is commonly regarded as an authoritative history of the engineers, suggests that the women left the industry more or less voluntarily.

> The dilutees ran, drifted or were eased out of the industry (Jefferys, 1970: 134.)

This is an extremely misleading statement given the efforts the engineering unions went to to obtain agreements that employers would expel newly introduced workers from the industry at the end of the war.

Most employers were willing to co-operate with the demands of skilled workers in order to ensure that production was not interrupted (Soldon, 1978: 100). The show of strength of the men's unions during the war over this issue must be considered an important factor in the employers relinquishing female workers at the end of the war. However, not all employers were willing to cease use of women workers. The Management Committee of the Engineering Employers' Federation discussed various requests from federated firms that they be allowed to employ women (Engineering Employers' Federation Minutes, Principal Series, vol. 17, 9 December 1918, p. 7, 28 March 1919, p. 65). The Committee considered that this was an issue which should properly be discussed with the unions and was not prepared to agree to the employment of women without the unions' approval.

> The question of the employment of women is one which will have to be the subject of negotiations with the unions. (Engineering Employers' Federation Minutes, Principal Series, vol. 17, 9 December, 1918, p. 7.)

This might be considered an extraordinary stance for the Federation to adopt since on the issue of the employment of unskilled men they had vehemently denied the right of the unions to interfere with the right of management to select workers. They had previously declared that:

> The machines are the property of the employers and they are solely responsible for the work turned out by them; they, therefore, will continue to exercise the discretion they have hitherto possessed of appointing the men they consider suitable to work them. (EFEA, 1897: 3.)

In 1897 and in 1922 the engineering employers locked out the engineers in massive confrontations over the issue of the manning of the machines. Yet on the issue of the employment of women, the engineering employers were prepared to defer to the demands of the unions. It can be seen that employers were much more prepared to concede the unions' demands for a male monopoly of engineering employment than they were to yield to the unions demands for a monopoly of the machines by skilled men; that is, they were more willing to concede the patriarchal demand than the class demand.

In view of the strength of the feminist movement in the early years of the twentieth century (see e.g. Strachey, 1978), it might have been expected that women workers would have resisted the attempts to expel them from skilled jobs at the end of the war. The interests of women workers were represented in several women's organizations, including the Women's Trade Union League and the National Federation of Women Workers. Yet these organizations did not resist the expulsion of women from their wartime jobs to make way for male workers. Indeed Mary MacArthur, of the National Federation of Women Workers explicitly stated that the women should give up their jobs for returning men (Hamilton, 1925).

The reason for this stance must be sought in the political compromises made by leaders of women trade unionists in order to obtain some support from the men's trade unions. MacArthur and other women leaders were so concerned not to alienate the men's trade unions that they were prepared in this instance to put jobs for male engineers before jobs for their own members. The reasons for this stance must be sought in the particular weakness of women workers, and the hegemony of a patriarchal labourist ideology within the trade union movement. The women trade unionists did not have the resources necessary to resist effectively this hegemony: women workers were organizationally and financially weak and feminist ideas on the division of interests between men and women did not have a sufficient base among them. Women workers did gain benefits from the occasional assistance of men trade unionists, and their leaders were not prepared to risk losing this, despite the immediate costs entailed for women war workers.

Not all women trade unionists were prepared to make such a compromise, as will be shown later in this chapter; however, the fact that their national leaders were prepared to do so had continuing effects for women workers.

The pre-war conditions were partially but not entirely recreated after the war. Employers had long sought to introduce machinery which used less skilled labour and some of the practices introduced during the war were retained. It is difficult to disentangle the effects of the war from these long-term pressures. Between 1914 and 1919 the percentage of skilled workers in engineering dropped from 60 to 50 while the percentage of semi-skilled workers rose from 20 to 30 and the percentage of unskilled workers remained static. The percentage of women in engineering rose from 6 in 1911 to 10 in 1921 (Jefferys, 1970: 134).

While the majority of women were pushed out of engineering at the end of the war, not all were. The decade 1911 to 1921 shows a large proportionate rise in the number of women in engineering. The jump from 6 per cent to 10 per cent is one of nearly double. Employers were determined to introduce a policy of admitting women to areas of work segregated from men's areas of employment (Drake, 1984: 222; Committee on Women in Industry, 1918, Cmd. 167, vol. 31, p. 648).

The strength of the men's trade unions combined with their access to state power and the need for the men's co-operation during the war, combined with little effective resistence to this by women whose trade unions were compromised under a patriarchal hegemony in the trades and labour movement, led to the expulsion of many, but not all, women from engineering at the end of the First World War. Employers' experience of women's capabilities and the specific nature of men's objections to women workers led to a policy of increased employment of women in a highly segregated workplace.

Clerical Work in the First World War

In the years from 1914–1918 women were substituted for male clerks called into the armed services. At the end of the war some of these women clerks were expelled from their positions (see e.g. Drake, 1984: 194). The expulsions met with objections from organized women clerks. The Association of Women Clerks and Secretaries protested at the wholesale removal of women clerks at the end of the war, while not objecting to making way for specific men returning from the front to claim an old job:

> Let it be understood, we do not claim the ex-service man's job. But the job to which no man is to return should be given to the woman who has carried it on for the last three or four years. Why is it that in offices which did not exist before the war the order has now gone forth that no more women are to be employed? Why is it that women are sacked in order to make room for youngsters from school? Why is it that we constantly see complaints that the men will not work beside the women in this or that office? (*The Woman Clerk*, 1919: 2.)

Temporary clerks of both sexes formed their own associations to protect their interests, such as the Public Services Temporary Clerks Association (Humphries, 1958: 100, 101).

Women were ejected from clerical work to a lesser extent than they were in other areas of employment. For instance, in 1914 there were only 1,000 women railway clerks, while in 1919, after the end of the war, there were 12,000 (Lockwood, 1958: 92) although, during the last part of the war the number of women clerks had risen to around 20,000 (Drake, 1984: 174). Here we see a considerable degree of exclusion of women at the end of the war, but not a return to the pre-war position. The continued employment of these extra 11,000 women was seen by some in the Railway Clerks Association as due to women's cheapness (Soldon, 1978: 152). This, however, is not a sufficient explanation, although it is part of it. The other important part of the explanation is the relative weakness of the men's unions in this area.

The Civil Service was another major employer of women clerks during the war. In 1914, 65,000 women were employed in the Civil Service, of whom 58,000 worked in the Post Office, while in 1919 there were 170,000. Many of these women were employed on a temporary basis, without the usual job security of civil servants, and confined to the lower grades. Nevertheless, there was to some extent a reduction in the severity of the sexual segregation (Martindale, 1938: 75–81; CSCA, 1952: 84).

At the end of the war numerous government committees considered both the position of temporary women clerks and also the place of women in a reorganized Civil Service. The Machinery of Government Committee and the Committee on the Organization and Staffing of Government Offices advocated expanding the employment of women clerks in the government service. The Gladstone Committee recommended the limited recruitment of women on separate lines to those of men. The War Cabinet Committee on Women in Industry recommended the abolition of separate grades and examinations for women and recommended leaving the decision on the number of women to individual departments (Martindale, 1938: 82–5). The Women's Advisory Committee of the Ministry of Reconstruction argued that women employed during the war should be able to present themselves for selection for positions and that these should not be reserved to returning servicemen. The same view was held by the Third Interim Report of the Treasury Committee on Civil Service Recruitment After the War (Ministry of Reconstruction, Women's Advisory Committee, 1919, Cmd. 199, vol. xxix, pp. 155–6). The Committees received evidence from a wide range of bodies. The National Union of Clerks extensively reported its own submissions in its journal (*The Clerk*, 1919: 49–51). This deluge of committee papers indicates how much the gender composition of the Civil Service was an issue of controversy and struggle.

Clerical work in the government service did not diminish at the end of the war in such a dramatic way as did work in engineering.

Expanded public services did not contract to the same extent as the munitions industry. Jobs remained for women clerks admitted during the war, and their expulsion at the end of the war did not occur to the same extent as in engineering. But this was only partly because the field of employment did not contract in the same manner. In addition, the men's unions in clerical work were not as strong as those in engineering and indeed had been unable to prevent the introduction of women to this area of work before the war.

The Inter-war Years

After a brief boom in the immediate post-war years there was a severe depression in the British economy barely broken by short-lived economic upturns. The depression was highly uneven in its impact on different industries and regions. Further, the growth of some new industries in this period was also very uneven (Alford, 1972). The depression entailed extremely high rates of unemployment and fierce competition for the jobs which remained.

The conventional approach to women's unemployment in the inter-war period is one which sees married women disappearing back into the home. They are considered to be peripheral members of the labour force and thus to simply drop out of it:

> . . . women resembled, in one sense only, the physically and mentally handicapped: except in areas like Lancashire, where women traditionally worked in the textile industry, they tended to be only marginal members of the labour force. Social custom encouraged women to work only when single. When job opportunities shrank in the depression many women simply dropped out of the labour market and ceased to register at the labour exchanges. (Constantine, 1980: 23.)

In this view women are barely pushed out of the workforce, but follow the promptings of 'social custom'. Similarly, the simple brand of the reserve-army thesis in both its Marxist (Beechey, 1977) and neo-classical economist (Mincer, 1966) versions suggests that women leave paid work in times of economic downturn with little fuss. This approach suggests that women quietly disappear back into the family and home.

On the contrary, there were strong, active attempts by patriarchal forces to give men's employment priority over women's, and these were met by women not with acquiescence but resistance. Women did not leave the paid work force quietly, but protested at these attempts at their exclusion. Women's resistance combined with employers' demand for women's labour ensured that women were not pushed out of paid employment during the inter-war period. The proportion of women in the workforce did not fall despite the patriarchal pressures on women. Popular impressions of this period are wrong.

Employment changes in the depression

Despite attempts to push women out of the paid work force, women's employment did not drop as much as that of men. In the depth of the depression, between 1929 and 1932, the number of men in employment fell by 868,450 or 11 per cent, as compared to only 96,690 or 3.1 per cent for women. In the slightly longer period between 1923 and 1933 the number of women with jobs increased by 16.7 per cent while men with jobs increased by only 0.5 per cent (Soldon, 1978: 135). Since this was a time of growth of the working population, the increase of 0.5 per cent was a drop in the rate of employment for men.

These gender patterns of employment should be understood as the outcome of competing capitalist and patriarchal forces. There was an intensification of certain forms of patriarchal exclusionary practices in this period. However, these were not successful in their ultimate goal of giving men's claims to employment priority over women's in the economy as a whole, because of employers' preference for women workers in the expanding sectors of the economy, and because of women's resistance. There were significant variations between industries, occupations and regions (see tables 6.1 and 6.2). While the South East had an increase of 2.6 per cent in its female activity rate, the North West had a decrease of 1.5 per cent. These regional changes appear to be partly the result of the growth or decline of employment in specific industries. Textile employment for women showed a significant decrease, and this was concentrated in the North West, while the growth of the personal service sector, commerce and finance and the professions were concentrated in the South East (Lee, 1979).

Table 6.1 Changes in Women's Economic Activity, by Industry, 1921-31

Standard Industrial Classification		Change in numbers	Percentage change
I	Fishing	−229	−14.0
II	Agriculture	−29,363	−34.4
III	Mining	−1,667	−15.4
IV	Bricks, pottery	310	+ 0.6
V	Chemicals	−34	− 0.1
VI	Metal	13,554	+ 5.5
VII	Textiles	−108,878	−16.1
VIII	Leather	1,447	+ 6.5
IX	Clothing	−7,100	− 1.4
X	Food and drink	6,609	+ 3.3
XI	Wood	3,591	+14.8
XII	Paper	14,192	+11.2
XIII	Building	1,328	+14.7
XIV	Other manufacturing	−5,422	− 7.6
XV	Utilities	−2,220	+48.3
XVI	Transport and communication	−606	− 1.5
XVII	Commerce and finance	92,215	+12.4
XVIII	Public Administration	−351	− 0.1
XIX	Professions	31,450	+13.0
XX	Entertainment	7,243	+17.7
XXI	Service	94,720	+ 6.2
XXII	Other	−59,162	−88.3
	Total	57,647	+ 1.1%

Source: calculated from UK census, Industry Tables for 1921 and 1931.

Table 6.2 Changes in Regional Female Employment, 1921-31

Region	Percentage change
South East	2.6
East Anglia	0.9
South West	−0.7
West Midlands	1.0
East Midlands	0.9
North West	−1.5
Yorkshire and Humberside	−0.4
North	1.1
Wales	0.3
Scotland	1.3

Source: calculated from Lee, 1979, *British Regional Employment Statistics*

Table 6.3 Percentage Changes in Men and Women's Employment, by Occupation, for England and Wales, 1921–31

Occupation			Percentage change Men	Percentage change Women
I		Fishing	– 6.5	–51.8
II		Agriculture	– 4.7	–33.0
III		Mining	– 9.0	–23.9
IV		Mine products	–10.0	–36.1
V		Bricks, pottery and glass	–21.8	–39.5
VI		Chemicals and paints	–33.2	–73.1
VII		Metal workers	–12.4	–11.9
VIII		Precious metals	–20.8	–24.4
IX		Electrical apparatus	+29.4	+39.4
X		Watches and clocks	–14.4	–35.9
XI		Leather	–16.1	+13.2
XII		Textiles	–18.9	– 5.0
XIII		Clothing	– 4.1	– 0.9
XIV		Food, drink and tobacco	–13.2	–25.6
XV		Wood and furniture	+ 0.8	–25.8
XVI	1921			
XVI, XVII	1931	Paper and publishing	+12.6	– 7.2
XVII	1921			
XVIII	1931	Construction	+37.5	–55.5
XVIII	1921			
XIX	1931	Painters and decorators	+27.5	(11-fold increase)
XIX	1921			
XX	1931	Other materials	– 9.7	–20.6
XX				
XXI		Gas, electricity and water	+38.5	(37-fold increase)
XXII		Transport and communication	+10.2	+ 8.4
XXIII		Commerce and finance	+36.1	+21.9
XXIV		Public administration and defence	–34.4	–96.0
XXV		Professions	+19.2	+ 7.4
XXVI		Entertainments and sport	+36.2	–20.1
XXVII		Personal services	+ 7.7	+14.9
XXVIII		Clerks and draughtsmen	+40.0	+35.0
XXIX		Warehouse and packers	+14.7	+21.0
XXX		Stationery engine	+ 0.5	(20-fold increase)
XXXI				

Source: calculated from UK census for England and Wales, Occupation Tables for 1921 and 1931.

1 Certain occupational classifications changed between the censuses of 1921 and 1931. This is the reason for an apparently large increase in classifications XIX, XXI and XXX. It is also the reason behind the renumbering of four occupations in 1931.

However, there was a further gender-related aspect to this restructuring. In the declining occupations the percentage decrease in women's employment was usually greater than that in men's, while in the expanding occupations women's employment increased more rapidly than men's (see table 6.3). So while women were being expelled from declining occupations more rapidly than men, they were drawn more rapidly into the growing ones. Women were not ejected from the work force during this part of the depression, but their position in it was substantially restructured. There were important occupational and regional variations in the strength of patriarchal organization. Male workers were more organized in trade unions in the traditional occupations which were declining than in the new ones (Soldon, 1978; Lewenhak, 1977).

A survey carried out by the TUC in 1923 shows that among trade unions which catered for women workers the proportion of women workers had declined. In all but four cases, the ratio of women to men in these trades had declined (Soldon, 1978: 117). In the occupations and hence regions where male-dominated trade unions were strong, women were more likely to be ejected from paid work and hence to become unemployed than in jobs and places where the men were not so well organized.

Three processes must be separated in explaining uneven rates of decline of employment for men and women. Firstly, the rates tend to be uneven in industries and occupations in which different sexes predominate: if male-typed forms of employment decline at different rates than female-typed forms, then this produces different rates of employment loss for each sex and differential unemployment rates. Secondly, the difference in rates can reflect the ejection of one sex more than the other from a particular type of employment: for instance, when well organized men have made women bear a disproportionate amount of employment loss. Thirdly, there are the uneven rates of increase in employment for women and men. All three processes were operating in the inter-war period, and they should be seen as interrelated, though distinct. When women's conditions of employment are depressed beneath those of men by patriarchal forces it is to be expected that employers developing new products will endeavour to devise forms of labour process and locational policies to take advantage of women's labour.

Gender struggles over access to work

Patriarchal attempts to exclude women from paid work focused on married women in particular. There was an increase in the already common practice of sacking women workers when they married (Lewis, 1980: 214). This was by no means a new practice, but one which became more widespread during the depression. Married women had long been banned from employment in the Civil Service and indeed in most white collar work with the support of both the employers and the unions (Lewenhak, 1977: 94). The spread of the practice was an attempt to deal with unemployment at the expense of women.

> There is a general resolve to attack the unemployment problem by the removal of women, and more particularly married women, from jobs. (*The Vote*, 1932: 52.)

The moves to sack married women were especially pronounced in areas of white collar work controlled by local authorities, such as teaching.

> It is becoming a practice on the part of the State, of Municipal Corporations and private employers, to arbitrarily dismiss a woman from her profession or employment on the day of her marriage. (*The Vote*, 1932: 129.)

The practice of denying employment to married women even spread to the Lancashire cotton textile mills where it was previously rare (Lewenhak, 1977: 215; *The Vote*, 1932: 58). In Sheffield too, firms which previously employed married women stopped doing so (*The Vote*, 1932, 15 April).

However, the spread of the marriage bar did meet with some resistance, and it was not uniformly implemented. In 1934, the Married Women's Right to Work Campaign sent a deputation representing 26 women's organizations to the London City Council, in support of the right of married women to paid work (*Women's Freedom League Bulletin*, 6 July 1934: 2). In 1932 there was a large conference of women's organizations and trade unions representing women on the position of married women in paid employment which passed resolutions on access to paid work and to unemployment benefit (*The Vote*, 1932: 349). Another enthusiastic meeting on married women's right to work was held at Central Hall, Westminster, in 1933 (*Women's Freedom League Bulletin*, 1 December 1933:1). While some authorities, such as Bury St. Edmunds, Finsbury and Cheshire, introduced or tightened up the marriage bar, others such as Worcester, while discussing its possible introduction, decided against it (*The Vote*, 1932: 29, 35; *Women's Freedom League Bulletin*, 1 December 1933, 19 January 1934: 1). The extent of women's organization was an important factor determining whether such a marriage bar was introduced. In Nelson where women were politically active no such bar was introduced, while in Lancaster and Preston, where women were much less politically organized, the marriage bar was introduced by the local authority (Mark-Lawson, Savage and Warde, 1985). Resistance to these patriarchal exclusionary attempts thus met with a certain amount of success, although this was not total. However, the resistance does indicate that women did not willingly give up their jobs to help the male unemployed, but rather were vigorously pushed.

State unemployment policy in the inter-war years

While there was no major legislation further restricting women's paid employment, state policy towards those married women who lost paid employment increasingly severely restricted their access to benefits on the same terms as men. Government policy on unemployment benefit in this period was discriminatory against women in that it tended to push unemployed women back onto the support of their husbands or other kin. Regulations, predicated on the assumption that married women were not long-term members of the work force, deprived them of unemployment benefit.

In much of the 1920s the 'not genuinely seeking work clause' had in practice operated to exclude many married women from claiming unemployment benefit. In 1931 the Unemployment Insurance (Anomolies) Act, brought in by the Labour government, introduced stringent new regulations which had the intention and effect of striking many married women (as well as seasonal and short-time workers) off the benefit register. These new regulations included one which laid down that a married woman had to have paid a certain number of contributions after she was married in order to be able to claim benefit. If a woman's contributions had been paid only before marriage then she was not allowed to claim benefit, however many years of contributions she had made, unless she was able very clearly to demonstrate that she was normally employed and could expect to find work in the district (Branson and Heineman, 1971: 22; Soldon, 1978: 131). The Anomalies Act was primarily directed at married women; by 1933 over 200,000 married women had been refused benefit as compared with only 45,000 seasonal workers and 5,000 intermittent workers (Deacon, 1979: 218). Its impact is further shown in that in September 1931 only 3.3 per cent of women on the unemployment register were not receiving benefit, while by March 1932 this had risen to 24.3 per cent (Deacon, 1979: 224). *The Vote* (1932: 58) complained about the case of a 42-year-old woman laundry worker, who had been employed 22 years at a firm of dyers and bleachers and 11 years at the Co-operative Society laundry, who was dismissed on marriage in 1931. At first she was able to claim unemployment benefit but when the Anomalies Act came into force later in that year her claim was disallowed and her benefit stopped despite the fact that her husband was unable to make provision for her. This discriminating legislation was introduced not by a Conservative administration, but rather by a Labour Government: the labour movement's party was no ally of feminists over the issue of women's employment. The possibility of women taking on patriarchal positions in the state is also demonstrated in this instance since the Act was the departmental responsibility of Margaret Bondfield, one-time leader of women trade unionists, and one of the first women cabinet ministers.

The Act was seen as a deliberate attempt at denying married women benefit, and was greeted with the protests of organized women. Women's organizations gathered evidence and presented their case to the Royal Commission on Unemployment Insurance in 1932 about the position of married women under the Anomalies Act. The organizations which made these representations included, among others, the Open Door Council, the Women's Freedom League and the National Union of Societies for Equal Citizenship. They demanded the right of married women to earn and their right to unemployment benefit (*The Vote*, 1932: 58). The Standing Joint Committee of Industrial Women's Organizations also gave evidence to this Commission and protested at the denial of unemployment benefit to married women (*The Vote*, 1932: 116). Several Preston trade unions representing women cotton textile workers protested at the wholesale disallowance of married women (*Cotton Factory Times*, 27 November, 1931: 1). *The Cotton Factory Times* argued against the new Act and told trade union officials to argue against it too (30 October 1931: 1).

Unions in the inter-war period

Many of the separate union organizations of women workers which had developed since the last quarter of the nineteenth century amalgamated with male-dominated unions in the inter-war period. This was the case for both of the federations of women workers (the National Federation of Women Workers and the Women's Trade Union League) and also many of the small trade unions representing women in particular trades, (although there are exceptions, for instance the Union of Women Teachers broke away from the National Union of Teachers because the latter union dragged its feet over demands for equal pay (Littlewood, 1984)). The merging of these bodies was eagerly pursued by some of the women's leaders as a development in which women moved into the mainstream of the labour movement and into a position whereby they could call upon the strength of a much larger group of workers to back demands against employers. The terms of the mergers often involved women having reserved seats on the executive bodies of the new amalgamation in what was hoped simply to be insurance against a failure of women to be elected. The National Federation of Women Workers (NFWW) merged in 1921 with the National Union of General Workers which was a large mixed union recruiting semi- and unskilled workers, especially in engineering trades. The NFWW was initially constituted as a separate women's district of the union with its own officers and hence some autonomy. The Women's Trade Union League merged with the Trades Union Congress in 1921, the TUC having just before created a women's sub-committee and reserved two seats on the General Council for women (Hamilton, 1925; Lewenhak, 1977; TUC annual report, 1930: 107–11).

While the terms of many of these mergers were for the women to retain some reserved seats and a limited degree of autonomy inside the amalgamation, these provisions often became diluted or eroded with time. For instance, the women's district of the GMWU was first demoted to a department with the women organizers to work under male organizers, then it was abolished altogether, leaving only the post of National Woman Officer, and, since the occupant of this post was selected by the male dominated executive when it fell vacant, this too was changed in character. Within the TUC structure there was a constant battle over the composition of the National Women's Advisory Committee: its members from the General Council were largely men since the only women on the General Council were the two holders of the reserved seats (themselves elected by the male dominated Congress rather than by the Women's TUC); the Women's TUC (or rather the conference for unions catering for women workers) several times demanded greater representation on this committee and there was a regular see-saw in which they would gain more members, giving the committee a majority of women elected by a largely female conference, followed by a male majority of General Council members (Lewenhak, 1977; see also TUC annual reports).

Should these mergers be seen as part of a tide of progress for women workers, in that they were accepted into the men's world and no longer excluded, or should they be seen as the catastrophic demise of women's organizations, and their incorporation as a subordinate group into organizations whose interests were in conflict with their own? This question poses a version of an age-old organizational issue for feminists: separate organization or integration with other 'progressive' forces. I believe it was disaster for women that organized women workers gave up their organizational independence; they gained little of significance and lost much. Indeed, in much of the following period, up to today, one of the major struggles of women workers has been to re-establish appropriate independent organizational forms. The inter-war period saw a struggle to establish an annual conference for women trade unionists, or rather of trade unionists from unions catering for women workers (a substantial minority of the delegates were male) and a network of women's committees attached to trade councils. There have been further struggles over the composition of the TUC's National Women's Advisory Committee – struggles over whether the TUC General Council was able to fill the Committee with men from the General Council, or whether women elected from the conference of trade unions catering for women workers are to be in the majority. It has been only in the 1980s that women within trade unions have been able to re-establish even semi-autonomous organizations at the level of individual trade unions (see TUC annual reports).

A further loss involved in the amalgamations was the position of union leader. This further entailed the loss of representation at the Congress and General Council, since, while women were leaders of women's unions, they were very rarely leaders of mixed unions, and it was generally the leaders–the General Secretaries–who spoke at Congress and were represented on the General Council. This was also the case at a more local level. With shop stewards unwilling to accept a woman convenor or even male workers a woman shop steward, women typically only reached such positions in an all-female section of the workforce.

The loss of the independence of organization for women trade unionists was a significant factor in the diminution of women's voices in industrial affairs. Its effects continued into the early post-war period as will be seen in the next chapter.

Scientific management and 'protective legislation'

The limitations on women's paid work introduced in the so-called protective legislation of the nineteenth century continued to have an effect into the twentieth century. In the inter-war period the effect of legislation which limited the hours women could work in factories was combined with new scientific management to further restrict women's access to paid work. The introduction of the Bedaux system of scientific management (Littler, 1980, 1982b), in the context of this restrictive legislation, tended to lead to the substitution of men for women workers. The Taylor system of scientific management was not taken up in Britain to any great extent, while that of Bedaux was being introduced by the Bedaux firm of management consultants. Part of the Bedaux system involved the systematic intensification of work and increased utilization of machinery by lengthening the working day and introducing a shift system (Littler, 1980). Women workers were replaced by men in order to achieve this because the 'protective' legislation prevented women from working long hours or night shifts. For instance, the introduction of the three-shift system in some clothing and textile factories led to the displacement of some women workers for this reason (Soldon, 1978: 125).

Women attempted to resist the introduction of the Bedaux system. Some of the largest and most successful strikes against it were by unorganized women workers. In 1932 there was a successful strike by 10,000 unorganized women against the systems at Lucas, a motor accessory plant, in Birmingham (Branson and Heineman, 1971: 82, 111).

In some of these disputes over the Bedaux system there was collusion between male trade unionists and employers against the women workers. An example of this occurred with the application of the Bedaux system to the Wolsey hosiery factory in 1930–34. Wolsey tried to introduce scientific management in its works in 1930–34 and employed the services of the Bedaux company and its engineers (Littler, 1980). The Wolsey management was faced with some worker resistance and was reluctant to use confrontational tactics. The evidence suggests that the Wolsey management obtained the co-operation of the trade union by offering to substitute male for female workers when implementing the scheme. At a Board meeting on 14th February 1933, the Wolsey management agreed that in its approach to the trade union it should

> emphasize that the company intended to use the service of men as opposed to women operatives as much as possible. (Littler, 1980: 457.)

Littler has a footnote which describes more fully the changes in process:

> I have attempted to strip away many of the details of the changes in the labour process in order to concentrate on essentials. In fact Bedaux proposed, and Wolsey implemented, a package of changes consisting of (a) the introduction of faster machines and the scrapping of many older machines, (b) a shift from female operatives to male workers in order to increase machine utilization, the men worked 55 hours per week compared to the women's 48 hours, (c) associated with (b), the introduction of shift working, which again only men were allowed to do, (d) stretch out (e) wage reductions, at least for the new workers brought into the plant. (Littler, 1980: 488.)

The existence of the protective legislation is in itself insufficient to explain its utilization in this manner. Rather, it was used in the context of a struggle between union and management. The management wanted to introduce their new scheme of scientific management in order to make the firm more profitable, while the male dominated union was prepared to allow this if management employed men in preference to women. Littler interprets this evidence as follows:

> Essentially the union acceded to management's proposals, partly because the additional male workers rather than women, provided a more stable union membership. (Littler, 1980: 457.)

However, to suggest that the Hosiery Worker's Union preferred men because they formed a 'more stable union membership' does not accord with other evidence Littler presents. Littler notes elsewhere that the average length of time a woman worker stayed at Wolsey was 12–14 years (Littler, 1980: 462). By no stretch of the imagination therefore can Littler suggest that the women constituted an unstable workforce. He says that they were 'treated as casual labour' (Littler, 1980: 462) but the reasons for this cannot be held to reside in the women themselves, but rather in the way in which management and union practice constructed their workforce participation. In Littler's calendar of events at Wolsey from 23 August 1930 to 12 February 1932, there are references to the practice of laying off and attempting to dismiss the married women workers in preference to other categories. (Littler, 1980: 467, 469).

At Wolsey it was the women workers who went on strike against the introduction of the Bedaux system, not the male workers, despite the fact that the women were largely non-unionized. The union was reluctant to take action in support of the women and was quick to compromise the women's interests. In this instance the union clearly represented patriarchal interests in its operations. The management was prepared to concede patriarchal employment practices in order to ensure union co-operation in the implementation of the Bedaux system of scientific management.

The existence of protective legislation preventing night work and long hours by women gave further pressure to the employment of men instead of women. Since the Bedaux system involved greater utilization of machinery (Littler, 1980: 488), the existence of this legislation meant that men were favoured for employment rather than women.

The Bedaux system of scientific management stands in an interesting contrast to the Taylor system. In the Taylor system there is a greater emphasis on the importance of breaking down work tasks to simpler processes which can be performed by cheaper labour (Braverman, 1974). This is likely to lead to management constructing jobs for cheaper female or immigrant labour. The increasingly deskilled labour processes are held to be more appropriate for women, who are more likely to be unskilled and unable to command high wages. Indeed, Braverman describes the changing sexual composition of the post-war American work force in this context. The participation rate of men was declining, while that of women was rising.

The Taylor scheme was not directly introduced into England, and the revised form which was introduced in the inter-war years, the Bedaux system, had some significant differences from it (Littler, 1982). There was less emphasis on the breaking down of the work tasks in the Bedaux system and more weight on work intensification and the increased utilization of machinery. Thus, the tendency to feminization of the work force which Braverman identifies in Taylor's system of scientific management is less likely in Bedaux's. Bedaux's system is more likely to facilitate the replacement of women by men than vice versa, as the Wolsey case illustrates (cf. Warde, 1982). Thus the introduction of scientific management in the USA and in Britain might be seen to have different effects on the gender composition of the workforce. The extent of the difference should not, however, be over-emphasized since the gender composition of the UK workforce has after all shifted in somewhat similar manner to that in the USA.

The existence of the 'protective' legislation fitted in with a constellation of other practices to reduce the employment opportunities for women. In the context of the Bedaux system's emphasis on work intensification and the utilization of machinery for longer periods, and the unions' preferences for the employment of men rather than women, protective legislation was used to justify the closure of employment openings for women. The effects of the varying interrelations of capitalist and patriarchal relation in different areas of employment will now be examined through the comparison of engineering, textiles and clerical work.

Cotton textiles in the inter-war years

After a short-lived post-war boom there was a prolonged depression in the cotton textile trade during the inter-war period. In March 1921 unemployment among cotton workers rose to 42 per cent and fluctuated between 7 and 20 per cent until 1930. In 1930 the rate of unemployment among cotton workers soared to 40.7 per cent for men and 45.5 per cent for women. This high level was sustained during the 1930s with 30.6 per cent unemployment in the cotton trade in 1932, not falling to 10.9 per cent until 1937 (Savage, 1982: 33). Weaving towns were particularly severely affected by unemployment, though most cotton workers were affected by unemployment at some time during this period. In Blackburn in 1930 87 per cent of insured women made a claim at the Labour Exchange as did 70 per cent of the men (Savage, 1982: 33, 34).

The particularly bad performance of the cotton industry in this period was due to factors in addition to the recession. Most Lancashire mills were technologically backward, especially in comparison with cotton factories in countries such as Japan. In Britain in 1930 42 per cent of looms and 30 per cent of mule and ring spinning spindles had been built before 1900 (Branson and Heineman, 1971: 92; Soldon, 1978: 133). The huge profits of the post-war boom had been handed out as dividends or recapitalized shares rather than invested in new plant, and union protests at this had only led to the introduction of welfare paternalism (Savage, 1982: 59). In 1929 rationalization in the form of amalgamations and forced closures were forced on the industry by creditors and bankers. One such new corporation, the Lancashire Cotton Corporation, formed through action by the Bankers' Industrial Development Company, acquired 70 companies in its first year and 26 in the next. The main strategy of this, and similar consolidations, was to increase profits through the scrapping of the least efficient plant and closing mills (Hannah, 1976: 84, 137).

The increasing competition for jobs encouraged patriarchal pressures to give priority to the claims of men to such jobs as did exist. Many firms introduced a marriage bar, at least in the form of no longer taking on married women (*The Vote*, 1932: 58; Lewenhak, 1977: 215). This exclusion of married women led to a much higher rate of unemployment among married women cotton workers than among those who were single. At a time when 25 per cent of single women cotton workers were unemployed, the rate among married women was 75 per cent (*The Vote*, 1932: 58). Such women who were dismissed on marriage found their claims to unemployment benefit disallowed under the terms of the Anomalies

Act, and so suffered additional hardship through the refusal of state agencies to accept that a married woman could be really unemployed.

Further problems for women arose when some textile factories introduced a night shift. Since legislation banned women from working nights, this further lessened their opportunities for textile work (Beauchamp, 1937: 18; Soldon, 1978: 125). There were attempts to further restrict women's hours of work when a Bill to this effect was introduced in Parliament in 1937. While it was welcomed by the *Cotton Factory Times*, the journal of the cotton unions, it was opposed by feminist organizations such as the Open Door Council (*Cotton Factory Times*, 1937, 12 February, p. 5, 19 February, p. 4, 26 February, p. 4).

So, women's jobs were disproportionately affected by the recession in the cotton textile industry because of the patriarchal forces which led to the introduction of the marriage bar in firms which had not previously operated one and by the so-called 'protective' legislation which prevented their night work. The loss of employment in textiles had a particularly serious effect on women's paid employment as a whole because cotton textiles was such a big employer of women.

Engineering in the Inter-war Years

The movement of women into engineering continued during the inter-war period, increasing from 10.5 per cent of the workforce in 1921 to 13.7 per cent in 1931. Women were employed in large numbers in the newly developing areas of light engineering, electrical engineering and motor and cycle manufacture. Electrical engineering increased its share of engineering employment from 5 per cent in 1907 to 15.4 per cent in 1924 and 22.5 per cent in 1935, while motor, cycle and aircraft manufacture increased its share from 7.4 per cent in 1907 to 20.4 per cent in 1924 and 28.5 per cent in 1935. These two areas of engineering in 1935 employed over half of the total engineering workforce. The importance of these sectors further increased in the years leading up the the Second World War as rearmament took place. This development also meant a locational change, as the new industry developed in the Midlands and around London, rather than in the old industrial areas of the North. The decay of the old engineering industries in the depression further exacerbated this regional shift in engineering employment (Jefferys, 1970: 196–200; Beauchamp, 1937: 24–5).

There was a continued development of new machinery which produced ever-higher quality goods at faster speed and permitted the use of less skilled labour. The proportion of skilled workers in engineering declined (from 60 per cent in 1914 to 50 per cent in 1921, 40 per cent in 1926, and 32 per cent in 1933), while the proportion of semi-skilled workers increased (from 20 per cent in 1914 to 30 per cent in 1921, 45 per cent in 1926, and 57 per cent in 1933), and the proportion of unskilled workers declined (from 20 per cent in 1914 to 11 per cent in 1933) (Jefferys, 1970: 207). This period saw a dramatic shift in the skill composition of the workforce, and the end of the time when the majority of people working in engineering had undergone an apprenticeship.

This decline in the proportion of skilled workers, who were organized in craft unions, opened the way for the recruitment of women. The control that male engineering workers had over the gender composition of the workforce was seriously weakened by the declining significance of apprenticeship as the route of entry into engineering.

In 1907 only 3 per cent of engineering operatives were women. Their numbers increased steadily, rising to 8.5 per cent in 1924, 10 per cent in 1930 and 13.2 per cent in 1935. This was not an even proportion, but varied enormously according to the age of the branch of engineering. In the old, established industry of shipbuilding, women were a small proportion of workers, being only 6 per cent even in 1935, while in the newly developing branch of electrical engineering women constituted 35 per cent of the workforce in 1935 (Jefferys, 1970: 207).

In the inter-war period the skilled men's unions still fought battles against the introduction of women and unskilled male workers on particular machines. In 1922 there was another lock-out over this 'machine question' which, yet again, the union lost (Frow and Frow, 1982: 80–1). There were also many local disputes over the question of what sort of labour should use particular machines. For instance, in 1932 the Amalgamated Engineering Union protested at the actions of the firm of Asquith at Halifax, which had introduced unskilled men onto what the engineering union considered to be the work of skilled fitters. They took the case through the various disputes procedures up to a 'Central and Special Conference' between themselves and the Engineering and Allied Employers' National Federation. A similar dispute took place at Laurence Scott and

Electro Motors, Norwich (Engineering and Allied Employers' National Federation, Central and Special Conference Minutes, 8 April 1932: 468–70, 485).

While some of the disputes were over the introduction of unskilled men, others were over the introduction of women. For instance, the Amalgamated Society of Engineers objected to the employment of women on Halliday's carburettors, Globe Patter steam and motor valves and No. 4 Herbert Capstan lathes and held protracted negotiations at local and national level on this issue. The Women's Engineering Society opposed the actions of the men's union and wrote to the firm supporting the women's right to work. In response to these pressures the Engineering Employers' Federation told its member firm, Armstrong and Whitworth's, to restrict the employment of women to carburettors, thus conceding part of the unions demands, although the union was not content with this solution (Engineering Employers' Federation Minutes, Principal Series, vol. 18, 21 November 1919: 14, 28 November 1919: 25, 19 December 1919: 51). In a further case in 1920 the Amalgamated Engineering Union went on strike against the employment of women on roller bearings at the Lancashire Ordnance Accessories Ltd. Stockport (Engineering Employers' Federation Minutes, Principal Series, vol. 19, 29 October 1920: 113, 26 November 1920: 140, 25 November 1920: 145).

The engineering craft unions did make some attempts to develop into more general unions in the period between the wars. The Amalgamated Society of Engineers opened its doors more fully to non-skilled workers and, after further amalgamations in which the Amalgamated Society of Engineers became the Amalgamated Engineering Union, this union created new sections to admit semi- and unskilled workers in 1926. Some members of the AEU National Committee argued for the need to admit all engineering workers to the union to prevent the undercutting of their position during further rationalization of production by employers. The proportion of union members who were skilled rapidly dropped during the inter-war period. By 1936–9 only just over half of the existing membership was skilled, while only one fifth of new workers joining the union in this same period were skilled. (*AEU Monthly Journal*, January 1930: 56; Jefferys, 1970: 208). However, despite this massive influx of semi-skilled and unskilled members, the bulk of the new mass production industries remained largely non-unionized (Branson and Heinemann, 1971: 110, 117).

Despite this opening up of the major engineering union to semi-skilled and unskilled workers, the union still refused to admit women to membership. The union's opposition to women workers was not based merely on their hostility towards semi- and unskilled workers, but was also based on hostility to women purely because they were women. Only 2 per cent of women in engineering were unionized, most of them in the National Union of General and Municipal Workers. However, this union took so little interest in its women members that it did not even know (in 1937) how many of its women members were employed in engineering (Beauchamp, 1937: 26).

The correlation between the absence of unions and the employment of women in engineering in this period is quite remarkable. It was in the new branches of engineering, in parts of the country where engineering unions did not have members, that the employment of women developed rapidly in certain segregated processes. The highest proportion of female metal machinists in the country, 18 per cent, was to be found in the Coventry motor vehicles industry which was weakly unionized. In comparison in the strongly unionized areas of the North East and Manchester, women constituted less than 4 per cent of this type of worker (Summerfield, 1984: 10). This correlation combined with the known hostility of the engineering unions to the employment of women in engineering is convincing evidence that in engineering the men's unions were a major force behind the limitation of women's employment.

The growth of women's employment only within relatively segregated areas was a consequence of the struggle between engineering employers and unions over the entry of women and over the skill classification of work. At the end of the First World War, leading engineering employers had stated that they intended to segregate women employees from men in order to facilitate women's employment. They had been impressed by women's work during wartime and intended to continue to utilize women workers. Segregation was seen as a way of allowing them to employ women cheaply while paying the men a wage sufficient to enable them to retain a dominant position in the family. Some of the representatives of employers' associations advocated such a policy. Mr John King and Mr F. Blackwell, representatives of one of the engineering employers' associations, gave evidence to this effect to a government committee investigating women's place in industry at the end of the war:

> Women should be educated for light repetition work, and men allocated to the heavier more skilled grades. The obligations on men supporting dependants should not be overlooked in determining the future relation of wages for the two sexes. There must always be a differentiation in rates for ordinary repetition work, skilled work and 'skilled plus heavy' work. (Committee on Women in Industry, 1918, Cmd. 167, vol. 31, p. 648).

Women were indeed paid cheaply, the average wage for women in engineering in 1931 being 27s. 6d. as compared to 52s. 6d. for men (Beauchamp, 1937: 26).

The employers were well aware of the hostility of the men to the employment of women in engineering. They were at pains to argue that the increased employment of women was not at the expense of men. Women were segregated from the men in order to bolster this argument. The employment of women was justified on the grounds that they were doing 'women's work'. In 1933 the Engineering and Allied Employers' National Federation issued a pamphlet on the problem of unemployment in order to support their claims. It stated that women were confined to a narrow range of employment that was particularly suitable for them and thus that they were not displacing men. In relation to work done by women on electric lamps it was stated that

> the work is of a nature which is peculiarly adapted physically to female labour (Engineering and Allied Employers' National Federation, 1933: 14).

By sex-typing the work in this way engineering employers were able to expand the employment of women while not directly confronting the men's unions.

Clerical work in the inter-war years

The depression of the inter-war years saw the intensification of certain patriarchal exclusionary practices, especially the marriage bar, in the field of clerical labour. Yet the proportion of clerks who were female did not decline. Between 1921 and 1931, the numbers of women clerks increased, while the ratio of women to men remained more or less stable at around 39 per cent. However, the decade 1921 to 1931 is the only decade since 1951 in which the gender composition of clerks does not shift substantially towards women.

Later in the inter-war period the proportion of women clerks begins to rise again. On government staffs the proportion of women white collar workers rose from 26 to 30 per cent between January 1928 and April 1934. In banking the proportion of low level women white collar workers rose from 29 to 37 per cent between 1926 and 1934. These were not absolute declines in the number of men, since the occupations themselves were growing; rather the increases in men's employment were simply much smaller than those of women. A large portion of the increase in women clerical workers was composed of women entering offices to use the new office machinery (Klingender, 1935; 88, 93–94; Beauchamp, 1937: 56; Lockwood, 1958: 91). Ninety per cent of the workers on these machines were women. As work was moved from hand workers to machine workers so was work effectively transferred from men to women. The manufacturers of the new machinery were involved in this process since they trained the young women to use these machines (Klingender, 1935: 88, 93–4).

In the Civil Service there were continuing disputes over the numbers and placing of women in the clerical grades. A serious and substantial reassessment of the organization of the Civil Service and its restructuring along new lines began at the end of the war and continued into the first half of the inter-war period. The main focus of the numerous committees considering the issue was the attempt to rationalize the disparate grading schemes used by the different government departments and replace them by a uniform structure. The majority of the committees also recommended expanding the employment of women clerks (Martindale, 1938: 82–5; Humphreys, 1958: 99–131).

The way that women should be incorporated was a matter for struggle between employers, male unions and women's unions. The continuation of the differentiation of men and women clerks was the outcome of this struggle. In this outcome women clerks were the losers in terms of pay and conditions, while male clerks largely retained their privileged position in the hierarchy and employers gained the labour of women cheaply.

The attempts by the women clerks to resist remaining segregated and unequal were largely unsuccessful. There were bitter disputes between the women's unions and other unions and management over the issue of whether there should be identical treatment for women on pay and recruitment. The Writing Assistants' Association, which was all-female because it represented a woman-only section, and the Federation of Women Civil Servants argued for equality of pay and the merging of men's and women's grades. The failure of the men's unions to support these demands effectively led the Federation of Women Civil Servants to withdraw from both the Staff Side and the Civil Service Alliance and then to repudiate the final settlement (Humphreys, 1958: 120–1).

However, there was some limited assimilation of men's and women's grades and a reduction in the rigidity of the segmentation of male and female clerks. In an attempt to prevent the women from undercutting men in the new assimilated grades, the all-male unions which had represented these grades began to admit women (Humphreys, 1958: 153). The process of assimilation proceeded slowly and unevenly in the different government departments with higher-level posts often remaining closed to women. In particular the process of aggregating seniority lists took a long time to be achieved. By the mid-1920s the assimilation of the middle clerical grades was achieved. However, the bottom grade of Writing Assistant remained all-female (Humphreys 1958: 182; Martindale, 1938: 93–101, 110).

The existence of this bottom grade of women's employment enabled de facto substitution by women for men through the

Table 6.4 Employment of Women in the Civil Service, 1928–34

Government staff	1 January 1928		1 April 1934	
	Men	Women	Men	Women
Administration	1,131	19	1,210	25
General executive	4,002	137	4,034	225
Other executive	10,243	480	11,123	519
General clerical	27,442	6,961	32,938	8,007
Other clerical	19,206	2,503	18,319	3,480
Writing assistants	–	4,914	–	7,336
Typing grades	120	6,980	76	8,904
	62,144	21,994	67,700	28,498

Source: F. W. Fox 'Introduction of Office Machinery into Government Departments' Institute of Public Administration, 1956.

expedient of transferring work from the mixed grades to the women's grade. Between 1924 and 1934 this female grade of writing assistant increased in size by 75 per cent, from 4,204 to 7,381 (Beauchamp, 1937: 58). Table 6.4 shows the distribution of employment in the Civil Service towards women in the lower grades, and indicates the extent of the vertical segregation.

Thus in clerical work the patriarchal controls on women's employment were not effective in preventing an increase in the proportion of women workers. Rather, employers were able to employ the cheaper women workers in the new and expanding areas of clerical work.

The Second World War

Like the First, the Second World War saw an expansion of women's employment followed by its contraction. Again, as in the earlier war, there are two main rival interpretations: one which argues that the war made an enormous and permanent improvement to the position of women (Marwick, 1968; Wright, 1968) and another which argues that the gains were rather small (Smith, 1981; Summerfield, 1984). I shall suggest that, while Summerfield is correct to argue that the reorganization of women's domestic labour was not as dramatic as Marwick and Wright believe, she underestimates the significance of the permanent restructuring of women's access to paid employment. In particular the removal of the marriage bar and the institutionalization of part-time working were of lasting importance. While Summerfield notes these changes, and indeed is the best source on the development of part-time working during the war, she does not sufficiently stress their significance for the further restructuring of the relations between women's paid and unpaid work. However, Smith (1981) is right to argue that little significant progress was made toward equal pay during the war considering the strength of the movement for equal pay. At the height of the war effort in 1943, 800,000 more women were in paid employment than in 1939. There was an increase of 1,500,000 women working in the essential war industries (Summerfield, 1984: 29). The end of the war saw some diminution in the numbers of women in paid employment, but proportionately much less than after the First World War. In 1948 there were 683,000 more women in paid employment than in mid-1939 (Soldon, 1978:

156–7). The new women workers were more likely than existing women workers to be married, and they were also older. In 1931 only 16 per cent of women in employment were married, while in 1943 the proportion was 43 per cent. In 1931 41 per cent of women paid workers were under 25 while in 1943 only 27 per cent were this young. The number of women aged 25 to 34 rose from 27 per cent to 31 per cent while those aged 35 to 44 rose from 16 to 26 per cent (Summerfield, 1984: 31, 196).

Collective solutions to domestic labour?

During the first year or so of the war there was little effort by the government to increase the numbers of women in paid work. Then with ever-increasing degrees of both assistance and coercion the government attempted to get more women into war work. There was an increase in the provision of nursery schools and day nurseries, with 1,550 nursery schools provided by 1944 (Lewenhak, 1977: 239). There was heightened provision of ready-cooked meals at the factories, with 10,000 factory canteens and 2,100 'British restaurants' in 1943 (TUC, 1955: 84).

Some have regarded the facilities provided as a major shift in policies towards women and domestic labour.

> These and many other measures, although they were conceived as emergency measures devised to meet the special circumstances arising from the common danger, denoted a profound departure from the old traditional attitude towards woman and her functions and responsibilities. (TUC, 1955: 84.)

However, there were serious limitations in the amount of collectivization of domestic labour during the war. Summerfield (1984) considers these limitations to be so serious that the notion that domestic labour was collectivized during the war is only 'feminist mythology'. She shows that while there were some nurseries provided, the majority of children of women in paid employment were cared for by grannies, other relatives or neighbours, and that less than 25 per cent of children under five were cared for in nurseries (Summerfield, 1984: 84). Further, while there had been an increase in factory canteens only a minority of meals, even during the working day, were eaten there (Summerfield, 1984).

One of the major sources of immediate opposition to the expansion of nurseries came from the Ministry of Health. It continuously placed obstacles in the way of the development of nurseries designed to assist women to take up paid employment. This opposition was expressed as a concern for 'standards', such as the ratio of staff to children (one staff to 3–4 children) and space allocation (while simultaneously holding back on funding for constructing the appropriate buildings). There were contradictions in policy both within the Ministry of Labour and between it and the Ministry of Health over such provision (Summerfield, 1984).

Here we see divisions and contradictions within the state which reflect rival demands on the use of women's labour. On the one hand there are the interests of the waged economy (supported by the Ministry of Labour), and on the other, the patriarchal interest in the maintenance of the privatized patriarchal organization of domestic labour in the household (supported by the Ministry of Health). In this situation the tensions between patriarchal and capitalist demands for women's labour are represented in the contradictions between the different policies of different departments of the state.

Cotton textiles in the Second World War

The cotton industry was affected by a shortage of male labour in spinning, which retarded production, yet there was still resistance to the employment of women in the mule room (Amalgamated Association of Operatives and Cotton Spinners and Twiners, 31 October 1939: 5–6, 31 January 1940: 6, 30 April 1940: 4, 31 January 1942: 4). The industry as a whole declined during the war, and the number of women employed declined from 656,000 in 1939 to 456,000 in 1943 (Summerfield, 1984: 30). However, within the spinning industry there was a disproportionate decline in the male-worked mule spinning as compared with the female-worked ring spinning. Mule spinning fell by more than half the earlier figure, while ring spinning fell by less than a quarter. By 1945 the spinning industry, previously a male stronghold, had a workforce which was 65 per cent female (Evershed Commission, 1945). This change in gender composition may be partly attributed to the shortage of male labour available for mule spinning, owing to the call-up into the armed forces, partly to the actions of employers disproportionately shedding the more expensive male labour on the mules, and partly to the increasing use of cheaper female labour in the ancillary occupations.

Engineering in the Second World War

Engineering was an area of employment which underwent considerable changes during the course of the war. The proportion of women employed in engineering increased from 97,000 or 10 per cent of the engineering workforce in 1939, to 602,000 or 34 per cent in 1943 (Summerfield, 1984: 29). After the war the numbers of women fell to a level half way between its pre-war and mid-war points so that in 1950 women constituted 20.5 per cent of the engineering workforce (Soldon, 1978: 365).

As in the First World War, the biggest barrier to the employment of more women in engineering was the opposition of the men's craft unions. During negotiations between the Amalgamated Engineering Union and the Engineering and Allied Employers' National Federation over increased wartime employment of women, Jack Tanner, the President of the AEU, stated

> We, as an organization are opposed to the introduction of women as a general principle. (Engineering and Allied Employers' National Federation, Central and Special Conference Shorthand Minutes, 8 April 1940, p. 430).

The AEU was prepared to countenance the employment of women in wartime as an 'unavoidable necessity', but demanded guarantees from the employers that this would be for the duration of the war only. They further wished to restrict women from taking on skilled men's work (Engineering and Allied Employers' National Federation, Central and Special Conference Shorthand Minutes, 8 April 1940, pp. 430–2). The final agreement concedes the first union demand in that the first clause states 'Women drafted into the Industry under the provisions of this Agreement shall be regarded as temporarily employed'. Here is the full text of the agreement:

> Memorandum of Agreement between Engineering and Allied Employers' National Federation and Amalgamated Engineering Union.

To Provide for the Temporary Relaxation of Existing Customs so as to Permit, for the Period of the War, the Extended Employment of Women in the Engineering Industry.

Whereby it is agreed that additional women may be drafted into the Industry for the purpose of manufacturing engineering products, with special regard for increasing output and to meet war-time emergencies:

1. Women drafted into the Industry under the provisions of this Agreement shall be regarded as temporarily employed.
2. An agreed record shall be kept of all changes made under this Agreement.
3. (a) The provisions of this Agreement will not affect the employment of women workers engaged on work commonly performed by women in Industry.

   (b) There shall be no objection to the extension of employment of women in establishments where women have not hitherto been employed on work commonly performed by women in the Industry, subject to the general undertaking contained in Clauses 1 and 2.
4. Women workers may be employed on suitable work hitherto performed by boys and youths under 21 years of age.
5. In the case of the extension of employment under Clauses 3(b) and 4, the National agreed scale of wages of women workers shall apply or the boys' and youths' schedule of wages shall be applied, whichever is the greater.
6. Women workers may be employed on work of a suitable character hitherto performed by adult male labour, subject to the following conditions:

   (a) Such women workers shall serve a probationary period of eight weeks at the women's national schedule of time rate and bonus.

   (b) At the end of the probationary period and for a further period of twelve weeks the women workers shall receive an increase as follows:

   (i) The basic rate shall be increased by one-third of the difference between the national women's schedule basic rate and the basic rate of the men they replace.

(ii) The national women's schedule bonus shall be increased in the same way by one-third of the difference between that bonus and the national bonus appropriate to the men they replace.

(c) At the end of the 20 weeks and for a further period of twelve weeks the women shall be paid:

(i) A basic rate equal to 75 per cent of the basic rate of the men replaced.

(ii) A national bonus equal to 75 per cent of the national bonus appropriate to the men replaced.

(d) Thereafter:

(i) In respect of women who are unable to carry out their work without additional supervision or assistance, the rate and bonus shall be negotiable and arranged according to the nature of the work and the ability displayed.

(ii) Women, however, who are able to carry out the work of the men they replace without additional supervision or assistance shall, at the end of the 32 weeks, receive the basic rate and national bonus appropriate to the men they replace.

(e) On payment by results the base rate and bonus paid shall be in accordance with Sub-Sections (a) to (d) of this Clause. When the work is carried out without additional supervision or assistance, the male workers' piece work price shall be given. When additional supervision or assistance is provided, the piece prices will be negotiable under the principles of Sub-Section (d) (i).

7. Notwithstanding anything herein provided, women who might enter employment fully qualified to perform without further training and without additional supervision or assistance work heretofore recognised as work done by male labour, shall be paid the rate and national bonus appropriate to the male labour they replace.

8. In the event of a question being raised in relation to the provision of this Agreement it shall be dealt with through the ordinary procedure for avoiding disputes, except that in the event of failure to agree locally the matter shall be dealt with expeditiously by a special central conference held in London.

Signed on behalf of
Engineering and Allied Employers' National Federation:
G. E. Bailey, Vice-President
Alexander Ramsay, Director
Alex. C. Low, Secretary
Amalgamated Engineering Union:
Jack Tanner, President
B. Gardner, Assistant General Secretary
22nd May, 1940
(Engineering and Allied Employers' Federation, Trade Union Agreements: National Agreements, no. 38.)

On the second demand of restricting women to semi- and unskilled work, the employers equivocated and talked at length of the variations of the industry and problems in applying such a restriction. The union was not successful in getting the restriction of women to unskilled and semi-skilled work written into the agreement.

The AEU's final demand, and one pursued tenaciously by the men, was that any unemployed men should be employed in preference to any woman (Engineering and Allied Employers' National Federation, Central and Special Conference Shorthand Minutes, 8 April 1940, pp. 434–48). They asked:

> That women will not be generally employed on work that has been done previously by men unless the unemployed males in the district can be said to have been absorbed. (P. 434.)

The employers prevaricated again, and denied the AEU's suggestion that they had already conceded this to other unions.

> I would like to qualify that when you talk about an understanding, we have had certain discussions and explored certain phases of this question, but you must realise that we have achieved nothing yet in the nature of an agreement. (P. 434.)

The AEU was clearly opposed to the employment of women *qua* women, not merely because they were likely to be unskilled or semi-skilled. Their preference for the employment of men, indeed any men, even men only 75 per cent fit, in preference to women is crystal clear in the minutes of this conference. They themselves note that the issue is not just one of skill and industrial relations, but a political one.

> I still want to get from you the position with respect to the employment of unemployed males before women are introduced. We want this matter clear because it has a political and social aspect, apart from the purely industrial one. (P. 445.)

The AEU pursued this point doggedly in the face of considerable employer resistance and absolutely refused to agree to admit women unless all unemployed men were taken in first. Finally, under considerable pressure, the employers conceded in the following interchange.

> Mr. Smith (A.E.U.): If a man has the same intelligence and is unemployed you would consider him first.
> The Chairman (E.A.E.N.F.): That, I think, is fundamental to the understanding. (P. 448.)

The Extended Employment of Women Agreement was concluded between the Engineering Employers Federation and the Amalgamated Engineering Union in 1940. It was followed from 1940 to 1942, by many similar agreements between the engineering employers and other unions (Engineering and Allied Employers' National Federation, Trade Union Agreements; National Agreements, nos. 71, 74, 75, 76, 78, 79, 87, 91, 92). A further agreement was the Restoration of Pre-War Practices Act, passed by the government in 1942, to further allay the fears of the skilled male workers. The Act guaranteed government support in ejecting women and restoring skilled work at the end of the war (Soldon, 1978: 154).

Despite this proliferation of pledges by the government and employers to restore pre-war privileges to skilled male workers, there was continuing opposition from men to women workers in some parts of engineering. There are repeated references in the literature to the hostility of the male workers to the female dilutees (Summerfield, 1984: 155; Inman, 1957: 28, 57, 58, 60–3; Frow and Frow, 1982: 155, 156, 171, 384; Lewenhak, 1977: 237; Soldon, 1978: 152). Some of these references are simply to the expressed dislike of men to the employment of women, especially at rates they thought too high for women (Inman, 1957: 28; Frow and Frow, 1982: 171; Lewenhak, 1977: 237; Soldon, 1978: 152), including attempts by the unions to negotiate with management the exclusion of women from skilled work (Frow and Frow, 1982: 155). Others are references to the informal sabotage of attempts to introduce women to skilled work by such tactics as hostility and refusal to train women in the necessary skills (Inman, 1957: 58; Frow and Frow, 1982: 384; Summerfield, 1984: 154–5). Still further forms of opposition included strikes and other industrial action (Inman, 1957: 57; Frow and Frow, 1982: 156). Indeed, opposition to the introduction of women in the sheet metal shops by the unions was fully successful for the duration of the war (Inman, 1957: 60–3).

Despite this opposition to the entry of women, there was a decisive shift in the policy towards women workers of the leading engineering union, the Amalgamated Engineering Union. During the war the AEU changed its policy towards women from predominantly one of complete exclusion of women from engineering, to one of accepting their presence in the industry and attempting to organize them. This change is indicated in the decision of the AEU to admit women to membership in the middle of the war, and the admission of 139,000 women in the first year of their eligibility in 1943 (Frow and Frow, 1982: 187). Yet as late as June 1940 the National Executive of the AEU had rejected a proposal to admit women by 25 to 14 (Soldon, 1978: 152).

The union was at last forced to recognize that women in engineering were not going to go away and that attempts to exclude them had failed. This change in strategy towards women was a consequence of employers' pressure to utilize cheaper women workers, the recruitment of these women workers by the general unions, and the introduction of new techniques of production which were not susceptible to forms of craft control. While the basic conditions for this change of policy had been building for a long time, the wartime situation acted as a catalyst to speed up the process. Women were rarely employed on the very skilled processes in large numbers during the war, but they were used extensively on semi-skilled work (Inman, 1957: 129). However, while there was a decisive shift in the national policy of the AEU, this did not mean that the local officials were enthusiastic about pushing the interests of the women workers. The following account is given by an AEU official who, when having a cosy chat in the office with the foreman, had his attention drawn to the fact that his union members were going on strike.

> I was in the office, and these girls were putting their coats on–they were going home, so the foreman asked me what was going on. But I didn't even know, because they hadn't told me mate, they were pissing off home. (Croucher, 1977: 129.)

Further the AEU had every intention of keeping these new women members under firm male control. Women were not allowed to stand for election to the offices of Branch Secretary, Branch President or Branch Treasurer (*AEU Monthly Journal*, September 1943: 321).

At the end of the war there was a considerable struggle between unions and employers over which work was to be done by men and which by women, and whether the men's or women's rates applied to it. Towards the end of the war there was an increase in the numbers of cases in which unions sought to register workers as temporary war workers on men's jobs in readiness for this struggle (Engineering and Allied Employers' Federation Minutes, Principal Series, vol. 43, 22 February 1945, GLM no. 101, p. 52–3). If this work was so registered then the unions had the right to demand the expulsion of the women workers. The relatively arbitrary allocation of certain tasks to men and others to women as a tactic to legitimate paying women at rates substantially beneath those of men, when combined with the discontinuities of employment brought about by the end of the war, made the task of defining 'women's work' very difficult for the unions (Summerfield, 1984).

> The enquiry [by the Engineering Employers' Federation] revealed, that although a good deal of the work had been done by juvenile male workers, work on each of the eight separate machines and on repetition viewing was performed to a considerable extent both by females and adult males, the work being done largely by females in one establishment and by adult males at another, and that in a small percentage of cases both females and adult males were found on the same work in the same establishment. (Royal Commission on Equal Pay, 1946, Cmd. 6937, vol. xi, p. 720.)

Since the allocation of a task to one sex or the other had little apparent rhyme or reason employers delighted in discovering that a task for which the unions claimed a man's rate was in fact performed by women somewhere else in the country. It thus provided them with legitimation for their claim that it was work 'commonly performed by women in the industry', and thus pay for it to be done at the women's lower rate. The employers and unions debated as to whether such tasks as 'sweeping up' were properly men's work or women's work and thus both who should do them and at what rate of pay (Summerfield, 1984). In 1947 the unions protested to the Engineering Employers' Federation that women should not be working on metal houses since it was the same as men's work. The employers countered that it was repetitious unskilled work requiring dexterity and thus 'women's work' (Engineering and Allied Employers' Federation Minutes, Principal Series, vol. 44, 27 February 1947, p. 85–6).

The unions' earlier strategy of collusion with the employers over the sex segregation of employment and the payment of women at lower rates thus backfired on the men. As a consequence of this, and the post-war expansion in engineering, the expulsion of women from this industry did not take place to the extent that a preliminary examination of the agreements would have predicted.

Clerical work in the Second World War

Clerical work expanded during the war, and the proportion of white collar workers who were women rose even faster, from 19 to 46 per cent between 1939 and 1943. The bulk of this increase was in local and national government where 540,000 more women were employed, while there were smaller increases elsewhere, such as of 50,000 in commerce (Summerfield, 1984: 30). The percentage of women in the non-industrial Civil Service rose from 25–26 per cent in April 1939, when there were 95,000 women as compared with 280,000 men, to 48 per cent in October 1944 when there were 320,000 women as compared to 350,000 men (Royal Commission on Equal Pay, 1946, Cmd. 6937, vol. xi, p. 670). As in the case of the First World War there was some evidence of a small decrease in sexual segregation of employment during the war (p. 748).

Women were not expelled wholesale from clerical work at the end of the Second World War. In particular many women stayed in the Civil Service, although there was a reduction in the number of staff who had temporary status. In 1944 there were 370,000 civil servants, this rising to 684,000 in 1946. Eleven years later, in 1957, there were 635,656, a reduction of not quite 50,000. However, there were redundancies among the temporary staff and the percentage of clerks with temporary status (who were largely, but not exclusively women) dropped from 72 per cent of the total staff in April 1947 to 30 per cent in 1955 (Humphreys, 1958: 187).

The main reason for the relatively small contraction of this area of employment at the end of the war was the slow run down of the war and the expansion of the social services by the new Labour government. Many of those in the wartime agencies transferred to the new growing government departments. Some of the temporary staff applied to transfer to the permanent staff under special schemes and were permanently incorporated into the Civil Service. However, there were some redundancies among the temporary staff, based on seniority, the nature of the job that was held and efficiency (Humphreys, 1958: 187). The Redundancy Agreement drawn up by the National Whitley Council Committee did not single out women for unequal discharge. Indeed it explicitly stated that 'no discrimination should be exercised against married women' or 'part-timers'. This was justified on the grounds that there was a continuing manpower shortage and a desire not to alienate those who had responded to government wartime appeals (CSCA, 1952: 342).

These three areas of employment: cotton textiles, engineering and clerical work show very different changes in their gender composition under the impact of the two wars and the depression. In the First World War, the male cotton spinners were able to resist pressures to substitute women for the men called up into the army, partly because of the strength of their union. However, in engineering, despite the equally strong engineering craft unions, women did enter the trade, albeit concentrated in the semi-skilled rather than skilled work. The main reason for the difference was the greater importance of increased engineering production for the war which led to government intervention. The terms of this intervention were clearly patriarchal in that they guaranteed the men the return of 'their' jobs at the end of the hostilities if they would let the women in for the duration of the war. This was possible because of the lack of political power of women at the level of the state. In clerical work the increase in labour demand was met by the recruitment of women with none of the state support for men that had occurred in engineering. Male clerks were badly organized as compared with engineers, and were not able to enlist state support on their own behalf.

The cotton industry was particularly badly hit by the inter-war depression and greatly reduced its need for labour of both sexes. The introduction of such patriarchal practices as sacking women on marriage led to higher unemployment rates among married women than other groups of cotton textile workers. The impact of the depression on the engineering industry varied by branch and by region. Some of the branches which were worst hit, for instance ship building, had the most exclusive employment of men, and the strongest unions, while the sections which grew in the inter-war period, for instance electrical engineering, did so in areas of lesser union organization and employed a higher proportion of women. Thus although there was no direct substitution of women for men, nonetheless there was an increase in the percentage of women in engineering in inter-war years. In these newer areas the weaker unions were less able to resist employers' attempt to employ cheaper female labour on some segregated processes. In clerical work there was also a small increase in the percentage of women employed, again on tasks which were segregated from those on which men were engaged.

The Second World War saw an increased proportion of women in all three areas of employment. In cotton spinning this occurred as a result of the call up of the men and the disproportionate decline in the male-dominated mule spinning rather than the cheaper female-worked ring spinning. The change in the balance of technologies thus side-stepped the men's resistance to the admission of women to spinning, which had been successful in the First World War. In engineering and clerical work the patterns were nearly the same as in the First World War as regards the entry of women. In the case of engineering, there was again state support for the exclusion of women at the end of the war, and again not in the case of clerical work. However, at the end of the war the guarantees given to the engineers proved less effective than after the First. This was largely because the limited employment of women before the war in highly varied patterns of segregation of male and female workers enabled employers to claim that a smaller number of jobs were 'really' men's jobs than the unions had expected. Further, the continued expansion of engineering meant that the decline in the number of jobs at the end of the war was not as great as before. In government clerical work the expansion of state services meant that many temporary female clerks retained their jobs.

These varied historical outcomes show the importance of not simply considering the relative strength of only one or two social forces in understanding changes in the gender composition of paid work. It is rather the complex interaction of a number of factors which must be considered: employer demand for labour, which is crucially affected by the product market; trade unions, which are critically differentiated by not only their overall strength, but also their policy towards gender relations; variations in the extent to which particular groups can mobilize the state; and the shifting relations between occupations due to changes in technology. Further these interactions take place not only in sequence through time but also in spatially differentiated social and political contexts.

7
Post-War Progress?

There has been a considerable increase in the proportion of women in paid employment after the Second World War. Women's activity rate increased from 26.9 per cent in 1951 to 36.5 per cent in 1971 and 47.2 per cent in 1983. Only in the recession after 1979 has the number of women in paid employment started to fall, from a peak of 9.5 million to 9.1 million in 1984. This increase has not occurred evenly over the country, but rather regions which had a very low female activity in 1951 have since had very sharp increases, while those regions which had a relatively high rate have experienced only small increases in female activity. Thus the most striking change of this period is the reduction of regional differences in women's employment and unemployment. Since we may take the wide regional variations in the early 1950s as indicative of substantial hidden unemployment among women in the regions with low female employment rates, the increase in these low rates is indicative of the reduction of women's unemployment in these areas. Between 1952 and 1979 an average increase of 6.5 per cent in the proportion of women in paid employment hid regional variations ranging from an increase of 10.8 per cent in East Anglia and one of only 2.3 per cent in the North West as table 7.1 shows.

There appear to be three reasons for this narrowing of regional differences in female employment rates. Firstly, there has been a relatively even spatial distribution of the increase in some of the types of service sector jobs in which women predominate. For instance, health, education and retailing became increasingly important sources of employment for women in all regions. Secondly, this convergence in regional employment rates for women is related to the overall changes in regional employment. The regions with the fastest growing employment are among the regions with the lowest rates of female employment at the beginning of the period (see table 7.1). Wales, East Anglia and the South West had particularly low rates of female employment and have experienced

Table 7.1 Changes in Regional and Female Employment Rates, 1951-79

Region	Changes in regional female employment rates, 1951–1979	Regional female employment rates, 1951–1979: Percentage of women in paid employment 1951	1979	Female activity 16+ 1981	Regional employment change, 1952–1979
East Anglia	+10.8	21.0	31.8	47.1	+43.5
North	+10.6	21.2	31.8	46.0	+ 9.4
Wales	+10.2	18.5	28.7	42.0	+10.0
South West	+10.1	21.7	31.8	44.1	+29.6
Scotland	+ 8.3	25.1	33.4	47.0	+ 1.5
East Midlands	+ 7.4	25.8	33.2	48.0	+21.0
South East	+ 5.7	28.9	34.6	48.2	+14.4
West Midlands	+ 5.2	29.6	34.8	48.4	+ 8.3
Yorkshire and Humberside	+ 5.0	27.8	32.8	47.3	+ 5.8
North West	+ 2.3	31.5	33.8	48.5	− 5.2
Great Britain	+ 6.5	26.9	33.4	47.2	

Source: calculated from census data in Lee (1979) and from Eurostat, 1981, *Labour Force Survey, 1979*.

above average rates of employment growth. Thirdly, declining industries are unevenly spread between regions, and where these have employed relatively large proportions of women, this contributes to a disproportionate decline in female employment in that region. An important instance of this was the decline of cotton textiles which is primarily located in the North West.

Women at Work in the Post-War Period

There were considerable changes in employers' policies towards women workers in the period. Many of the bars to women's employment, and especially to married women's employment were removed. However, positive attitudes and practices towards women were far from uniformly introduced. Hunt's (1975) survey of management attitudes towards employing women shows the existence of considerable ignorance and prejudice about the productive abilities of women workers. Further it was widely reported that the employers' federations including the Engineering Employers' Federation and the British Paper Box Federation issued written advice to its member-employers on how best to evade the implications of the Equal Pay Act of 1970 (TASS, n.d.: 213; TUC, 1970: 412).

There were significant changes during the course of this period. In 1973 the Confederation of British Industry (CBI) accepted the case for legislation to make discrimination on the grounds of sex illegal (Snell et al., 1981: 10), and in 1979 issued a statement and code on equal opportunities to all its members (CBI, 1979). In this 1979 statement the CBI not only supported the principle of equal opportunities, but also detailed some of the organizational steps necessary to implementing such policies. In 1982 the CBI and Equal Opportunities Commission jointly ran a conference on employers' attempts to introduce equal opportunities policies (EOC, 1982b). It should not be assumed, of course, that policy statements by the CBI are the same as grass-roots practices.

Married part-time women

The post-war period thus saw a large increase in women in paid employment, but with a highly uneven distribution. A considerable part of this increase involved the employment of married women working part-time. The proportion of women working part-time in the UK is higher than in all other European countries except Denmark. Since the rapid economic expansion of the post-war years was an experience common to all European countries, an explanation of the increase in part-time work among British women in terms of the increased demand for labour cannot be a sufficient explanation. Rather, the distinctive experiences of wartime Britain are crucial. During the war, part-time employment was specifically introduced to assist in the mobilization of women who had domestic commitments involving the care of dependents. This experience was important in the post-war years as the basis on which married women were recruited into paid work during this latter period of labour shortage.

As the wartime shortage of labour continued into the post-war period so did the distinctive ways devised in Britain to facilitate the employment of women. The post-war economic conditions were quite unlike those after the First World War. There was a slower winding down of the war effort, rather than the sudden lay-offs of the previous period (Soldon, 1978: 155). The development of the social services by the newly elected Labour government further helped to sustain employment (Humphreys, 1958: 187). There was a continuing high demand for labour during the post-war reconstruction and the government attempted to sustain the wartime employment of women to a considerable extent, retaining the conscription of women for some years after the war (Lewenhak, 1977: 244). The implementation of the Restoration of Pre-War Practices Act was postponed, and only in 1947 did the government announce that it was to be implemented in the beginning of 1948 (Engineering and Allied Employers' National Federation Minutes, Principal Series, Management Board, 26 June 1947, p. 169). The less extensive and less sudden expulsion of women from paid work after the Second World War as compared with the First, together with the continuing demand for labour facilitated the continuity of employment practices introduced to encourage women to take paid work during the work. Many practices introduced during wartime to facilitate the employment of women were continued into peace time. One of the most important of these was the continued utilization of the labour of married women.

The ending of the marriage bar and its discrimination against women had long been fought for by women's organizations. This campaign was conducted both inside and outside of Parliament, including a deputation from all parties to the Chancellor of the

Exchequer in 1945 (*Women's Bulletin*, 16 March 1945, pp. 2–3). Many, although not all, employers took on married women after the war, in stark contrast to their pre-war practices. In 1946 the Civil Service abolished its marriage bar (Soldon, 1978: 157; CSCA, 1952: 91).

The changing employment practices at Peak Freans illustrates these developments. Before the Second World War this biscuit manufacturer refused to employ married women, and female employees were discharged on marriage. The labour shortage during the war forced the company to reconsider its marriage bar and from 1941 it started to employ married women. This employment practice continued in the post-war period because of labour shortages. By 1955 three-quarters of the firm's workers were female and four-fifths of them were married. Three-quarters of the women workers worked part-time, most of these being married (Social Science Department, LSE, 1960: 8).

However, the continued employment of married women was far from uniform. Some unions were successful in obtaining the reimposition of the marriage bar (Soldon, 1978: 266), while in many other cases married women were more vulnerable to dismissal, when a firm contracted its employment, than other categories of workers (MacKay et al. 1971: 376; Soldon, 1978: 265). This was often initially the policy of trade unions, which expected management to concur (Soldon, 1978: 265–6).

Employers' reasons for the employment of part-timers included the relative unavailability of full-time workers and the usefulness of part-timers in covering fluctuations in demand (CBI, 1967: 26–8; Klein, 1965: 129). More recent research has also suggested the advantages to management of various kinds of flexibility involved with employing part-time workers (Perkins, 1983; Beechey and Perkins, 1986; Bruegel, 1979; Robinson and Wallace, 1984). These advantages of part-time workers for employers were further consolidated over the post-war period by their exemption, if they worked beneath a certain number of hours, from various Acts relating to security from dismissal and redundancy payments. Further advantages accrued from the threshold for the payment of National Insurance contributions (Manley and Sawbridge, 1980).

The consequences of the lack of both trade union and legislative protection of part-time workers was that such workers are more liable to lose their employment than other categories of workers. The numbers of part-time workers within particular industries showed greater fluctuations than those of full-timers (Bruegel, 1979). Since part-time workers were almost entirely married women, this differentiation of the conditions and security of part-time and full-time workers was effectively the differentiation of the conditions of a large proportion of married women from those of the rest of workers.

Part-time work thus represented the new form of the compromise between patriarchal and capitalist interests. The expansion of part-time work and the consolidation of the distinction between it and full-time work during the post-war period saw the continuation of this patriarchal and capitalist accommodation. Women's labour was made available to capital, but on terms which did not threaten to disrupt the patriarchal status quo in the household, since a married woman working part-time could still perform the full range of domestic tasks.

Women and trade unions

While employers were increasingly seeking women workers in the post-war period, the trade unions were forced to rethink their position on gender related questions. There was a major shift in the strategy of unions towards women during the twentieth century although there remained in parts hostility to women taking *particular* types of jobs, especially in the immediate post-war period. For instance, the TUC openly argued that it was necessary for the unions to struggle for segregation by sex in order to protect men's pay:

> The trade unions have been compelled not only to uphold, but to promote, a clear demarcation between men's and women's work–where such demarcation was possible–in order to protect the men's and thus indirectly the women's rates of pay . . . There can be no question that where industries are well organised such demarcation is strongly upheld both by custom and to some extent by specific agreement between the employers and the trade unions. (TUC annual report, 1945: 467.)

This submission to the Royal Commission on Equal Pay goes on to detail segregation by sex in a range of industries, and the trade union opposition to women taking 'men's jobs' in: cutting rooms in the clothing trade; clicking, press, lashing and finishing in the boot and shoe trade; printing; pottery; wood; and upholstery in the furniture trade (TUC annual report, 1945: 480–4). An example of successful trade union opposition to women is embodied in the national agreement signed by the Incorporated Federated Association of Boot and Shoe Manufacturers of Great Britain and Ireland and the National Union of Boot and Shoe Operatives. Clause 10 of this agreement states:

> It is undesirable that females should be employed amongst male operatives in the clicking, press, lashing and finishing departments in which male labour is now almost exclusively employed. (TUC annual report, 1945: 481.)

There were divisions within the unions over the employment of women. In some cases, while national union officials accepted that women should not be barred from paid employment, the rank and file did not agree. In 1950 there was a four day strike of 14,000 London transport workers in which one of the demands was that there should be no further employment of women conductors. The national officials of the Transport and General Workers Union refused to make this strike official (Allen, 1957: 170–1).

There have been two major changes in the response of trade unions to women workers since the onset of the Second World War. The first was the consolidation of the practice of segregating their work from men's so that the conditions and wages for men were not undermined. This is shown particularly clearly in the changed response of the leading engineering union, the AEU, to women. Having admitted women to their union in 1943, they urged on the TUC the policy of organizing women, albeit under a patriarchal hegemony. In 1952, the AEU welcomed a new TUC paper thus:

> The TUC have started something with this 'Notebook' and if they make it brighter and talk in women's language, then we are certain that the danger to the male trade unionists that there has been over a number of years will be eliminated and the women will come in. We do not want the statements that the trade unions have no time for women, but we have reached the stage where women, in their fight for equality, have the same right to be organised and the right to an equal position with our men members. (TUC annual report, 1952: 337.)

Here we see patronizing attempts to recruit women (women apparently needed pictures to make them read this publication) expressed simultaneously as in the interests of male trade unionists and in terms of equality between the sexes. Tension between these two themes runs throughout the union's responses to women in the post-war period.

By the late 1960s the second strand, that of equality between the sexes, begins to take on greater importance under pressure from women unionists. This has led to the adoption of policies by most of the major unions overtly urging equality of opportunity between men and women workers, and, in some cases, the setting up of special committees and appointment of special officers to implement these policies. However, these new policies are usually limited to equality of opportunity, and rarely go as far as affirmative action programmes which might directly challenge male interests.

The causes of these changes are complex. Women had been trying to alter union policies for many long decades, as previous chapters have described; so the issue is why these changes occurred at the time that they did, rather than why they occurred at all. I think it was the result of the combination of the following seven factors.

Firstly, there had been a significant growth in the number of women in paid work, which led to their increased proportionate importance for trade unions, both in terms of their potential subscriptions and their enhanced voting power.

Secondly, there had been a significant growth in the number and proportion of women in trade unions. The wartime peak of women in trade unions was regained and surpassed in the 1960s and increased steadily in the 1970s. The percentage of women members in unions affiliated to the TUC rose from 15 per cent in 1950 to 29 per cent in 1978 (WTUC annual report, 1978: 40). Simultaneously the number of unions affiliated to the TUC which had no women members fell from 44 out of 117 in 1967 to 17 in 1978 (p. 32).

Thirdly, the continuing attempts at growth by many of the larger more general unions led to a competition for members, which benefited women workers.

Fourthly, the renewal of industrial militancy among women unionists, especially in the engineering unions, such as that by the women at Fords and in the 1968 engineering pay round, gave women workers more influence.

Fifthly, there was a resurgence of political militancy of women throughout the country on a wide range of issues; that is, the emergence of the second major wave of feminist agitation had an important influence. This had significant impacts on trade unions in a variety of ways: some women were directly involved in both trade unions and the women's liberation movements and drew confidence and support in the overlap between these political and industrial activities; the media coverage of feminist events generally raised the political consciousness and determination of women unionists to fight on their own behalf; women's liberation groups sometimes provided direct support to women unionists in struggle, such as in the cases of the night cleaners campaign and the Grunwick's strike, this alliance providing not merely practical support, but also radicalizing ideas.

Sixthly, the nature and strength of the opposition to women's demands has changed and weakened. The rhetoric of equal opportunity is now so firmly established that the ideological terrain is slanted in women's favour. Arguments that women's place is in the home are no longer so credible and protestations as to men's superior productivity do not constitute arguments against mere equality of opportunity. Blocking devices of 'the time is not right' or 'the country cannot afford it this year' do not carry the same force. That is, women have utilized liberal ideology most effectively to undercut the previous patriarchal hegemony of the trade union movement.

Seventhly, the readoption of forms of organizing which had previously been effective for women was important. That is, there was a development of women's caucuses at many levels in many unions, and their institutionalization into women's committees within the unions. During the first feminist wave women had also had forms of union organization which were independent from those of men, but these had mostly been amalgamated with those of men in the inter-war period with consequent loss of an independent voice for women unionists. The rebirth of women's committees in the last decade or so within trade unions has done much to give women's voices a chance to be heard at policy making levels.

There was a long struggle for changes within the TUC to gain greater representation of the views of women. The TUC body which was most sensitive to the views of women has been the annual Women's TUC conference, which started as an annual conference for unions catering for women workers in 1930. This conference selects about half of the members of the Women's Advisory Committee, the other half being from the General Council; usually all the delegates from the Women's TUC have been female, while all bar two of the members from the General Council have been men. The Congress itself is a heavily male-dominated body whose gender composition does not reflect that of the membership in the unions themselves. The General Council is the most male-dominated body of all, and it is this committee which has been most significant in blocking demands from women workers which had reached the national level of the TUC.

There had been a committee for women on the General Council of the TUC since 1921, a time when the first major feminist wave was still influential. Between 1921 and 1930 there were five members of the General Council (GC) on this committee (WTUC annual report, 1978: 2), and, since there were usually only two women on the GC itself, this meant a male majority. In 1930 a special TUC conference was held on the organization of women workers at which the women's committee of the GC called for special committees for women at a local and national level and annual conferences for unions catering for women workers (TUC annual report, 1930: 108–9). The women's group on the GC was transformed into the Women's Advisory Committee and included delegates from the annual Women's TUC conference (TUC annual report, 1930: 108–9; WTUC annual report, 1978: 21). There were various attempts to establish women's committees at local, trades council level (TUC annual reports, 1945: 38, 1952: 123–4), although these did not become successfully established (TUC annual report, 1959: 128).

During the 1970s there was a concerted campaign to change the gender composition of the General Council so that it might more accurately reflect that of the membership, together with attempts to slant the composition of the Women's Advisory Committee towards women by increasing the proportion of its members elected from the Women's TUC rather than from the General Council. In 1975, the Women's TUC conference called for an increase in the number of women's seats on the General Council, which responded by saying merely that it would consider the matter further (WTUC annual report, 1977: 5–6). In 1977 the Women's TUC conference called for ten women to be elected to the Women's Advisory Committee (which at that time had a male majority) by the Women's TUC and for seven more seats for women on the General Council

(WTUC annual report, 1978: 1–21). While the first demand was partially conceded, in that the Women's Conference was allowed to elect eight (not ten) members of the WAC, the General Council resisted the change to its own composition more strongly. The General Council said that they had consulted member unions about the composition of the General Council and that the majority of them wanted the abolition of the women's seats altogether (WTUC annual report, 1978: 3).

The Women's Advisory Committee acted as something of a go-between in relation to the Women's Conference and the General Council, albeit appearing to side with the General Council over the issue of women's seats on the General Council. When the General Council refused to increase the number of women's seats, the Women's Conference passed a motion 'deploring' their action despite opposition from the WAC which tried to remit or defeat this motion (WTUC annual report, 1978: 69–71). In 1981, however, the General Council conceded an increase in the number of women's seats from two to five (not the seven asked for) (WTUC annual report, 1981: 4), and a further increase to six in 1983 (WTUC annual report, 1983: 2). By 1983 there was a Women Workers' Bulletin published by the TUC and a new Charter for Women (WTUC annual report, 1983: 2) and by 1984 every Regional Council in England and Wales had, or was establishing, a Women's Advisory Committee (WTUC annual report, 1984: 5).

During the last few years there have been substantial changes in the gender relations within trade unions. The following are some examples of such developments. The General and Municipal Workers' Union (GMWU) set up a system of annual regional and national equal rights conferences in 1975. This was followed by the appointment of an Equal Rights Officer in each region in 1977, a working party to examine the position of women in the union in 1978, and an Equal Rights Advisory Committee in 1980 (GMWU, 1981: 32–3). The Technical, Administrative and Supervisory Section of the Amalgamated Union of Engineering Workers (TASS) appointed a Women's Officer in International Women's Year (TASS, n.d.: 2). The National Association of Local Government Officers (NALGO) set up an Equal Rights Working Party which reported in 1975 and conducted a survey comparing the position of its women members with its men (NALGO, 1981). Special working parties, committees or sub-committees for women or equal rights were set up by several other unions during the 1970s including the Association of Scientific, Technical and Managerial Staffs in 1975, the Association of Professional, Executive, Clerical and Computer Staff, the British Actors Equity, the National Association of Teachers in Further and Higher Education, the National Union of Bank Employees (now BIFU), and the National Union of Teachers (Ellis, 1981: 50) and Union of Construction Allied Trades and Technicians in 1982 (Ellis, 1985: 19). A survey of trade unions by the Equal Opportunities Commission (EOC) in 1980 found that out of the 52 respondents 21 had examined their structure for barriers to women members and 13 had set up special committees to deal with equality issues (EOC, 1983e: 17, 24).

The importance of these special equal opportunity structures is suggested by the fact that ten of the 13 unions found by the EOC to have special committees had special policies for women on a wide range of issues, while 19 out of those which had no such committees did not (EOC, 1983e: 25). However, it is possible that these are both the consequence of a different cause, rather than the committee causing the policy. Further, it should be noted that ony a minority of unions have introduced special committees and policies.

Legislating for equal opportunity

The Equal Pay and Sex Discrimination Acts represent significant turning points in state actions on gender relations. They are the first positive attempts to improve women's position in paid employment across the country as a whole by the state. While they are widely believed to have had only a marginal effect on women's labour market position (cf. Gregory, 1982, 1985; Snell, 1979; Snell et al., 1981), nonetheless, they constitute an important change in the direction of state policy, from one constraining women's paid employment to one which, at least symbolically, encourages it.

The evidence on the effects of the legislation is ambiguous. Only a very low proportion of complaints made under the Sex Discrimination Act have been successful. In 1979 of 141 complaints brought by women under this Act, only 15 culminated in favourable decisions at Industrial Tribunals. The Tribunals dismissed 32 claims, while 49 were withdrawn for unknown reasons, and 45 reached some kind of out-of-court settlement (*Employment Gazette*, 1980: 385–6). Nevertheless, there is evidence of a decline in sexual segregation in employment in the years immediately following the Act. Hakim suggests that the decline in sexual segregation in the years 1973–7 is four times that which would be expected on the basis of the trend she discovered in the years 1901–71 (Hakim, 1981: 529). The causes of this legislation are primarily those seven changes just described which wrought such significant alterations in the position of women within the trade union movement.

In the end, when the legislation was being considered by Parliament in the late 1960s and early 1970s. there were no major institutional forces explicitly ranged against the legislation. Organized women, the Trades Union Congress, the Confederation of British Industry, the Labour party and the Conservative party were all in support of some such legislation. The focus here is on the Equal Pay Act, since it was around this that most agitation had centred, and the Sex Discrimination Act followed on more smoothly five years later.

The TUC first gave formal approval to the demand for equal pay in 1888 (Drake, 1984: 227). The history of its prevarication over putting any resources into the pursuit of this claim is one of simultaneous lip service to liberal ideology together with a tenacious patriarchal practice. I argued in chapter 6 that the amalgamation of women's with men's unions led to a serious decline in the representation of the interests of women workers, which was not compensated for by the increased overall power of the larger amalgamations. The failure of the campaign for equal pay until 1970, may be at least partially attributed to this.

During the Second World War there had been a very strong campaign for equal pay (Smith, 1981). Yet despite a TUC policy for equal pay since 1888 and a Labour government from 1945, the TUC refused to push for this demand in the immediate post-war period, saying that this should be left to individual unions. Despite a resolution of the Congress in 1947 to 'use its full resources to engage without delay in vigorous co-ordinated activity to secure equal pay' the General Council found it 'impracticable for the TUC at the present time to extend these activities to include the holding of a series of large public meetings throughout the country' (TUC annual report, 1948: 275–6). Again in 1949 the General Council refused to push equal pay on the government because of: the economic situation; the unlikelihood that the government would change its mind; and the need for counter-inflationary policy (TUC annual report, 1949: 252). The same happened in 1950 when three resolutions for equal pay from the Women's TUC met with resistance from the general TUC, due to the 'current economic circumstance' (TUC annual report, 1950: 255). In these instances, and throughout the 1950s, grass roots pressure for action on equal pay was consistently blocked by the General Council of the TUC, even when the women had managed to get their motions through the Congress itself.

While the TUC prevaricated, and found it 'impracticable' to hold large public meetings, women workers did not. In 1951, after yet another refusal by the government to grant equal pay, 3,000 people, largely women, held a protest meeting in London, and hundreds from this meeting descended on Parliament in a mass lobby. This protest was sufficiently large and vociferous that it staggered and bewildered the police, who closed the doors of Parliament and brought in mounted police to disperse the chanting demonstrators (*Civil Service Opinion*, August 1951: 121). It appears that the women did not have adequate forms of representation; only one woman speaker was on the platform of this mass meeting; and there were clear suggestions that the representatives of the workers, or staff side, had not pushed very hard in the negotiations over pay. The grass roots pressure by women was not institutionalized in forms of representation at a national level and sometimes found expression in relatively spontaneous, disorderly protest. The greatest activity by the TUC came when it backed the limited demand for equal pay for government employees to the extent of writing to, and then visiting, the Chancellor of the Exchequer (TUC annual report, 1953: 262; 1954: 307). This demand was finally granted by the 1954 Conservative government.

Motions calling for equal pay continued to be put from the Women's TUC to the TUC throughout the 1950s and 1960s with little further success. The popular image of no feminist activity in Britain in this period is contradicted by the continuing efforts of trade unionists representing women workers to push for equal pay and other feminist demands. In 1963 a six-point Charter for Women was passed by Congress which called for equal pay, equality of opportunity and better training for women and girls (TUC annual report, 1963: 134).

During the 1960s the changes in the position of women in the labour movement, in paid work and as political actors transformed the political climate. However, the TUC was not at the forefront of the battle for equal pay. Of the unions behind this campaign

(National Association of Local Government officers (NALGO), National Union of Teachers, (NUT), Civil Service Clerical Association (CSCA), Institute of Professional Civil Servants (IPCS) and Society of Civil Servants (SCS)), only the CSCA was affiliated to the TUC. Pressure to ratify two international treaties on equal pay provided further impetus for governments. In 1951 ILO Convention 100 was adopted. Article 119 of the Treaty of Rome also required legislation for equal pay if Britain were to join the Common Market. By the mid-1960s both Labour and Conservative parties had committed themselves to equal pay in election manifestos. Equal pay was one of the broken promises of the 1964 Labour government (Snell et al. 1981). Yet even as late as 1968, Roy Hattersley, as Joint Parliamentary Secretary to the Ministry of Labour, was procrastinating on equal pay on the grounds of 'present economic circumstances' (*The Clerk*, February 1968: 6).

The final pressures leading to legislative action included increasing militancy by women workers and, in particular, the Ford machinists' strike in 1968. The presence of a woman, Barbara Castle, as the relevant Minister of State is also of significance. She was openly sympathetic to the demands of the women workers and had long backed women's claims to equal pay, for instance in 1960 pressing for equal pay for women civil servants in Hong Kong. She then expressed exasperation with the blocking tactics of the men when she declared that women

> were getting tired of having this stale old trick foisted on them of appointing an all-male committee in order to establish that there is no case for giving women equal pay with men. (*Woman Teacher*, January 1961: 45.)

The final haggling focused on two issues: definition–equal work, same work or work of equal value; and timing–seven years or two. The more progressive stance was taken by the TUC, while the CBI took the more conservative one. The TUC backed the wider definition of equal pay for work of equal value preferred by the women unionists, rather than the more restrictive equal pay for equal work. This followed a TUC enquiry which showed that some unions (representing altogether 54,000 women members) said they would not wish to go beyond equal pay for equal work, while 27 unions (with 880,000 women members) wanted equal pay for work of equal value (TUC, 1970: 4). This report noted that the position of the trade unions varied 'according to whether their main aim was to safeguard the position of their male members, or to gain parity for their women members' (p. 5). The most important changes then were: firstly, the increased strength of women in trade unions, due to both an increase in their numbers and organizational factors; and, secondly, the granting of the vote to women–women were now constituted as citizens whose views had to be taken account of, at least to some extent, in party politics; thirdly international pressure, especially through the EEC.

Women in this period had greater power to realize their interests than in the earlier period of employment legislation in the nineteenth century; this strength was due both to their organization in the labour market and to increased power at the level of the state. There were other political factors also, the most important of which was the international context, in which Britain was enmeshed. The Sex Discrimination Act quickly followed on from the Equal Pay Act. This was again supported by both major parties. The 1972 publication of the Labour Party Study Group, set up in 1967, recommended making discrimination on grounds of sex illegal and the setting up of an independent enforcement body. The Conservative party's Committee of Enquiry set up in 1969, the year after Labour's, led to a series of recommendations including one of introducing a law to remove discrimination. This was included in their 1970 manifesto, two years before the Labour party committee reported. It was a Conservative government which took the first active steps on this when in office in 1973, with the publication of a consultative document containing the above recommendations, and a Bill embodying these was in preparation when the Conservative party was defeated in 1974. The incoming Labour government published a White Paper on similar lines, which led to a Bill that year and the Sex Discrimination Act of 1975. This act was somewhat wider in scope than the Conservative model and the enforcement body was granted wider powers but, unlike the Conservatives, Labour did not propose the repeal of the 'protective' legislation, merely that the new Equal Opportunities Commission should review it (Snell et al., 1981).

Both the CBI and the TUC eventually accepted the case for sex discrimination legislation. Prior to 1972 the TUC did not want such legislation, but was persuaded in 1972; the CBI agreed in 1973, although wishing for a narrow definition of discrimination. It is clear that the differences between the Labour party and the Conservative party on their policies and practices are very slight, Labour policy is perhaps slightly stronger. The unanimity of all these diverse forces, which on issues relating to conventionally defined class relations were so far apart, might be considered quite remarkable. The feminist case had been accepted by the representatives of a wide range of class forces; gender issues were truly a cross-class issue.

Ethnicity and gender

In the post-war period there had been a shift in the ethnic composition of the paid workforce as a consequence of immigration. The employment of ethnic minorities has some different features from that of the native white population (further, it should not be forgotten that there are white ethnic minorities, such as the Irish, who were resident in Britain long before this period). The shifting ethnic composition is of relevance to my argument in two ways: firstly, in that the employment experiences of the various ethnic groups are significantly different; secondly, because immigration affected the existing gender patterns of employment.

The diversity of employment experience by ethnicity is itself complex and affects men and women differently. Among men, whites systematically do better than all blacks, in many different ways (Brown, 1984). Among women, Asian women systematically do worse than white women; however, the data on West Indian women is much more ambiguous. West Indian women earn on average more than white women, although if only the age range of 25–54 is considered (that is, omitting the older women earning low wages who are to be found disproportionately among whites), then this is changed to a slight white advantage (Brown, 1984: 215). However, West Indian women suffer significantly higher rates of unemployment than white women: 20 per cent, as compared to 13 per cent of white women, are unemployed (registered and unregistered) (calculated from Brown, 1984: 156).

The distribution of different ethnic groups across industry sectors and socio-economic groups can be seen in tables 7.2 and 7.3 These show that there is segregation in employment by ethnicity as well as by gender. The distribution across industry is one of the reasons why those West Indian women who do obtain employment do not fare as badly as we might have expected given the disadvantages they

Table 7.2 Persons Aged 16 and Over in Employment by Ethnic Origin, Industry Division and Sex, Great Britain 1981

Percentages

Ethnic origin and sex	Industry Divisions											
	Agriculture, forestry and fishing	Energy and water supply	Extraction of minerals and ores	Metal goods, engineering and vehicles	Other manufacturing industries	Construction	Distribution, hotels and catering, repairs	Transport and communications	Banking, finance and insurance	Other services	No reply/ inadequately described/ working outside UK	*All industries (thousands = 100%)*
	0	1	2	3	4	5	6	7	8	9		
Men												
White	3.6	4.9	5.3	16.4	10.9	10.7	14.5	8.5	6.8	17.2	1.3	*13,325*
West Indian or Guyanese	0.0	1.3	5.0	27.4	11.2	10.6	10.9	18.0	3.2	11.3	1.1	*120*
Indian	0.0	0.8	4.7	24.4	15.4	4.0	21.1	11.3	6.5	10.8	0.9	*174*
Pakistani or Bangladeshi	0.4	0.0	6.4	15.2	23.3	–	29.7	11.9	4.0	7.3	1.8	*69*
Chinese, African, Arab, mixed or other	0.4	1.5	3.1	16.8	7.4	4.3	27.0	9.5	7.5	20.1	2.4	*114*
Not stated	0.9	1.4	1.4	4.1	3.2	2.8	2.7	1.8	1.8	4.7	75.3	*161*
All ethnic origins	3.4	4.7	5.2	16.5	10.9	10.4	14.6	8.6	6.7	16.9	2.2	13,962
Women												
White	1.1	1.1	2.3	6.6	11.4	1.3	24.6	2.8	8.9	38.4	1.5	*8,945*
West Indian or Guyanese	0.0	0.5	0.7	7.8	8.4	0.5	10.2	5.7	6.3	57.7	2.2	*107*
Indian	0.5	0.2	3.2	12.0	28.7	1.0	20.9	4.2	7.7	21.8	0.0	*93*
Pakistani or Bangladeshi	0.0	2.4	4.4	12.0	29.5	0.0	11.7	0.0	10.7	29.2	0.0	*10*
Chinese, African, Arab, mixed or other	0.0	1.2	1.5	5.6	11.7	1.3	26.7	2.9	3.7	38.9	1.5	*70*
Not stated	0.2	0.0	0.7	2.1	1.9	0.0	7.2	0.5	2.5	15.1	69.8	*102*
All ethnic origins	1.1	1.1	2.3	6.6	11.5	1.2	24.2	2.9	8.8	38.2	2.2	9,328

Source: OPCS, 1982, *Labour Force Survey 1981*, Table 4.24.

Table 7.3 Persons Aged 16 and Over in Employment by Socio-Economic Group, Ethnic Origin and Sex, Great Britain 1981

Percentages

Ethnic origin and sex	Socio-economic group: Professional	Employers, managers	Other non-manual	Skilled manual	Semi-skilled manual	Unskilled manual	Armed forces/ inadequately described/and not stated	*All groups (thousands = 100%)*
Men								
White	6.1	16.2	17.9	38.0	15.7	4.7	1.4	*13,325*
Non-white	6.6	10.4	14.6	36.7	24.0	6.7	1.0	*476*
West Indian or Guyanese	1.7	4.0	7.3	48.6	26.6	10.8	1.1	*120*
Indian	9.0	10.5	16.9	36.7	21.8	4.8	0.3	*174*
Pakistani or Bangladeshi	4.2	15.4	7.9	31.7	31.8	8.6	0.4	*69*
Chinese, African, Arab, mixed or other	9.7	14.0	22.9	27.3	19.7	4.2	2.3	*114*
Not stated	1.7	3.3	4.9	10.0	3.7	1.4	75.0	*161*
All ethnic origins	6.0	15.9	17.0	37.7	15.8	4.7	2.2	13,962
Women								
White	1.1	6.6	53.0	7.4	23.4	8.1	0.3	*8,945*
Non-white	1.7	2.9	47.2	8.4	33.5	5.6	0.6	*281*
West Indian or Guyanese	0.2	1.9	50.0	4.4	34.5	8.4	0.7	*107*
Indian	2.9	4.2	41.1	13.0	35.3	3.4	0.0	*93*
Pakistani or Bangladeshi	6.7	2.3	39.9	14.1	34.3	0.0	2.7	*10*
Chinese, African, Arab, mixed or other	1.8	2.8	52.2	7.7	29.5	5.1	1.0	*70*
Not stated	0.3	2.5	16.1	1.7	8.3	2.1	69.1	*102*
All ethnic origins	1.1	6.5	52.5	7.3	23.6	7.9	1.1	9,328

Source: OPCS, 1982, *Labour Force Survey 1981*, table 4.25.

face as a result of racist practices. This is possibly because of the significance of their employment by the public sector and in particular the NHS. During the 1950s and 1960s, due to a labour shortage in the UK, there was deliberate recruitment of overseas workers, especially from the West Indies, for jobs in the health service. This is a highly unionized area of employment, with conditions of employment which are better than many of those faced by women in the private sector. Asian women on the other hand have been employed largely in the private sector with additional disadvantageous consequences for their conditions of employment.

The second major way in which ethnicity is important for an analysis of the distribution of the sexes in employment is the effect it has upon that distribution. Within the three areas of employment which are the focus of this book the most dramatic is in textiles and will be considered below, after a consideration of the impact of the recent recession on gender divisions in employment.

The current recession

An understanding of women's employment in the current recession requires an examination of the same three processes as were examined for the inter-war depression. These were: the differential rate of job loss among men and women in the same industries and occupations, the differential rate of employment decline in industries and occupations in which one sex or the other predominates, and lastly, the differential rate of increase in new employment opportunities for men and women.

The current recession and high levels of unemployment might have been expected to set off similar patriarchal pressures on women's employment as they did in the inter-war depression. Yet while there have been some similar statements from men advocating that married women should leave the labour market (Coote and Campbell, 1982: 84–7), there has not been such a direct attack on women's right to paid work as before. However, there does seem to have been some increase in the sexual segregation of the workforce during the recession (Hakim, 1981: 526–7).

One way in which women typically lose their jobs more easily than men is because of the particular forms of job loss which may be negotiated. Most forms of negotiated job loss attempt to give priority to the claims of the longest serving workers. Women may lose their jobs more often than men in situations of job loss, because of their vulnerability as part-time workers, or because of their lack of seniority or negotiating power.

A study of job loss

I devised the study described below to address such questions of gender relations in the process of job loss. The research aimed to discover whether women were more or less likely than men to lose employment at times of job loss. It also aimed to uncover the immediate factors behind the decisions as to *how* jobs are shed. A study at the level of the establishment was felt to be necessary to investigate these issues, which can be easily obscured by aggregate figures. Further, the actual process of job loss can best be studied at the establishment level, particularly the respective contributions of managers, trade unions, and female and male workers.

Thirty employment establishments were examined, all in the North West of England. The reason for this was primarily to cut down on travelling time and to facilitate contacts. The process of job loss was investigated by interviewing management and unions in each of the 30 establishments. The fieldwork was undertaken between March 1981 and July 1982 and managers and trade unionists were asked questions about the preceding two years. Thus the period of job loss covered by this report extends over 1979–82, a period of high job loss both regionally and nationally.

Unemployment rates in the area had been higher than the national average for some time, and management and unions were typically familiar with the issues surrounding job loss. Almost all the establishments that were contacted had experienced recent contraction of some form or another, thus eliminating the need to search for such firms.

The intention of the research was to ascertain why particular strategies of job loss were adopted and whether these had a differential effect on the men and women employed. Characteristics which might be pertinent to processes of job loss were identified, therefore, and establishments were quota-sampled to ensure that there were some with each characteristic. The 30 establishments were drawn from manufacturing and services; they varied in size and in occupational mix; they had different patterns of ownership and levels of unionization; and they employed men and women in different

Table 7.4 Number of Establishments, by Most Severe Form of Job Loss Employed

	Total	Compulsory redundancy	Voluntary redundancy	Natural wastage/ temporary contracts	None of these
Sector					
Manufacturing	14	9	1	3	1
Service	16	4	4	5	3
Occupational mix					
Wholly manual	4	0	0	4	0
Mainly manual	15	11	3	0	1
Even manual/ non-manual mix	1	0	0	1	0
Mainly non-manual	10	2	2	3	3
Size					
Small (less than 100 employees)	13	4	1	5	3
Medium (100–999)	13	8	2	2	0
Large (1000+)	4	1	2	1	1
Gender mix					
Mainly male	8	5	2	1	0
Even	10	5	3	2	0
Mainly female	12	3	0	5	4
Ownership					
State-owned	7	0	3	4	0
Multinational corporation	7	4	1	0	2
National capital	10	7	1	1	1
Local capital	6	2	0	3	1
Unionization					
Unionized	24	10	5	6	3
Non-unionized	6	3	0	2	1
Total	30	13	5	8	4

proportions. Table 7.4 shows the distribution of the characteristics of the establishments in the sample by the most severe form of job loss experienced.

Compulsory redundancy is only one of several types of job loss, even if the most visible variety. Indeed its high visibility probably accounts for an undue concentration by researchers on this form of job loss. Other major forms include voluntary redundancy, early retirement and natural wastage. Yet other ways of cutting back on labour include the use of temporary contracts and cutting down the number of hours worked by each employee.

Each of the major types of job loss takes a variety of forms. In

Table 7.5 Distribution of Types of Job Loss in the Sample of Establishments

	Number of Establishments[1]
Compulsory redundancies	13
induced by:	
least essential tasks or skills	6
last-in, first-out	5
least efficient	4
part-timers first	4[2]
near or over retirement age	3
least personal hardship	1
disliked by management	1
Voluntary redundancies	10
induced by:	
financial benefit (state minimum)	5
geographical redeployment (only alternative)	2
financial benefit (above state minimum)	1
internal redeployment (only alternative)	1
change of hours (end of twilight shift)	1
Natural wastage	20
of which:	
simple	16
delays in reappointment	3
enhanced	1
Early retirement	9
induced by:	
financial benefit (above state minimum)	4[3]
internal redemployment (only alternative)	4
geographical redeployment (only alternative)	2
hours cut	1
bonus cut	1
financial benefit (state minimum)	1

[1]Some establishments used more than one type of job loss; hence the numbers come to more than 30.
[2]Not all these cases unambiguously belonged to this category.
[3]In one case there was a dual inducement of both financial benefit above state minimum and the threat of internal redeployment.

situations of compulsory redundancy the pattern and distribution of job loss is significantly affected by the criteria used to select people for dismissal. The following types of criteria were identified from this study: part-timers first; those near or over retirement age first; last-in, first-out; least efficient; those with the least essential tasks or skills; those who might suffer the least personal hardship; and those disliked by management.

Voluntary redundancies were never totally voluntary, but involved pressure of some kind. For instance, the only alternative to redundancy was sometimes internal or geographical redeployment, a change of hours or a loss of bonus. Voluntary redundancy sometimes involved a positive inducement of some kind, usually in the form of a financial benefit. Early retirements were likewise not entirely voluntary and involved a similar range of pressures and inducements. Natural wastage was sometimes not a simple category, but various changes were made in the conditions of employment which might be said to 'enhance' it. Table 7.5 sets out these various forms of job loss and their occurrence in the sample.

Compulsory redundancy is not a form of job loss which of itself necessarily has a greater consequence for one sex than the other. Its effect on the balance between male and female employment depended on the selection criteria used in relation to departmental divisions within the establishment. Examples of direct discrimination against women as women seemed to be very rare; in fact, it was found on only one occasion. It should be added, however, that since such discrimination would be unlawful, and since the interviews were confined to those responsible for decisions relating to redundancy–that is, management and unions–the lack of evidence does not actually prove that such discrimination does not occur. Nevertheless, the research does suggest that direct sex discrimination is not the common and overt practice which writers in earlier periods have reported (cf. MacKay et al., 1971).

It is possible, however, that the selection criteria used for compulsory redundancy could lead to indirect discrimination against women; that is, that criteria are used which are more likely to select women for redundancy than men. The research threw up an interesting illustration of how the particular pressures and inducements used by employers could have a disproportionate effect on one sex. In two establishments the offer of a job in a neighbouring locality as an alternative to redundancy had led to relatively greater job loss among women than among men, except where the costs of this were borne by the employer. This was largely because the women were less likely to be earning a wage which made the ensuing travel worthwhile. It can be seen that existing features of women's employment, such as relatively low pay, can have a knock-on effect in the job-loss process.

The distribution of voluntary redundancies was affected by the sex segregation of the workforce in the same way as compulsory redundancies. Where early retirements took place with the incentive of service-related payments there was a tendency for more men to go than women. This may be explained by the greater benefits men typically derive from such schemes as compared with women, because of their greater likelihood of having long unbroken service. As in the other forms of job loss, the segregated nature of employment is often of significance in the sex composition of early retirers.

More than half of the establishments in the sample were using natural wastage in order to reduce the size of their work forces. While in a third of these this was the only method used, in the remaining two-thirds it was used alongside more precipitate forms of job loss. Where it was possible to distinguish the effects of natural wastage alone it was found to result in a slightly greater loss of women's jobs than those of men. This was to be expected because of the marginally higher turnover rates in the jobs typically occupied by women. The process of natural wastage was sometimes enhanced, retarded or otherwise shaped by the management. For instance, in one case the withdrawal of holiday play schools and nursery places 'encouraged' the disproportionate 'wastage' of women. Thus, while natural wastage in itself tended to produce a greater loss of women's jobs than men's, in practice there existed ways of shaping this process, with varying effects on the gender distribution of job loss.

This account has so far focused primarily on the variations in the methods of job loss and their impact. However, the distribution of job loss itself across the range of employers has a significant effect on the distribution of job loss between men and women. The establishments with the greatest contractions in employment were predominantly in the manufacturing sector and employed a relatively high proportion of men, whilst those with the smaller contractions were predominantly in the service sector and employed a relatively high proportion of women (see table 7.4). The sample of 30 establishments reflected the behaviour of the national economy in this respect. Across the spread of the sample, men were more likely to lose their jobs than women despite the fact that, in many job-loss situations, the practices employed were more likely to lead to the loss of a higher proportion of women's jobs. The concentration of women in the sector of the economy least affected by the current recession has thus protected women's employment as a whole. So, for instance, while part-timers, who were almost exclusively married women, were more likely to lose jobs than full-timers in a particular job-loss situation, the bulk of part-time jobs were in the service sector which was the sector undergoing least job loss. There existed simultaneously two distinct sets of processes, one of which, at the establishment level, meant that women were more likely to become unemployed than men, and the other, at the sectoral level, which meant that women were less likely to become unemployed than men. The aggregate figures of male and female unemployment and employment must then reflect the continued effect of these two contrary processes.

At establishment level, some commonly used forms of job loss do mean that women are sometimes more likely to lose their jobs than men. For instance, in situations of 'compulsory redundancy' the use of 'part-timers first' and 'last-in, first out' selection criteria lead to a higher proportion of women than men losing their jobs. Other examples of 'semi-voluntary' forms of job loss showed that the offer of geographical redeployment without travelling expenses as an alternative to 'voluntary' redundancy leads to a higher proportion of women losing their jobs than men. The use of natural wastage also leads to a slightly greater proportion of women's jobs being lost.

This situation is primarily the outcome of women's structural position in the labour market which tends to be reaffirmed in union–management negotiations and remains relatively undisturbed by Industrial Tribunal decisions. Women's occupation of jobs with higher turnover rates leads to a higher rate of natural wastage than for men, while their generally lower rates of pay make travelling long distances to work economically less viable for them than for men. Similarly, women are slightly more likely to be dismissed when 'last-in, first-out' is used as the selection criterion for compulsory redundancy, because they are likely to have held their jobs for a shorter time than men. Part-time workers suffer from a relative lack of representation by trade unions and a tendency for their work to be seen as less important than that of full-timers. Most of the forms of job loss which disadvantage women *vis à vis* men thus appear to stem from giving priority to the employment claims of those who have been in specific jobs the longest, a category of worker which is also the best represented in workplace discussions and negotiations. Thus women's disadvantaged position in society tends to be reflected at the workplace in the processes of job loss.

The picture was nevertheless immensely complex, with many

variations and exceptions. The process of job loss takes many forms, which are the result of much negotiation, and the application of which is open to much flexibility and discretion. In such situations women are often disadvantaged relative to men, though not inevitably so (for a fuller account of this study see Walby, 1985a).

There have been suggestions that women are particularly likely to lose their jobs because of the new technology. Huws (1982) suggests that the occupations to which women are confined will be very severely reduced in size by the introduction of the microchip.

Table 7.6 Changes in Men's and Women's Employment by Industry Group, 1979–81

	Women		Men	
	Actual change (thousands)	Percentage change	Actual change (thousands)	Percentage change
Agriculture, forestry and fishing	−11	12	50	12
Energy and water supply industry	6	6	44	7
Extraction of minerals, manufacture of metals and chemicals	−92	30	−307	−30
Metal goods, engineering and vehicle industries	−163	−21	−530	−19
Other manufacturing industries	−105	−9	−61	−4
Construction	−7	−6	−202	−12
Distribution, hotels and catering, repairs	144	7	0	0
Transport and communications	−8	−3	−142	−11
Banking, finance and insurance, business services and leasing	81	11	89	10
Other services	−1	0	−12	−1
No reply/inadequately described/working outside UK	84	68	124	70
All industries	−52	−1	−945	−6

Sources: calculated from Eurostat, 1981, *Labour Force Sample Survey 1979*, table 60; OPCS, 1982, *Labour Force Survey 1981*, tables A3 and A4.

However, while this may lead to a disproportionate employment decline for women in the future, this had not happened as late as 1981. The proportionate changes in employment for each sex in each industry grouping has been remarkably even (see table 7.6). The only significant differences in the changes in men's and women's employment are the greater decrease of female employment in 'other manufacturing industries'; the greater decrease of male employment in 'construction' and 'transport and communications'; and the female increase in 'distribution, hotels and catering, repairs'. However, these result in the decrease in female employment being substantially lower than the decrease in male employment.

Regional differences in changes in female activity rates are quite marked as in the earlier post-war period (see table 7.7). Again those regions which had the lowest female activity rates are among the ones with the highest percentage increases in 1979–81, thus leading to a further diminution of the differences between regional female activity rates. Despite the problems women have in keeping hold of jobs, their overall employment rate was not affected by the recession as much as men's, falling by only 1 per cent as compared to 6 per cent

Table 7.7 Regional Changes in Women's Activity Rates, 1979–81

	Numbers of economically active women (thousands) 1979	1981	Change in numbers of economically active women (thousands) 1979–81	Percentage change in economically active women 1979–81
North	550	563	13	2
Yorkshire and Humberside	889	916	27	3
North West	1,240	1,248	8	1
East Midlands	682	714	32	5
West Midlands	969	972	3	0
East Anglia	323	348	25	8
South East	3,182	3,274	92	3
South West	760	778	18	2
Wales	452	470	18	6
Scotland	994	954	−40	−4
Northern Ireland	224	244	20	9
Britain	10,044	10,237	193	2
UK	10,265	10,481	216	2

Sources: calculated from Eurostat, 1981, *Labour Force Sample Survey 1979*, table 60; OPCS, 1982, *Labour Force Survey 1981*, table 4.5.

for men. This further indicates that it is the newly developing areas of employment that are important in protecting women from greater unemployment. The evidence suggests that women are not substituted for men, but rather that they take a higher proportion of new jobs in expanding industries in locations where their activity rate was previously relatively low.

While the economy as a whole has experienced a period of prolonged growth (although marked by periods of stop–go economic management) followed by one of deep recession, the three areas of employment on which I have been focusing experienced quite different patterns.

Cotton Textiles in the Post-War Period

After a brief resurgence in the immediate post-war period the cotton textile industry suffered a serious and escalating decline. Total employment rose between 1945 and 1951 from 175,040 to 285,750 and plummeted to 165,390 in 1960, 83,580 in 1970, 32,440 in 1980 and 22,290 in 1983 (ATWU, 1983: 25). While some writers have argued that the collapse of the British cotton textile industry was due to entrepreneurial failure, in particular a problem of a lack of investment despite the large profits of earlier years, others have argued that it is a result of the shift of competitive advantage from the industrialized to the industrializing nations in processes requiring the particular mix of skill, technology and capital involved in cotton textiles (Sandberg, 1974). This decline of the cotton textile industry is not unique to Britain, but affects other industrialized European countries as well. Indeed, the West German textile industry has been taken as a key example in an analysis of the new international division of labour between countries at different levels of development in the world economic system (Fröbel et al., 1980).

Despite the brief post-war recovery of cotton in Britain, the industry's decline was rapid and severe for most of the period since the war. Reductions in employment took place alongside increasing mechanization, speed-up and mill closures. The 'more looms' developments of the inter-war years progressed so that fewer weavers were required to look after the same number of looms. The loss of jobs took place despite protests from the workers (Lewenhak, 1977: 263). There was a substantial decline in the proportion of women in the cotton industry. This occurred for two main reasons: firstly, the increase in shift working from which women were barred by the 'protective' legislation, and their substitution by Asian men; secondly, the combined efforts of male workers and employers in implementing the recommendations of the all-male Evershed Commission. It would appear that black male labour was indirectly substituted for white female labour in textiles. Table 7.8 shows a decline in the proportion of women in textiles during the latter part of the period after the Second World War (cf. Fevre, 1984, on the woollen industry). This occurred at the same time that the employers were recruiting Asian men. It appears that the employers introduced night-shift working in order to more efficiently utilize their machinery at a time of declining competitiveness of the British textile industry within an increasingly internationalized world economy. Women were prevented from working night-shifts by the restrictive 'protective' legislation unless complex exemptions were arranged.

Table 7.8 Employment in Cotton Textiles, 1970–82

	Total	Male	Female	% Female
June 1970	150,000	73,900	76,000	50.7
June 1975	98,200	54,800	43,500	44.3
June 1980	69,500	39,100	30,500	43.9
June 1982	50,600	29,300	21,300	42.1

Source: calculated from *Department of Employment Gazette*, 1970–79, and *Employment Gazette*, 1980–2, table 1.4.

The exact figures on employment in the cotton textile industry are impossible to deduce from official government statistics because of the classifications used. The nearest approximation is to add together SIC MLH 412 'spinning and doubling on the cotton and flax systems' and SIC MLH 413 'weaving of cotton, linen and man-made fibres'. This is on the one hand an overestimate as a consequence of the inclusion of flax, linen and man-made fibres, and on the other an underestimate since I have omitted 'narrow fibres' and 'textile finishing'. However, it is the best that can be derived using statistics classified according to the Standard Industrial Classification. Given that man-made fibres might be expected to be more buoyant than the older cotton industry these figures might have a tendency to understate the decline of the cotton industry.

Native white male labour could not be obtained at the rates of pay the textile employers were prepared to offer; black male labour immigrating into Britain could be. This was in a general context in which the wages which black people could obtain, for reasons which included racial discrimination, were lower than those of whites, for whom a wider and better range of job opportunities existed.

A Commission was set up at the end of the war to investigate wages and work organization in cotton spinning. It was an all-male committee despite the fact that 65 per cent of the workers in the industry at that time were female and the committee was supposed to be composed half and half of employer and worker representatives with an 'independent chairman'. It was set up under government auspices–in particular those of the Board of Trade and the Ministry of Labour and National Service (Evershed, 1945). The Commission saw the problem of a good labour supply as one of much importance for the industry. They proposed a restructuring of wages and occupational segregation so as to ensure greater employment of men at the expense of the women:

> Such wage arrangement will in practice tend towards the greater employment of male adult labour which, as already indicated, we regard as highly desirable in the interests of the industry. (Evershed Commissison, 1945: 18.)

The Commission rationalized this collusion between employers and male-dominated unions in two ways: firstly, women were held to be guilty of greater casual absenteeism than men and of being less likely to remain permanently in the industry. Secondly, women were doing work which was considered by these men as inappropriate for women, especially in that it was too heavy. They stated that 'women have been employed to a greater extent and for heavier types of work than is in our view desirable or justifiable' (p. 18). They saw women as having been introduced owing to their cheaper labour and because of the wartime labour shortage. Women were not present on the committee so there was no account of women's views on this issue.

It is interesting to note a shift in the terms of rationalizing the exclusion of women since the nineteenth century: rationalization is no longer in terms of women's supposed place at home. Rather it is articulated largely via the supposed requirements of the industry, women being held to be less competent, and partly by a minor theme of protecting women. The heavy weights theme combines both of these: women are either not able or less able than men to do such work, and they should be protected from it.

The Commission provided a classification of occupations according to sex and advocated the removal of women from some of those areas of employment they designated as male.

There was a curious combination of principles on rates of pay involving both the notion of the rate for the job and also that of the rate for the sex. The Commission's procedure was to fix which occupations were for men and which for women, and then to fix the rate for the job. In the detailed sections there are clear references to the fixing of some rates as suitable for a married man (p. 20), and indeed of packing it was said, 'we think the work must be regarded as appropriate to men and the wages fixed accordingly' (p. 34). It was explicitly recommended that adult male labour should be substituted for female in certain occupations. Further even unskilled men were to be paid more than women.

> We are anxious that the status and quality of the operatives shall approximate throughout the industry to that of the stripper and grinder and to this end we recommend that employment in the blowing room should henceforth be regarded as a male occupation, the necessary changeover taking place as vacancies occur.

and again

> By providing for blowing room work being done by men the proposals will also bring to an end the practice of employing women and girls in this department, a practice which is more prevalent in fine spinning mills than elsewhere but which we unanimously deprecate on the grounds that the handling of laps and the supervision of the blowing room plant is altogether unsuitable for women and girls. (Evershed Commission, 1945: 20.)

Indeed they argued overall that

> the industry should be organized on the basis of providing primarily for adult occupations and so as to increase the

> opportunities for employment at all stages of production (save such categories of work which by reason of their lightness or otherwise, are particularly adapted for female or juvenile labour) of adult male operatives. (P. 37).

Here we see a committee which considers itself as representative of the interests of those involved in the spinning industry not merely ignoring the interests of the majority of the workforce, but making recommendations which run directly counter to them. It is an explicit instance of patriarchal collusion between unions and employers; the patriarchal interests cross-cutting the class division between the employers and unions. The state is a party to this, in that it had influence over the composition of the Commission, and the recommendations carry extra legitimacy in coming from a government body. In some ways it is a good example of the development of post-war corporatism in its involvement of employers, unions and state to sort out a perceived problem in industry. It also raises the question of whether 'patriarchal conspiracy' is indeed an appropriate term to describe the actions of men against women on some occasions.

Women lost ground in their representation on the trade union committees, which further hindered their claims to employment. The composition of the Rossendale Weavers' Association altered from a female majority to a male majority, while women disappeared from the Accrington Weavers' Committee and the North East Lancashire branch committees of the Card Blowing and Ring Room Operatives Union (Lewenhak, 1977: 264). There were a series of amalgamations of unions, since the rapidly declining membership could not support the existing union structure. By 1975 all textile unions, bar the overlookers, had joined the new Amalgamated Textile Workers Union, while talks of mergers with larger general unions including General Municipal Boilermakers and Allied Trades Union (GMBATU) were underway (ATWU, 1983: 6–7, 22). The overlookers, an all-male group of supervisors (Savage, 1982), retained their exclusion of women even after the Sex Discrimination Act, and reported no women members to an Equal Opportunities Commission survey in 1980 (EOC, 1983e: 38). Both the Executive and the District Secretaries of the new amalgamations had substantial male majorities (ATWA, 1983).

So in cotton textiles, not only was there a loss of employment for women, since less labour was needed due to technological development and the overall contraction of the industry, but women also lost jobs because of their displacement by male workers. The cotton textile industry was a major employer of women in the North West so the decline of employment for women in this industry is a major reason why the employment of women there has not grown at the same rate as in other areas of the country. The major decline in skilled manual employment for women in the post-war period is accounted for to a considerable extent by the decline of women's employment in cotton textiles. This decline accelerated in the last decade as the cotton textile industry collapsed.

Engineering in the Post-War Period

In the first part of the post-war period, engineering experienced a growth in employment rising from just over 3.5 million employees in 1951 to well over 4.5 million in the late 1960s (Lee, 1979; Croucher, 1977: 136). During the same time the proportion of women increased slowly from 19 to 23 per cent. However, after the late 1960s the number of workers in engineering rapidly decreased until by 1982 they were nearly a million beneath the 1951 level (calculated from Lee, 1979 and *Employment Gazette*, 1982: Table 1.4). The proportion of women employees also declined, so that in 1982 this had gone back to the 1951 level of 19 per cent (calculated from *Employment Gazette*, 1982: Table 1.4).

Table 7.9 shows that the proportion of women in the various branches of the engineering industry remained remarkably constant over the 30-year period, and the small increases and the decreases in the percentage of women in engineering as a whole largely reflects the fortunes of the sectors which had high or low rates of female employment – in particular the growth and decline of employment in electrical and mechanical engineering which were the largest employers of women. There were reports of discouragement, and indeed refusal, to employ women in certain branches of the industry. Unions continued to make an impact on employment practices. Indeed the majority of engineering establishments reported in a survey that they were prevented from organizing labour in their plants in the way that they wished, with 96 per cent of employers reporting that trade unions were 'a restrictive factor in arranging their labour

Table 7.9 The Proportion of Women in Engineering, 1951–82

Standard Industrial Classification		1951	1961	1971	1982
VI Metal	T[1]	570,565	625,940	550,790	29,700
Manufacturing	%F[2]	10.9	11.5	12.4	10.5
VII Mechanical	T	932,198	1,128,300	1,124,850	694,300
Engineering	%F	14.9	17.1	16.6	14.6
VIII Instrument	T	111,483	143,940	145,260	119,000
Engineering	%F	31.3	34.5	35.0	34.0
IX Electrical	T	557,260	757,120	843,920	608,400
Engineering	%F	38.0	35.8	37.7	33.0
X Shipbuilding and Marine	T	276,803	236,600	180,420	137,400
Engineering	%F	3.8	4.6	6.1	7.8
XI Vehicles	T	734,616	837,710	788,830	566,100
	%F	13.5	13.2	13.3	11.3
XII Metal Goods not specified	T	503,627	524,960	585,980	409,300
elsewhere	%F	33.4	32.9	28.6	24.9
VI–XII All	T	3,686,552	4,254,570	4,217,050	2,823,400
Engineering	%F	19.3	20.7	21.5	19.4

Source: calculated from census data for 1951, 1961, 1971. Census figures taken from C. H. Lee, 1979, *British Regional Employment Statistics*, and from Department of Employment data for 1982 from *Employment Gazette*, 1982, table 1.4.
[1]T: total
[2]%F: percentage of women

force' (although 29 per cent saw this only to a small extent) (Marsh et al., 1971: 101).

The hostility of engineering to women was well known. In a survey of the public's views on engineering as a profession, many of the people who considered that it was a good career for a woman 'expressed reservations about women being accepted' (*Employment Gazette*, 1980: 26). One girl who applied to seven firms to be a trainee technician in this period received three replies which explicitly stated that they did not take girls, while a further three did not reply at all (Coote, 1979: 9). A discouraging atmosphere in most branches of engineering and outright refusal to employ women in some firms is reported by Galenson (1973: 39). In the mid-1960s a negligible number of women were members of professional engineering associations.

In this context the greater vulnerability of women than men to job loss is no surprise. MacKay et al. report that women, and in particular married women, were sacked before men in the engineering plants that they studied in 1959–66 (1971: 376). However there was a shift in the policy of the main engineering union, now the Amalgamated Union of Engineering Workers, away from directly exclusionary policies towards women. This was a continuation of the policy adopted during the war to recruit women in engineering. The reasons for the wartime change of policy–the shortage of labour, determination of employers to take on women and the changes in technology which assisted the growth of semi-skilled tasks–continued into peace-time. The opening of membership of the union to women during the war was retained. The unions did attempt to use The Extended Employment of Women Agreement to eject women at the end of the war, but, as the previous chapter suggested, these attempts were not always successful. By the early 1970s such attempts to utilize this agreement had long fallen into disuse (Dey, 1979: 82–3).

However, while directly exclusionary policies were no longer followed, the evidence suggests that men's claims to employment were still given priority over those of women in much of the post-war period. Women remained confined to the less skilled types of work, both at the height of engineering employment (Sear, 1968: 36) and right up to the present day (EOC, 1983c, 1983d).

The Amalgamated Engineering Union took seriously its commitment to organize women workers in engineering, albeit in ways which enabled the men to retain control of the union. The AEU formally backed the demand for equal pay, set up a newspaper for women engineering workers, and organized annual conferences of women workers. This sounds a major turn around in union policy, until the reasons for this, as stated in the women's paper by a male member of the National Committee, are understood:

> So long as women are paid at lower rates they represent to employers a reserve of cheap labour which can threaten the existing rates of men. (*Woman's Angle*, June 1952: 3.)

Further, the women were not left to organize themselves around their own perceptions of their own interests, as this description of the 'woman's' conference suggests:

> Facing this solid phalanx of men on the platform and arranged in a horse shoe were the women delegates. All very formal and

> impressive, but somewhat formidable, with all the women in the body of the hall, and nary a one among the officers. (*Woman's Angle*, April 1953: 2).

Even the 'women's' paper usually contained statements by the male members of Executive on the front page (together with their photographs). The union was proud of its endeavours on the behalf of women, and hailed as a great achievement an agreement with Vauxhall's at Luton in 1968 in which it was agreed that the range of women's employment would be expanded, slightly, subject to the following conditions.

> (a) Women will not be engaged if suitable men are available.
> (b) Existing male employees will not be replaced with women.
> (c) Women will be employed only on jobs broadly specified and agreed.
> (d) Rates for women will be 92% of the equivalent male rate (where applicable). (*AEU Journal*, May 1968: 231–2.)

Contemporary readers will be forgiven for not immediately understanding which part of this agreement was supposed to be a great victory for women.

There were significant differences between unions on the representation of women's interests. The General and Municipal Workers' Union prided itself on its support for women engineering workers and in 1968 backed its Woman's Officer (a position due to the amalgamation with the National Federation of Women Workers in the inter-war period) in her fight with other unions and employers in the annual pay round. Marion Veitch held her ground in these negotiations and caused a crisis by refusing to agree to the widening of the differential between unskilled men and all women. She was praised for her stand against other engineering unions on behalf of women by her own union bosses and the union's paper (*GMWU Journal*, November 1968: 7, January 1969: 3; GMWU, 1969: 188).

Industrial militancy among women engineering workers grew in the late 1960s and included the battle of the women machinists at

Fords for regrading, which developed into an issue of equal pay (*GMWU Journal*, January 1969: 3).

While discussion of much of the post-war period is concerned with the expansion of women's employment, this is not the case for the end of this period. Some writers have suggested that the introduction of the new technology is likely to have a disproportionate impact on the low-level jobs held by women (Huws, 1982; EOC 1983d). However, Cooke et al. have pointed to the growth of female workers in the new semiconductor industry, albeit at low levels of skill. In this industry women are employed particularly in the regions receiving state aid, and slightly less so in the non-assisted areas. In the former women constitute 74 per cent of the manual production workers in semiconductors, and only 48 per cent in the latter (1983: 13).

Rather than consider these to be competing interpretations I think they should be seen to relate to different areas of engineering employment. While women's employment in the more established engineering industries may be liable to disproportionate reduction, women are increasingly being employed in the newer branches of electrical engineering in the peripheral regions. The net outcome of these contrary trends has led so far only to a very small drop in the proportion of women in the engineering workforce.

Clerical Work in the Post-War Period

Clerical workers increased in numbers in the post-war period and the proportion of these workers who were women also increased. Between 1951 and 1971 the number of clerks increased from 240,400 to 347,900 while the proportion who were female rose from 59 to 71 per cent (Routh, 1980: 24). The proportion of the different types of clerical work did not change very greatly over this period with shorthand typists and typists decreasing from 23.8 to 22.8 per cent, office machine workers rising from 3.4 to 5 per cent and 'others' staying more or less unchanged at between 72 and 73 per cent. The number of typists reached a peak in the mid-1960s and then started to decline (Routh, 1980: 25; Vinnicombe, 1980: 7). Within these categories there were some changes as the percentage of bookkeepers, estimating clerks and costing clerks fell from 54 to 38 per cent (Routh, 1980: 26).

The category of typists, shorthand writers and secretaries is almost entirely female so the size of this group is important for the number and proportion of women in clerical work. The proportion of women in this category rose from 97 per cent in 1951 to 99 per cent in 1971 (Vinnicombe, 1980: 71). Other job categories with particularly high proportions of women were telephone operators at 83 per cent in 1971 and office machine workers at 86 per cent in 1971 (McNally, 1979: 44). The expansion of clerical work in the post-war period has been largely one of filling relatively menial positions with women (Crompton and Jones, 1982: 140).

One of the largest changes in restrictions on women entering clerical work in the post-war period was the general removal of the marriage bar after the war. This was recommended by the Royal Commission on Equal Pay for the Civil Service in 1946 and this was one of its recommendations which was acted on (Royal Commission on Equal Pay, 1946 Cmd. 6937, vol. xi, p. 651; Humphreys, 1958). However, some trade unions tried to insist that they should be retained. Indeed, the Union of Post Office Workers ensured its operation in the Post Office until 1963 (Lewenhak, 1977: 265).

Clerical workers, especially women clerical workers, are often thought as quiescent rather than militant workers. Yet organized clerks in the Civil Service were an important force behind the pressure for equal pay and against other forms of sex discrimination, and clerks in the banking unions were among the first to set up special equal opportunity committees in the 1970s (*Civil Service Opinion*, August 1951: 121, 138–140; *Civil Service Whip*, March 1951: 11, November 1951: 47; *The Clerk*, November/December 1946: 88, 89, January 1968: 4, 7, May 1968: 8, March 1973: 1, 3; *Banking Insurance and Finance Union Report*, November 1977; 4, 8, December 1977: 8, June 1978: 11, January 1984: 9, October 1983: 14).

The post-war period saw the removal of barriers to women entering clerical work and large increases in the numbers of women so employed. However, there are suggestions that at the end of the post-war period there is the beginning of a decline in women's clerical employment because of the introduction of the new technology into offices (Coote and Campbell, 1982: 71–3; Downing, 1980: 276; Huws, 1982: 23–27; Rhee, 1968: 167, 171–4; Werneke, 1985). It is claimed by these writers, that the new technology eliminates a higher proportion of jobs done by women than by men, and that a higher proportion of the new jobs brought about are performed by men than the old. Werneke (1985) suggests that it is the lower skilled clerical and first-line management jobs which will be most affected, most of which are held by women. An example of this was the reduction of women staff from 44 to 22 in a section of Bradford Council which introduced word processors (Downing, 1980: 276). A typical estimate of the reduction in office workers which will occur as a result of the new technology is between 25 and 30 per cent (Huws, 1982: 25).

However, Crompton and Jones (1982: 140) have suggested that women's employment opportunities are likely to improve in the future. They suggest that the increasing tendency of women to gain qualifications and to interrupt their paid working careers by domestic work to a lesser extent will lead to more women succeeding in clerical work. However, Crompton and Jones have addressed themselves here more to the issue of the level which women reach in paid work than their numbers.

The post-war period saw a reduction in the unemployment and underemployment of women in the regions of Britain where these had previously been most marked. The period as a whole showed an average increase in women's paid employment which, to a considerable extent, was a result of this process of levelling up the rate of women's (especially married women's) employment between the regions. The regions with the highest women's employment rate at the end of the war experienced little increase in this over the next three or four decades.

The new rounds of industrial development fixed new, distinctive patterns of gender relations as a result of the interaction of capitalist and patriarchal structures in new circumstances. Wartime innovations of employing married women part-time were continued into peace-time under pressure from the shortage of labour. While the employment of married women met with some opposition and was thought to be liable to engender major social problems, such as juvenile delinquency, the resistance to their employment was less trenchant and less effective than in similar circumstances in the nineteenth century. The patriarchal aspect of union strategy was now not to demand the total exclusion of women from paid work, but instead merely to ensure that men continued to retain the higher-graded positions, or rather that men's work should continue to be graded higher than women's. In these circumstances–the dominance of this newer patriarchal strategy in the trade unions together with increasing demand for labour–the employment of women proceeded apace.

Employers seeking increasing numbers of clerical workers provided a major source of paid employment for women, as did employers in the newer branches of engineering. Disproportionate contractions in the number of women workers in the older branches of engineering and in cotton textiles were not sufficient to affect the overall picture of increase in women's paid employment.

8 Conclusion

Gender inequality cannot be understood without the concept of patriarchy. Criticisms of the concept for its inability to grasp historical variation are misplaced; on the contrary, the notion of changing forms of patriarchy is indispensible to the understanding of historically varying forms of gender inequality.

Patriarchy does not exist in isolation; its intersection with capitalist and racist institutions significantly affects the nature of the consequent gender relations. The complex tensions between these systems of social relations cannot be understood outside of an analysis which recognizes their analytic independence, as well as their historical and empirical interlinkages.

Chapters 5–7 of this book have shown the importance for explaining the contemporary pattern of gender relations in employment, of examining variations in the nature of patriarchal relations in the workplace and of considering the specific ways that they interact with capitalist relations. Patterns produced at one historical moment build on previous patterns and the sexual division of labour at any one time is the result of the accumulation of these rounds of restructuring gender relations.

Particularly important patriarchal institutions which affect gender relations in the paid workplace include trade unions as well as employers and the state. Indeed the importance of a cross-class alliance of these entities must not be underestimated. However, there is a paradox in that the intensity of patriarchal intervention in the organization of paid work has diminished somewhat since the end of the nineteenth century, while the power of one of these, the trade unions, has increased substantially over the period (even if it has suffered a recent decline). For patriarchal relations in employment to decline while one of the main agencies responsible for them increases in influence might at first sight appear to be contradictory. However, this paradox is resolved when the significance of the differences in patriarchal strategies pursued over time is realized.

There are two main strategies: firstly, that of excluding women from paid employment; and secondly, that of confining women to jobs which are graded lower than those of men. From the last quarter of the nineteenth century an increasing proportion of trade unions used grading and segregation as their response to women's employment, rather than the exclusionary strategy. This shift has taken place both within unions and in connection with the growth of newer unions which have only ever adopted the second strategy. The Amalgamated Society of Engineers changed its exclusionary strategy to one of grading and segregation in 1943 (when it had become the Amalgamated Engineering Union), while the National Union of Clerks had followed a grading strategy from its inception at the end of the nineteenth century. Both of these were typical of unions in their sector of employment. It is almost never the case that a union which included men did not follow one of these two patriarchal strategies. The nearest to an exception that can be found is that of the weavers who supported a system in which men and women worked side by side for the same piece work rate. However, this is not a pure exception because promotion to overlooker (supervisor) was confined by the overlookers' union to men, and the men on average obtained higher wages because they were more likely to work on the fancy weaves and to have more looms. Nevertheless, the three areas of employment examined in this part of the book do effectively demonstrate the importance of the different patriarchal strategies.

The decision of which strategy to follow was determined by a variety of factors, most importantly by the extent of continuity of the labour process and worker organization with the related pre-factory forms of labour. Thus the gradual movement of engineering from small-scale craft production to the factory assisted the maintenance of strong craft-based organizations of the workers, who adopted a policy of exclusion in order to retain the scarcity of their labour, and thus the price at which it could be sold. This general exclusionary strategy facilitated the adoption of a patriarchal strategy based upon exclusion, rather than the one based on grading. In the case of clerical work the absence of strong organization among the male clerks precluded an effective exclusionary strategy against women when clerical work began to expand rapidly at the end of the nineteenth century. Although there are indications that this was tried, these attempts rapidly gave way to the strategy of confining women to work which was graded lower than that of men.

While exclusion and grading with segregation were two strategies used generally by unions to raise the price of their members' labour power, and while there is some convergence between the use of these strategies in general and their specific use in relation to women, this was by no means total. The discrepancy between the use of the grading strategy in, for instance, the organization and grading of semi-skilled and unskilled men, while simultaneously attempting to exclude women completely, demonstrates the independence of patriarchal relations from those between capital and labour. Many unions at the end of the nineteenth century excluded women from membership and tried to exclude them from areas of paid work even though they recruited semi- and unskilled men.

While trade unions were one of the most important agencies involved in patriarchal strategies in the workplace, they were not the only source of patriarchal intervention. The state has also played an important role in supporting such practices, especially before 1919. During the nineteenth century a series of legislation attempted to restrict women's access to paid work. This legislation was fought for by an alliance of patriarchal interests including male workers and bourgeois philanthropists, against the opposition of many, though not all, manufacturers. This political struggle by those patriarchal forces was not entirely successful since women's employment in the cotton textile mills, which was their primary focus, did not diminish in that century. Nevertheless, this struggle should be seen as one in which the state acted in the maintenance of patriarchal interests. Further instances of such action include the moves of the state in restoring patriarchal employment practices which were suspended for the duration of the wars. The state should not, however, be seen as the direct instrument of the patriarchal workplace organizations. Rather these actions were the outcome of struggles on the political level which have a degree of autonomy from economic interests. Patriarchal actions by the state on issues of women's unemployment and employment are less intense today than they were previously. The legislation which currently exists supports women's access to paid employment, although this is not vigorously implemented. The political struggles of women were important in changing this policy of the state, and these improvements should not be seen as the result of some inevitable drift of progress.

These varying sets of patriarchal relations interacted with capitalist relations to produce the various gender patterns of employment.

There was not a once and for all fixing of these relations, but rather at each new phase of capitalist development new struggles with patriarchal relations produced a set of gender relations in the new industry. These patterns in industries remained relatively fixed within specific industries until these industries were subjected to further change because of technological innovation or other causes of expansion or contraction such as war or depression. Each new fixing of the sex-typing of employment was built on the foundations of previous rounds of restructuring, and was significantly affected by it.

These patterns of inclusion and exclusion have given rise to the contemporary situation where women are more often to be found in industries which are contracting their labour requirement less than those industries in which men are primarily located. This is the essential background to explaining the paradox that women, despite being more likely to lose their jobs in any particular situation of job loss than men are, nevertheless, not substantially more liable to unemployment than men.

This paradox is reflected in the study of 30 employment establishments described in chapter 7. This showed that many, although not all, methods of job loss led to a higher proportion of women than men losing employment opportunities, yet that women were concentrated in the least depressed industries. The greater loss of women's jobs in any given establishment was largely a consequence of the interaction of women's generally disadvantaged position in the labour market with particular job loss strategies, which in themselves did not directly discriminate against women. This included cases where women earned a level of wages so low as to preclude the option of travelling to employment with the same firm in a different town because of the expense involved, and cases where slightly more women than men left under the 'last-in, first out' redundancy selection criterion because of a slightly higher rate of turnover in the lower-grade jobs in which women are more often to be found than men. The study showed that those workers with a relatively depressed position in employment, who were more often women than men, were more likely to lose their jobs in a situation of diminishing employment opportunities in any particular establishment.

This analysis of gender and employment has shown the strength of the model of patriarchy developed in chapter 3. The various sets of patriarchal relations, especially those of patriarchal workplace organizations and the state, have all contributed significantly to the determination of gender patterns of employment while not being reducible to one base. Patriarchy, then, is composed not only of a patriarchal mode of production, but also of sets of patriarchal relations in the workplace, the state, sexuality and other practices in civil society.

The independence of patriarchal relations from capitalist ones has also been demonstrated, as, indeed, has the conflict and tension between patriarchal and capitalist interests. There is no harmonious fit between the two sets of interests, but rather considerable antagonism and rivalry over the exploitation of women's labour. At certain times the struggle is particularly overt as was the case during the struggle in the nineteenth century over factory legislation, or over the restoration of patriarchal practices in employment which had been partially suspended for the duration of war (especially after the First World War), or over access to employment in the depths of the inter-war depression. At some other times there appears to be quiescence in this struggle as a result of compromises hammered out. The relative lack of political agitation in the second half of the nineteenth century may be partially attributed to a compromise between these rival interests over women's labour. Part-time work for married women since the Second World War is similarly a result of a compromise between patriarchal and capitalist demands for women's labour, arrived at during the war. Nevertheless, the tension between patriarchy and capital remains. Other analyses which attempt to reduce gender inequality to the workings of capitalism–or those which assert that patriarchy simply reinforces capitalist social relations–cannot account for such conflicts.

This book has put forward a model of patriarchy composed of interdependent yet relatively autonomous sets of patriarchal relations by analysing the conflict and tension between patriarchy and capital. The conflict is not only between patriarchy and capital, but between particular groups of men and women as well. Some groups of men struggled to prevent women from entering their areas of work. Neither did women docilely withdraw from paid work when men wanted them to, on marriage, or at the end of wars, or during depressions. They were pushed vigorously, and vigorously resisted. Many social historians, sociologists and economists write as if such patriarchal practices as the marriage bar never existed. Yet, almost universally in the better jobs, before the Second World War women had no option; on marriage they were sacked. The dropping of the marriage bar during the war was the single most important effect of the war on gender relations.

It is with such evidence in mind that I dispute the theories of those who argue that it is women's position in the family which leads them to choose a lesser form of engagement in paid work than men. Rather the issue is, why do women suffer such appalling conditions of work in the family as many do? Why do women marry on such terms? The answer is that the options for most women in paid work are not much better, because men have usually been successful in excluding women from the better forms of work. Hence housework is as good as anything else a woman is likely to get.

Men's attempts either to exclude women from paid work or to confine them to separate areas which are graded lower leave a divided workforce which can be taken advantage of by employers seeking cheaper labour. However, there have been significant changes in the orientation of the British labour and trade union movement towards gender relations: first there was a movement away from the exclusionary to the segregating form of patriarchal strategy, and, more recently, in a limited number of instances, under pressure from women, unions have sought greater equality between male and female workers.

Appendices

Appendix I Women's Membership of the Principle Trade Unions, 1870–1918

Name of union	Established	Women first admitted	Women on Executive committee	Women organizers	Main occupation of female members	Normal trade union restrictions on women's labour
Engineers Unions						
Amalgamated Society of Engineers	1851	1943				
Miners Unions						
Lanarkshire Miners' Union	1897	1897	0	0	pithead labourers, coal pickers, drawers-off, saw-millers	campaign to abolish female labour about collieries
Metal Unions						
Iron and Steel Trades Confederation	1886	1906	0	0 (ten women branch secretaries)	tin-place workers, cold rollers, etc.	prohibited in smelting processes
Textile Unions – Cotton						
Northern Counties Amalgamated Association of Cotton Weavers	1884 (Earliest 1850)	1884	0 (women on local committees)	0	weavers, warpers, winders	none
Amalgamated Association of Beamers, Twisters, Drawers-in	1890 (Earliest 1860)	1890	0 (women on district committees)	1	twisters and drawers-in	prohibited as twisters and drawers-in in certain districts
Amalgamated Association of Card and Blowing Room Operatives	1886	1886	0 (women on local committees)	0	card and blowing room operators, ring-spinners	definite demarcation between men's and women's work
Amalgamated Cotton Spinners Association	1837 (Bolton Association)	1837	0	0	Piecers	prohibited as spinners, or as piecers some districts

Appendix I (continued)

Name of union	Established	Women first admitted	Women on Executive committee	Women organizers	Main occupation of female members	Normal trade union restrictions on women's labour
Textile Unions – Wool and Worsted Goods						
General Union of Textile Workers	1881	1881	3	2	weavers, warpers, winders, condenser-minders, menders, knitters, burlers	men and women employed in different departments, except weavers
National Society of Wool-combers and Kindred Trades	1890	1900	0	0	machine minders and feeders	prohibited on men's machines and night work
Textile Unions – Textile Dyeing, Bleaching, Finishing, and Warehousing						
Amalgamated Society of Dyers, Bleachers, Finishers and Kindred Trades	1878	1912	0 (women on district committees)	0	light processes in warehouse, dyeing processes in Scotland	prohibited on wet and on men's dry processes
National Society of Dyers and Finishers	1851	1900	0 (women on district committees)	0	light processes in warehouse, 'knotters' and 'burlers' in Huddersfield	prohibited on wet processes and on men's dry processes
Bolton Amalgamated Society of Bleachers, Dyers and Finishers	1866	1900	0	0	light processes in warehouse men's dry processes	prohibited on wet processes and on

Appendix I (continued)

Name of union	Established	Women first admitted	Women on Executive committee	Women organizers	Main occupation of female members	Normal trade union restrictions on women's labour
Female Workers in the Shipping Industry	1908	1908	all, except President and Secretary	0	stitchers, cutters, markers-off, parcellers etc., hookers and stampers	prohibited on men's processes
Textile Unions – Hosiery						
Leicester Amalgamated Hosiery Union	1885	1885	1	0	knitters, menders, etc.	prohibited on Cotton's patent frames
Textile Unions – Flax and Jute						
Dundee and District Jute and Flax Workers	1906	1906	10	0	spinners and preparers, weavers, warpers, winders and reelers	prohibited as tenters and mechanics
Dundee and District Mill Factory Operatives	1885	1885	12 out of 20	woman secretary	spinners and preparers, weavers, warpers, winders and reelers	none
Textile Operatives of Ireland	1893	1893	all	all women officials	spinners, weavers, makers-up and warehouse women	none (prohibited in 'roughing' by men's society)
Other Textile Unions						
Kidderminster Power Loom Carpet Weavers	1866	1917	4	4 women assistant secretaries	weavers and other textile workers	prohibited on 'Jacquard' looms

Name of union	Established	Women first admitted	Women on Executive committee	Women organizers	Main occupation of female members	Normal trade union restrictions on women's labour
Newmilns and District Textile Workers' Union	1890	1890	0; women's auxilliary committees	women branch secretaries	lace and madras workers	men and women employed on different machines
Amalgamated Society of Textile Workers and Kindred Trades (Leek)	1919	1919	3	1	silk sorters, spinners weavers, winders, finishers, makers-up etc. Various other textile workers	Prohibited in some districts as weavers and twisters
Clothing Unions						
United Garment Workers' Trade Union	1915	1915	1 (majority of women on local committees)	16 (mostly local)	tailoresses, factory operatives, dress-makers, milliners, corset makers	none, provided that women receive men's wages
Amalgamated Society of Tailors and Tailoresses	1866	1900	0 (women on local committees)	1	tailoresses, factory operatives, dress-makers, milliners, corset makers	prohibited on best cutting and pressing
National Union of Boot and Shoe Operatives	1874	1885	1	0	closing and stock-room operatives	prohibited in clicking, press, lasting and finishing departments
Amalgamated Felt Hat Trimmers and Wool Formers	1886	1886	11 plus 4 men (branch officials)	0 (man secretary)	hat trimmers and wool formers	prohibited by allied men's union in felt processing

Appendix I (continued)

Name of union	Established	Women first admitted	Women on Executive committee	Women organizers	Main occupation of female members	Normal trade union restrictions on women's labour
Transport Unions						
National Union of Railwaymen	1913	1915	0	0	porters, cleaners, ticket-collectors etc.	prohibited on railways except as cleaners or charwomen
London and Provincial Licensed Vehicle Workers	1894	1916	0	0	conductresses (7 or 8) women drivers	prohibited on public conveyances and as van drivers
Amalgamated Tramway and Vehicle Workers	1889	1915	0	0	Conductresses (some women drivers)	prohibited on public conveyances and as van drivers
Printing Unions						
National Union of Printing and Paper Workers	1840	1904	3 (two places reserved to London Women's Branch)	5 (also financial secretary)	folders, sewers, stitchers, pagers, layers-on, assistant warehouse women, paper makers, paper bag and box makers	discouraged on cutting machines; prohibited by Typographical Association as compositors or machine operatives
National Union of Bookbinders and Machine Rulers	1836	1917	4 (places reserved to women in proportion to membership)	0 (women local officials)	folders, sewers stitchers, pagers	prohibited in skilled branches of book-binding

Appendix I (continued)

Name of union	Established	Women first admitted	Women on Executive committee	Women organizers	Main occupation of female members	Normal trade union restrictions on women's labour
Woodworking Unions						
National Amalgamated Furnishing Trades Association	1902	1911	0	0	French polishers, upholsterers, aircraft and other munition workers during war	prohibited on edge tools and wood-cutting machines
Chemical and Pottery Unions						
Amalgamated Society of Male and Female Pottery Workers	1906	1906	0 (4 women on district committees)	1	transferers, decorators, potters' attendants, flat-makers, warehouse women	prohibited as dippers, placers, and on making or casting large pieces
Food and Tobacco Unions						
Amalgamated Union of Operative Bakers	1861	1915	0	1	confectioners, bakeresses (tea-cakes, etc.)	prohibited on bread making
National Union of Cigar Makers	1835	1895	3	1 (Nottingham)	cigar-makers	none, provided women receive men's wages
Distributive Unions						
National Amalgamated Union of Shop Assistants, Warehousemen and Clerks	1891	1891	1	4 full-time women district secretaries	shop assistants	none
Amalgamated Union of Co-operative Employers and Commercial Workers	1891	1891	0	1 (3 in 1919)	shop assistants, factory workers	none

Appendix I (continued)

Name of union	Established	Women first admitted	Women on Executive committee	Women organizers	Main occupation of female members	Normal trade union restrictions on women's labour
Clerks						
National Union of Clerks	1890	1890	1	0	general clerks, typists, shorthand typists, bookkeepers, secretaries	none
Railway Clerks' Association	1897	1897	0	0	Booking-clerks; accounting, invoicing and general clerks	none
Union of Post Office Clerks	1920	1920	5	1	telegraphists, telephonists, sorting clerks	none
small societies affil. to Civil Service Federation and Civil Service Alliance	–	–	women on executive committees of Civil Service Federation and Civil Service Alliance	–	–	–
General Labour Unions						
National Federation of Women Workers	1906	1906	all	50	metal workers, engineering (mainly sub. women), asbestos workers, brass foundry workers, electric lamp,	prohibited by men's engineering unions in skilled processes

Appendix 1 (continued)

Name of union	Established	Women first admitted	Women on Executive committee	Women organizers	Main occupation of female members	Normal trade union restrictions on women's labour
					cable, needle, nail, nut and bolt, optical instrument, small tool and chain makers	
National Union of General Workers	1889	1889	0	1 (women temporary staff in addition)	hollow ware workers	–
Workers' Union	1898	1898	0	16	rope and net workers	–

Sources: Drake (1984) table II; Jefferys (1946), pp. 29, 260.

Appendix II

Industrial and Employment Appeals Tribunals Affecting Women

Industrial Tribunal (1977), Noble, Wood and Jacovow, David Gold and Son (Holdings) Ltd, nos. 38926/76/D, 38927/76/D, 39133/76/D. Decision: 6 May 1977.

Industrial Tribunal (1981), Clarke and Powell v. Eley (IMI Kynoch) Ltd, no. 16146/81, 21019/81. Decision: 15 December 1981.

Industrial Tribunal (1982), Grace, Pray, Webb, Barker, Hampson, Cox, Halfpenny and Williams v. Kraft Foods Ltd, nos. SX14553/81, SX14554/81, SX17462/81, SX17463/81, SX17465/81, SX17466/81, SX17467/81, SX17468/81. Decision: 15 February 1982.

Employment Appeals Tribunal (1978), Noble and Others v. David Gold and Son (Holdings) Ltd, no. EAT/411/77. Judgment: 16 January 1978.

Employment Appeals Tribunal (1982), Clarke and Powell v. Eley (IMI Kynoch) Ltd, nos. EAT 50/82, EAT 71/82. Judgment: 22September 1982.

Appendix II

Main Statistical Sources

Census of England and Wales, 1921, (1924), Occupation Tables.
Census of England and Wales, 1931, (1934), Occupation Tables.
Census of England and Wales, 1981, (1984), Occupation Tables.
Department of Employment Gazette, (1969–79).
Employment Gazette (1980–3).
Eurostat (1977), *Labour Force Sample Survey: Methods and Definitions*, Luxembourg, Statistical Office of the European Communities.
Eurostat (1980), *Labour Force Sample Survey 1973, 1975, 1977*, Luxembourg, Office for Offical Publications of the European Communities.
Eurostat (1981), *Labour Force Sample Survey 1979*, Luxembourg, Office for Official Publications of the European Community
International Labour Office (1977), *Yearbook of Statistics*, Geneva.
Lee, C. H. (1979), *British Regional Employment Statistics, 1841–1971*, Cambridge, Cambridge University Press.
Office of Population Censuses and Surveys, *General Household Survey*, London, HMSO.
Office of Population Censuses and Surveys (1982), *Labour Force Survey 1981*, London, HMSO.
Routh, Guy (1980), *Occupation and Pay in Great Britain 1906–1979*, London, Methuen.

References

Abercrombie, Nicholas and Urry, John (1983), *Capital Labour and the New Middle Classes*, London, Allen and Unwin.

Acker, Joan (1973), 'Women and Social Stratification: A Case of Intellectual Sexism' in Joan Huber (ed.) *Changing Women in a Changing Society*, Chicago, University of Chicago Press.

Alford, B. W. E. (1972), *Depression and Recovery? British Economic Growth 1918–1939*, London, MacMillan.

Allen, Sheila (1982), 'Gender, inequality and class formation' in Anthony Giddens and Gavin Mackenzie (eds) *Social Class and the Division of Labour: Essays in Honour of Ilya Neustadt*, Cambridge, Cambridge University Press.

Allen, V. L. (1957), *Trade Union Leadership: Based on a Study of Arthur Deakin*, London, Longmans.

Allin, Paul (1982), 'Women's activity rates and regional employment markets', British Society for Population Studies Conference: Population and regional labour markets, OPCS Occasional Paper no. 28.

Althusser, Louis (1971), *Lenin and Philosophy and Other Essays*, London, New Left Books.

Althusser, Louis and Balibar, Étienne (1977), *Reading 'Capital'*, London, New Left Books.

Amir, Menachem (1971), *Patterns in Forcible Rape*, Chicago, Chicago University Press.

Amos, Valerie and Parmar, Pratibha (1984), 'Challenging Imperial Feminism', *Feminist Review*, no. 17, 3–20.

Amsden, Alice H. (ed.) (1980), *The Economics of Women and Work*, Harmondsworth, Penguin.

Anderson, Gregory L. (1976), *Victorian Clerks*, Manchester, Manchester University Press.

Anderson, Gregory L. (1977), 'The Social Economy of Late-Victorian Clerks' in Geoffrey Crossick (ed.) *The Lower Middle Class in Britain 1870–1914*, London, Croom Helm.

Anderson, Michael (1971), *Family Structure in Nineteenth-Century Lancashire*, Cambridge, Cambridge University Press.

Anderson, Michael (1976), 'Sociological History and the Working-class Family: Smelser Revisited', *Social History*, vol. 1, no. 3, 317–34.

Andrews, Irene O. (1918), *Economic Effects of the War upon Women and Children in Great Britain*, Assisted by Margaret A. Hobbs, Carnegie Economic Studies of the War, New York, Oxford University Press.

Anthony, Sylvia (1932), *Women's Place in Industry and Home*, London, G. Routledge & Son.

ASE (1886–98), 'Engineering Trade Lock-Out' in *Amalgamated Society of Engineers, Miscellaneous Documents 1886–1898*, Amalgamated Society of Engineers.

Aspin, C. (1964), *James Hargreaves and the Spinning Jenny*, Helmsmore, Helmsmore Local History Society.

Atkinson, Ti-Grace (1974), *Amazon Odyssey*, New York, Links Books.

ATWU (1983), *Ninth Annual Report*, Rochdale, Amalgamated Textile Workers' Union.

Aydelotte, William O. (1973), 'Parties and Issues in Early Victorian England' in Peter Stansky, (ed.) *The Victorian Revolution: Government and Society in Victoria's Britain*, New York, New Viewpoints, Franklin Watts.

Banks, Olive (1981), *Faces of Feminism: A Study of Feminism as a Social Movement*, Oxford, Martin Robertson.

Barker, Diana Leonard (1978), 'The Regulation of Marriage: Repressive Benevolence' in Gary Littlejohn, Barry Smart, John Wakeford and Nira Yuval-Davis (eds) *Power and the State*, London, Croom Helm.

Barrett, Michèle (1980), *Women's Oppression Today: Problems in Marxist Feminist Analysis*, London, Verso.

Barrett, Michèle and McIntosh, Mary (1979), 'Towards a Materialist Feminism?', *Feminist Review*, no. 1.

Barrett, Michèle and McIntosh, Mary (1980), 'The "Family Wage": Some Problems for Socialists and Feminists', *Capital and Class*, no. 11, Summer, 51–72.

Barron, R. D. and Norris, G. M. (1976), 'Sexual divisions and the dual labour market' in Sheila Allen and Diana Leonard Barker (eds), *Dependence and Exploitation in Work and Marriage*, London, Longmans.

Beauchamp, Joan (1937), *Women Who Work*, London, Lawrence and Wishart.

Beechey, Veronica (1977), 'Some notes on female wage labour in capitalist production', *Capital and Class*, no. 3, Autumn, 45–66.

Beechey, Veronica (1978), 'Women and production: a critical analysis of some sociological theories of women's work', in Annette Kuhn and Ann Marie Wolpe (eds) *Feminism and Materialism: Women and Modes of Production*, London, Routledge and Kegan Paul.

Beechey, Veronica (1979), 'On Patriarchy', *Feminist Review*, no. 3, 66–82.

Beechey, Veronica and Perkins, Tessa (1986), *A Matter of Hours: An Investigation of Women's Part-Time Employment*, Cambridge, Polity.

Beneria, Lourdes (1979), 'Reproduction, production and the sexual division of labour', *Cambridge Journal of Economics*, vol. 3, 203–25.

Benston, Margaret (1970), 'The Political Economy of Housework', in Leslie B. Tanner (ed.) *Voices from Women's Liberation*, New York, Signet.

Bergmann, Barbara R. (1980a), 'Occupational Segregation, Wages and Profits when Employers Discriminate by Race or Sex' in Amsden (1980).

Bergmann, Barbara R. (1980b), 'Curing High Unemployment Rates Among Blacks and Women' in Amsden (1980).

Beteille, André (1977), *Inequality among Men*, Oxford, Basil Blackwell.

Binney, Val, Harkell, Gina and Nixon, Judy (1981), *Leaving Violent Men: A Study of Refuges and Housing for Battered Women*, Leeds, Women's Aid Federation, England.

Blackburn, R. M. and Mann, Michael (1979), *The Working Class in the Labour Market*, London, MacMillan.

Bowers, John (1970), *The Anatomy of Regional Activity Rates*, National Institute of Economic and Social Research Regional Papers 1, Cambridge, Cambridge University Press.

Bradby, Barbara (1975), 'The destruction of natural economy', *Economy and Society*, vol. 4, no. 2, 127–66.

Branson, Noreen and Heinemann, Margot (1971), *Britain in the Nineteen Thirties*, London, Weidenfeld and Nicolson.

Braverman, Harry (1974), *Labor and Monopoly Capital: The Degradation of Work in the Twentieth Century*, New York, Monthly Review Press.

Braybon, Gail (1981), *Women Workers in the First World War: The British Experience*, London, Croom Helm.

Britten, Nicky and Heath, Anthony (1983), 'Women, Men and Social Class' in Eva Gamarnikow, David Morgan, June Purvis and Daphne Taylorson (eds) *Gender, Class and Work*, London, Heinemann.

Brown, Colin (1984), *Black and White Britain: The Third PSI Survey*, London, Heinemann.

Brownmiller, Susan (1976), *Against Our Will: Men, Women and Rape*, Harmondsworth, Penguin.

Bruegel, Irene (1979), 'Women as a reserve army of labour: a note on recent British experience', *Feminist Review*, no. 3, 12–23.

Bullock, Paul (1973), 'Categories of Labour Power for Capital', *Bulletin of the Conference of Socialist Economists*, Autumn, 82–99.

Bullock, Paul (1974), 'Defining Productive Labour for Capital', *Bulletin of the Conference of Socialist Economists*, Autumn, 1–15.

Burniston, Steve, Mort, Frank and Weedon, Christine (1978), 'Psycho-analysis and the cultural acquisition of sexuality and subjectivity' in Women's Studies Group, Centre for Contemporary Cultural Studies, University of Birmingham, *Women Take Issue: Aspects of Women's Subordination*, London, Hutchinson.

Burstyn, V. (1983), 'Masculine dominance and the state' *Socialist Register*.

Byrne, Eileen, M. (1978), *Women and Education*, London, Tavistock.

Carby, Hazel (1982), 'White woman listen! Black feminism and the boundaries of sisterhood' in Centre for Contemporary Cultural Studies, University of Birmingham, *The Empire Strikes Back: Race and Racism in '70s Britain*, London, Hutchinson.

Catlin, Harold (1970), *The Spinning Mule*, Newton Abbot, David and Charles.

CBI (1976), *Employing Women: The Employer's View*, London, Confederation of British Industry.

CBI (1979), *CBI Members' Bulletin*, Industrial Relations section, 13 July.

Chapman, S. D. (1972), *The Cotton Industry in the Industrial Revolution*, London, Macmillan.

Clark, Alice (1982), *Working Life of Women in the Seventeenth Century*, London, Routledge and Kegan Paul (first published 1919).

Cockburn, Cynthia (1981), 'The Material of Male Power', *Feminist Review*, no. 9, Autumn, 41–58.

Cockburn, Cynthia (1983), *Brothers: Male Dominance and Technological Change*, London, Pluto Press.

Cohen, Stanley (1973), *Folk Devils and Moral Panics: The Creation of the Mods and Rockers*, St. Albans, Paladin.

Cole, G. D. H. (1955), *An Introduction to Trade Unionism*, London, Allen and Unwin.

Comer, Lee (1978), 'The Question of Women and Class', *Women's Studies International Quarterly*, vol. 1, no. 1, 165–73.

Connelly Patricia (1978), *Last Hired, First Fired, Women and the Canadian Work Force*, Toronto, The Women's Press.

Constantine, Stephen (1980), *Unemployment in Britain between the Wars*, London, Longman.

Cooke, Philip, Morgan, Kevin and Jackson, David (1983), 'New Technology and Regional Development in Austerity in Britain: The Case of the Semiconductor Industry', Paper presented at 4th Urban Change and Conflict Conference, University of Essex, Clacton.

Coote, Anna (1979), *Equal at Work? Women in Men's Jobs*, London, Collins.

Coote, Anna and Campbell, Beatrice (1982), *Sweet Freedom: The Struggle for Women's Liberation*, London, Picador.

Coveney, Lal, Jackson, Margaret, Jeffreys, Sheila, Kay, Leslie and Mahoney, Pat (1984) *The Sexuality Papers: Male sexuality and the social control of women*, London, Hutchinson.

Craig, Christine, Garnsey, Elizabeth and Rubery, Jill (1985), *Payment structures in smaller firms: women's employment in segmented labour markets*, Department of Employment Research Paper no. 48, London, Dept. of Employment.

Craig, Christine, Rubery, Jill, Tarling, Roger and Wilkinson, Frank (1982), *Labour Market Structure, Industrial Organisation and Low Pay*,

University of Cambridge, Dept. of Applied Economics, Occasional Paper no. 54, Cambridge, Cambridge University Press.

Crompton, Rosemary and Jones, Gareth (1982), 'Clerical "Proletarianisation": Myth or Reality', in Graham Day, Lesley Caldwell, Karen Jones, David Robbins and Hilary Rose (eds) *Diversity and Decomposition in Labour Markets*, Aldershot, Gower.

Crossick, Geoffrey (1977), 'The Emergence of the Lower Middle Class in Britain: A Discussion', in Geoffrey Crossick (ed.) *The Lower Middle Class in Britain 1870–1914*, London, Croom Helm.

Croucher, Richard (1977), *Communist Politics and Shop Stewards in Engineering 1935–46*, Ph.D. dissertation, University of Warwick.

CSCA (1952), *The Civil Service Clerical Association Compendium: 1952*, London, Civil Service Clerical Association.

Curtis, Lyn A. (1976), 'Present and Future Measures of Victimization in Forcible Rape' in Marcia J. Walker and Stanley L. Brodsky (eds) *Sexual Assault: The Victim and the Rapist*, Lexington, Lexington Books.

Davies, Margery (1979), 'Women's Place is at the Typewriter: The Feminization of the Clerical Labour Force' in Zillah R. Eisenstein (ed.) *Capitalist Patriarchy and the Case for Socialist Feminism*, New York, Monthly Review Press.

David, Miriam (1980), *The State, the Family and Education*, London, Routledge and Kegan Paul.

Davis, Angela (1981), *Women, Race and Class*, London, The Women's Press.

Deacon, Alan John (1979), *Genuinely Seeking Work: A Study of Unemployment Insurance in Britain 1920–1931*, Ph.D. thesis, University of London.

Deacon, Alan John (1981), 'Unemployment and Politics in Britain since 1945' in Brian Showler and Adrian Sinfield (eds), *The Workless State: Studies in Unemployment*, Oxford, Martin Robertson.

Deem, Rosemary (1978), *Women and Schooling*, London, Routledge and Kegan Paul.

Deem, Rosemary (ed.) (1980), *Schooling for Women's Work*, London, Routledge and Kegan Paul.

Delphy, Christine (1977), *The Main Enemy*, London, Women's Research and Resources Centre.

Delphy, Christine (1981), 'Women in stratification studies' in Helen Roberts (ed.) *Doing Feminist Research* London, Routledge and Kegan Paul.

Delphy, Christine (1984), *Close to Home: A materialist analysis of women's oppression*, London, Hutchinson.

Dey, Ian (1979), *A study of the formulation and implementation of policies relating to redundancy and unemployment by the AUEW district committee, Bristol, 1970–72*, Ph.D. thesis, University of Bristol.

Dobash, Rebecca Emerson and Dobash, Russell (1980), *Violence Against Wives: The Case Against the Patriarchy*, Shepton Mallet, Open Books.

Doeringer, Peter B. and Piore, Michael J. (1971), *Internal Labour Markets and Manpower Analysis*, Lexington, Mass., Lexington Books.

Donnison, David with Soto, Paul (1980), *The Good City: A Study of Urban Development and Policy in Britain*, London, Heinemann.

Downing, Hazel (1980), 'Word Processors and the Oppression of Women' in Tom Forester (ed.) *The microelectronics revolution: the complete guide to the new technology and its impact on society*, Oxford, Basil Blackwell.

Drake, Barbara (1984), *Women in Trade Unions*, London, Virago (originally published by Labour Research Department and Allen and Unwin, 1920).

Dworkin, Andrea (1981), *Pornography: Men Possessing Women*, London, The Women's Press.

Edholm, Felicity, Harris, Olivia and Young, Kate (1977), 'Conceptualising Women' in *Critique of Anthropology*, vol. 3, 101–30.

Edwards, M. M. and Lloyd-Jones, R. (1973), 'N. J. Smelser and the Cotton Factory Family: A Reassessment', in N. B. Harte and K. G. Ponting (eds) *Textile History and Economic History*, Manchester, Manchester University Press.

Edwards, Richard (1979), *Contested Terrain: The Transformation of the Workplace in the Twentieth Century*, London, Heinemann.

Edwards, Richard C., Gordon, David M. and Reich, Michael (1975), *Labour Market Segmentation*, Lexington, Mass., Lexington Books.

EFEA (Employers' Federation of Engineering Associations) (1897), *The 'Machine' Question: Correspondence and Report of Proceedings at Conference*, Employers' Federation of Engineering Associations.

Ehrenreich, Barbara and English, Deirdre (1979), *For Her Own Good: 150 Years of the Experts Advice to Women*, London, Pluto Press.

Eichler, Margrit (1980), *The Double Standard: A Feminist Critique of Feminist Social Science*, London, Croom Helm.

Eisenstein, Zillah R. (1979), 'Developing a Theory of Capitalist Patriarchy and Socialist Feminism' in Zillah R. Eisenstein (ed.) *Capitalist Patriarchy*, New York, Monthly Review Press.

Eisenstein, Zillah R. (1981), *The Radical Future of Liberal Feminism*, New York, Longman.

Eisenstein, Zillah R. (1984), *Feminism and Sexual Equality: Crisis in Liberal America*, New York, Monthly Review Press.

Elger, Antony (1979), 'Valorisation and deskilling–a critique of Braverman', *Capital and Class*, no. 7, Spring, 58–99.

Ellis, Valerie (1981), *The role of trade unions in the promotion of equal opportunities*, Manchester, Equal Opportunities Commission.

Ellis, Valerie (1985), 'Current trade union attempts to remove occupational segregation in the employment of women', paper presented to Segregation in Employment Symposium, University of Lancaster, July 1985.

Engels, Frederick (1940), *The Origin of the Family, Private Property and the State*, London, Lawrence and Wishart.

EOC (Equal Opportunities Commission) (1979), *Health and Safety Legislation: Should we distinguish between men and women?*, Report and Recommendations of the Equal Opportunities Commission, submitted to the Secretary of State for Employment in March 1979, Manchester, Equal Opportunities Commission.

EOC (Equal Opportunities Commission) (1982a), *Sixth Annual Report, 1981*, Manchester, Equal Opportunities Commission.

EOC (Equal Opportunities Commission) (1982b), One Day Conference on Positive Action 'The Key to the Future', Thursday, 11th February 1982, Manchester, Equal Opportunities Commission.

EOC (Equal Opportunities Commission) (1983a), *Seventh Annual Report, 1982*, Manchester, Equal Opportunities Commission.

EOC (Equal Opportunities Commission) (1983b), *Women and Sport*, Manchester, Equal Opportunities Commission.

EOC (Equal Opportunities Commission) (1983c), *Equal Opportunities in Craft, Design and Technology*, Manchester, Equal Opportunities Commission.

EOC (Equal Opportunities Commisssion) (1983d), *News Release*, 22 September.

EOC (Equal Opportunities Commission) (1983e) *Women and Trade Unions: A Survey*, Manchester, Equal Opportunities Commission.

Evershed Commission (1945), *Report of the Evershed Commission on Wages and Conditions of Employment in the Spinning Industry*, HMSO.

Faderman, Lilian (1981), *Surpassing the Love of Men: romantic friendship and love between women from the Renaissance to the present*, London, Junction Books.

Fairbairn, Zoe (1979), 'The Cohabitation Rule–Why It Makes Sense', *Women's Studies International Quarterly*, vol. 2, no. 3, 319–27.

Fasteau, Marc Feigen (1975), *The Male Machine*, New York, Delta.

Fee, Terry (1976), 'Domestic Labor: An Analysis of Housework and its Relation to the Production Process', *Review of Radical Political Economy*, vol. 8, no. 1, 1–8.

Fevre, Ralph (1984) *Cheap Labour and Racial Discrimination*, Aldershot, Gower.

Field, Frank (ed.) (1977), *The Conscript Army: A Study of Britain's Unemployed*, London, Routledge and Kegan Paul.

Fine, Ben and Harris, Laurence (1976), 'Controversial Issues in Marxist Economic Theory', *Socialist Register*, 141–78.

Firestone, Shulamith (1974), *The Dialectic of Sex: The Case for Feminist Revolution*, New York, Morrow.

Foster, John (1969), 'The Making of the First Six Factory Acts', *Society for the Study of Labour History Bulletin* V, no. 18, Spring.

Foster, John O. (1974), *Class Struggle and the Industrial Revolution*, London, Weidenfield.

Fothergill, Stephen and Gudgin, Graham (1982), *Unequal Growth: Urban and Regional Employment and Change in the UK*, London, Heinemann.

Fraser, Derek (1973), *The Evolution of the British Welfare State: a history of social policy since the Industrial Revolution*, London, MacMillan.

Freud, Sigmund (1977), *On Sexuality: Three Essays on the Theory of Sexuality and other Works*, Harmondsworth, Penguin.

Friedman, Andy (1977), 'Responsible Autonomy versus Direct Control over the Labour Process', *Capital and Class*, no. 1, 43–57.

Fröbel, Folker, Heinrichs, Jürgen and Kreye, Otto (1980), *The New International Division of Labour: Structural unemployment in industrialised countries and industrialisation in developing countries*, translated by Pete Burgess, Cambridge, Cambridge University Press.

Frow, Edmund and Frow, Ruth (1982), *Engineering Struggles: Episodes in the story of the shop stewards' movement*, Manchester, Working Class Movement Library.

Gagnon, John H. and Simon, William (1973), *Sexual Conduct: the social sources of human sexuality*, Chicago, Aldine.

Galenson, Marjorie (1973), *Women and Work: an international comparison*, New York, State School of Industrial and Labour Relations.

Gardiner, Jean (1975), 'Women's Domestic Labour', *New Left Review*, 89, 47–58.

Gardiner, Jean, Himmelweit, Susan and MacKintosh, Maureen (1975), 'Women's Domestic Labour', *Bulletin of the Conference of Socialist Economists*, vol. 4, 1–11.

Garnsey, Elizabeth (1978), 'Women's Work and Theories of Class Stratification', *Sociology*, vol. 17, 223–43.

Gelles, Richard J. (1972), *The Violent Home: a Study of Physical Aggression between Husbands and Wives*, Beverley Hills, Sage.

Gershuny, Jay I. (1983), *Social Innovation and the Division of Labour*, Oxford, Oxford University Press.

Giddens, Anthony (1979), *Central Problems in Social Theory, Action, Structure and Contradiction in Social Analysis*, London, MacMillan.

Gittins, Diana (1982), *Fair Sex: Family Size and Structure, 1900–1939*, London, Hutchinson.

Glass, D. V. and Hall J. R. (1954), 'A Description of a Sample Inquiry into Social Mobility in Great Britain' in D. V. Glass (ed.) *Social Mobility in Britain*, London, Routledge and Kegan Paul.

GMWU (1981), *Equality at Work: A GMWU Guide for Negotiations: The Way Forward*, Esher, Surrey, General and Municipal Workers Union.

Goldthorpe, John (1983), 'Women and class analysis: a defence of the conventional view', *Sociology*, 17, 465–88.

Goldthorpe, John H., Lockwood, David, Bechhofer, Frank and Platt, Jennifer (1969), *The Affluent Worker in the Class Structure*, Cambridge, Cambridge University Press.

Goldthorpe, John H. with Llewellyn, Catriona and Payne, Clive (1980), *Social Mobility and Class Structure in Modern Britain*, Oxford, Clarendon Press.

Goode, William J. (1971), 'Force and Violence in the Family', *Journal of Marriage and the Family*, vol. 33, pt. 4, 624–36.

Gordon, David M. (1972), *Theories of Poverty and Underemployment: Orthodox, Radical and Dual Labor Market Perspectives*, Lexington Mass., Lexington Books.

Gordon, Linda (1977), *Woman's Body, Woman's Right: A Social History of Birth Control in America*, New York, Penguin.

Gordon, Linda (1979), 'The Struggle for Reproductive Freedom' in Zillah R. Eisenstein (ed.) *Capitalist Patriarchy*, New York, Monthly Review Press.

Gough, Ian (1972), 'Marx's Theory of Productive and Unproductive Labour', *New Left Review*, December, 76, 47–72.

Gough, Ian (1973), 'On Productive and Unproductive Labour – A Reply', *Bulletin of the Conference of Socialist Economists*, Winter, 68–73.

Gough, Ian (1975), 'State Expenditure in Advanced Capitalism', *New Left Review*, no. 92, 53–92.

Gregory, Denis (1980), 'Low Pay and No Pay in Wales' in Gareth Rees and Teresa Rees (eds) *Poverty and Social Inequality in Wales*, London, Croom Helm.

Gregory, Jeanne (1982) 'Equal Pay and Sex Discrimination: why women are giving up the fight' *Feminist Review* no. 10, Spring.

Gregory, Jeanne (1985) 'Discrimination at Work: Equality through legislation' Paper presented to Segregation in Employment Symposium, Lancaster University, July 1985.

Gray, Robert (1981), *The Aristocracy of Labour in Nineteenth-century Britain, c. 1850–1914*, London, MacMillan.

Greenwood, Victoria and Young, Jock (1976), *Abortion in Demand*, London, Pluto.

Hakim, Catherine (1978), 'Sexual Divisions in the Labour Force', *Employment Gazette*, November.

Hakim, Catherine (1979), *Occupational Segregation: A comparative study of the degree and pattern of the differentiation between men and women's work in Britain, the United States and other countries*, Department of Employment Research Paper, London, Department of Employment.

Hakim, Catherine (1981), 'Job Segregation: trends in the 1970s', *Employment Gazette*, December, 521–9.

Hamilton, Mary Agnes (1925), *Mary MacArthur: A Biographical Sketch*, London, Leonard Parsons.

Hanmer, Jalna (1978), 'Violence and the Social Control of Women' in Gary Littlejohn, Barry Smart, John Wakeford and Nina Yuval-Davis (eds) *Power and the State*, London, Croom Helm.

Hanmer, Jalna and Saunders, Sheila (1983), 'Blowing the Cover of the Protective Male: A Community Study of Violence to Women' in Eva Gamornikow, David H. J. Morgan, June Purvis and Daphne Taylorson (eds) *The Public and the Private*, London, Heinemann.

Hanmer, Jalna and Saunders, Sheila (1984), *Well-Founded Fear: A community study of violence to women*, London, Hutchinson.

Hannah, Leslie (1976), *The Rise of the Corporate Economy*, London, Methuen.

Harrison, John (1973a), 'Productive and Unproductive Labour in Marx's Political Economy', *Bulletin of the Conference of Socialist Economists*, Autumn, 70–82.

Harrison, John (1973b), 'The Political Economy of Housework', *Bulletin of the Conference of Socialist Economists*, Winter, 35–52.

Hartmann, Heidi (1979a), 'Capitalism, Patriarchy and Job Segregation by Sex' in Zillah R. Eisenstein (ed.) *Capitalist Patriarchy and the Case for Socialist Feminism*, New York, Monthly Review Press.

Hartmann, Heidi (1979b), 'The Unhappy Marriage of Marxism and Feminism: Towards a More Progressive Union', *Capital and Class*, no. 8, Summer, 1–33.

Hartmann, Heidi (1981), 'The Unhappy Marriage of Marxism and Feminism: Towards a More Progressive Union' in Lydia Sargent (ed.) *Women and Revolution: The Unhappy Marriage of Marxism and Feminism*, London, Pluto Press.

Hay, Alex, Soothill, Keith and Walby, Sylvia (1980), 'Seducing the public by rape reports', *New Society*, no. 924, July, 214–15.

Hewitt, M. (1958), *Wives and Mothers in Victorian Industry*, London, Rockliff.

Himmelweit, Susan and Mohun, Simon (1977), 'Domestic Labour and Capital', *Cambridge Journal of Economics*, vol. 1, nol. 1, 15–31.

Hindess, Barry and Hirst, Paul Q. (1977), *Pre-Capitalist Modes of Production*, London, Routledge and Kegan Paul.

History of the Ministry of Munitions (1976), vols. I–XII, Brighton, Harvester Microfilm.

Hite, Shere (1981), *The Hite Report: a nationwide study of female sexuality*, London, Corgi.

Hobsbawn, E. J. (1968), *Labouring Men: Studies in the History of Labour*, London, Weidenfeld and Nicolson.

Holcombe, Lee (1973), *Victorian Ladies at Work: Middle Class Working Women in England and Wales 1850–1914*, Newton Abbot, David and Charles.

Holcombe, Lee (1983), *Wives and Property: Reform of the Married Women's Property Law in Nineteenth Century England*, Oxford, Martin Robertson.

Hooks, Bell (1982), *Ain't I a Woman?*, London, Pluto Press.

Humphreys, Betty V. (1958), *Clerical Unions in the Civil Service*, Oxford, Blackwell and Mott.

Humphries, Jane (1977a), 'Class Struggle and the Persistence of the Working Class Family', *Cambridge Journal of Economics*, September.

Humphries, Jane (1977b), 'The Working Class Family, Women's Liberation and Class Struggle: The Case of Nineteenth-Century British History', *The Review of Radical Political Economy*, vol. 9, no. 3.

Humphries, Jane (1981), 'Protective Legislation, the Capitalist State, and Working Class Men: The Case of the 1842 Mines Regulation Act', *Feminist Review*, no. 7, Spring, 1–33.

Humphries, Jane (1983), 'The "Emancipation" of Women in the 1970s and 1980s: From the latent to the floating', *Capitalist and Class*, no. 20, Summer, 6–28.

Hunt, Audrey (1975), *Management Attitudes and Practices Towards' Women at Work*, London, HMSO.

Hutchins, B. L. (1915), *Women in Modern Industry*, London, G. Bell and Sons.

Hutchins, B. L. and Harrison, A. (1911), *A History of Factory Legislation* (2nd edn), London, P. S. King & Son.

Huws, Ursula (1982), *Your Job in the Eighties: A Woman's Guide to New Technology*, London, Pluto Press.

Inman, P. (1957), *Labour in the Munitions Industries*, London, HMSO.

Jackson, Stevi (1978a), *On the Social Construction of Female Sexuality*, London, Women's Research and Resources Centre.

Jackson, Stevi (1978b), 'The Social Context of Rape: Sexual Scripts and Motivation', *Women's Studies International Quarterly*, vol. 1, no. 1, 27–38.

Jacoby, Robin Miller (1976), 'Feminism and Class Consciousness in the British and American Women's Trade Union Leagues, 1890–1925' in Berenice A. Carroll (ed.) *Liberating Women's History: Theoretical and Critical Essays*, Urbana, University of Illinois Press.

James, Selma and Dalla Costa, Mariarosa (1973), *The Power of Women and the Subversion of the Community*, Bristol, Falling Wall Press.

Jefferys, J. B. (1970), *The Story of the Engineers, 1800–1945*, New York, Johnson Reprint Corporation (first published 1945).

Jenkins, Mick (1980), *The General Strike of 1842*, London, Lawrence and Wishart.

Jessop, Bob (1982), *The Capitalist State: Marxist theories and methods*, Oxford, Martin Robertson.

John, Angela (1984), *By the Sweat of their Brow: Women Workers at Victorian Coal Mines*, London, Routledge.

Joseph, Gloria (1981), 'The incompatible ménage à trois: Marxism, Feminism and Racism' in Lydia Sargent (ed.) *Women and Revolution: The Unhappy Marriage of Marxism and Feminism*, London, Pluto Press.

Joyce, Patrick (1980), *Work, Society and Politics: The Culture of the Factory in Later Victorian England*, London, Methuen.

Kalven, Harry Jnr. and Zeisel, Hans with Callahan, Thomas and Ennis, Philip (1971), *The American Jury*, Pheonix edition, Chicago, University of Chicago, Phoenix.

Keat, Russel and Urry, John (1973), *Social Theory as Science*, London, Routledge and Kegan Paul.

Kinsey, Alfred C., Pomeroy, Wardell, Martin, Clyde, Gebhard, Paul (1953), *Sexual Behaviour in the Human Female*, Philadelphia, W. B. Saunders.

Kirkpatrick, Clifford and Kanin, Eugene (1957), 'Male Aggression on a University Campus', *American Sociological Review*, 22 February, 52–8.

Klein, Viola (1965), *Britain's Married Women Workers*, London, Routledge and Kegan Paul.

Klemmack, Susan, Klemmack, H. and David L. (1976), 'The Social Definition of Rape' in Marcia J. Walker and Stanley L. Brodsky (eds) *Sexual Assault: The Victim and the Rapist*, Lexington, Mass., Lexington Books.

Klingender, Francis D. (1935), *The Condition of Clerical Labour in Britain*, London, Martin Lawrence.

Koedt, Anne (1973), 'The Myth of the Vaginal Orgasm', in Anne Koedt, Ellen Levine and Anita Rapone (eds) *Radical Feminism*, New York, Quadrangle.

Kramer, Stella (1927), *The English Craft Guilds: Studies in their Progress and Decline*, New York, Columbia University Press.

Kreckel, Reinhard (1980), 'Unequal opportunity structure and labour market segmentation' *Sociology*, vol. 4, 525–50.

Kuhn, Annette (1978), 'Structures of Patriarchy and Capital in the Family', in Annette Kuhn and Ann Marie Wolpe (eds) *Feminism and Materialism: Women and Modes of Production*, London, Routledge and Kegan Paul.

Kuhn, Annette (1982), *Pictures of Women: Feminism and Cinema*, London, Routledge and Kegan Paul.

Lakoff, Robin (1975), *Language and Woman's Place*, New York, Harper and Row.

Land, Hilary (1976), 'Women: Supporters or Supported?', in Sheila Allen and Diana Leonard Barker (eds) *Sexual Divisions in Society: Process and Change*, London, Tavistock.

Law Enforcement Assistance Administration (1972), *San Jose Methods Test of Known Crime Victims*, National Institute of Law Enforcement and Criminal Justice, Statistics Div. SD STR 124P, Washington DC.

Lazonick, W. (1979), 'Industrial Relations and Technical Change: The Case of the Self-Acting Mule', *Cambridge Journal of Economics*, September, 231–62.

Lee, C. H. (1972), *A Cotton Enterprise 1795–1840: A History of McConnel and Kennedy Fine Cotton Spinners*, Manchester, Manchester University Press.

Lee, C. H. (1979), *British Regional Employment Statistics 1841–1971*, Cambridge, Cambridge University Press.

Leeds Revolutionary Feminist Group (1981), 'Political Lesbianism: The Case Against Heterosexuality' in *Love Your Enemy? the debate between heterosexual feminism and political lesbianism*, London, Onlywomen Press.

Lewenhak, Sheila (1977), *Women and Trade Unions: An Outline History of Women in the British Trade Union Movement*, London, Ernest Benn.

Lewis, Jane (1980), 'In search of real equality; women between the wars' in Frank Gloversmith (ed.) *Class, Culture and Social Change: A New View of the 1930s*, Sussex, Harvester Press.

Liddington, Jill and Norris, Jill (1978), *One Hand Tied Behind Us: The Rise of the Women's Suffrage Movement*, London, Virago.

Littler, Craig R. (1980), *The Bureaucratisation of the Shop-Floor: the development of the modern work system*, Ph.D. thesis, University of London.

Littler, Craig R. (1982), *The Development of the Labour Process in Capitalist Societies: a Comparative Study of the Transformation of Work Organization in Britain, Japan and the USA*, London, Heinemann.

Littlewood Margaret (1984), 'Makers of men: the anti-feminist backlash of the National Association of Schoolmasters in the 1920s and 1930s', *Trouble and Strife*, no. 5, 23–9.

Lockwood, David (1958), *The Blackcoated Worker: A Study in Class Consciousness*, London, Allen and Unwin.

London Rape Crisis Centre *(1984) Sexual Violence: The Reality for Women*, London, The Women's Press.

Loveridge, Raymond and Mok, Albert L. (1979), *Theories of Labour Market Segmentation*, University of Aston Management Centre Working Paper no. 166, Birmingham, University of Aston Management Centre.

MacDonagh, Oliver (1973), 'The Nineteenth-Century Revolution in Government: A Reappraisal', in Peter Stansky (ed.) *The Victorian Revolution: Government and Society in Victoria's Britain*, New York, New Viewpoints, Franklin Watts.

McDonough, Roisin and Harrison, Rachel (1978), 'Patriarchy and relations of production' in Annette Kuhn and Ann Marie Wolpe (eds) *Feminism and Materialism: Women and Modes of Production*, London, Routledge and Kegan Paul.

McIntosh, Mary (1978), 'The State and the Oppression of Women' in Annette Kuhn and Ann Marie Wolpe (eds) *Feminism and Materialism: Women and Modes of Production*, London, Routledge and Kegan Paul.

MacKay, D. I., Boddy, D., Brack, J., Diack, J. A. and Jones, N. (1971), *Labour Markets Under Different Employment Conditions*, London, George Allen and Unwin.

MacKinnon Catherine A. (1979), *Sexual Harassment of Working Women: A Case of Sex Discrimination*, New Haven, Yale University Press.

MacKinnon, Catherine A. (1982), 'Feminism, Marxism, Method and the State: An Agenda for Theory' in Nannerl O. Keohane, Michelle Z. Rosaldo and Barbara C. Gelpi (eds) *Feminist Theory: A Critique of Ideology*, Brighton, Harvester Press.

McNally, Fiona (1979), *Women for Hire: a study of the female office worker*, London, MacMillan.

Manley, P. and Sawbridge, D. (1980), 'Women at Work', *Lloyds Bank Review*, 29–40.

Mappen, Ellen (1985), *Helping Women at Work: the Women's Industrial Council 1889–1914*, London, Hutchinson.

Mark-Lawson, Jane, Savage, Michael and Warde, Alan (1985) 'Gender and local politics: struggles over welfare policies' in Linda Murgatroyd, Mike Savage, Dan Shapiro, John Urry, Sylvia Walby and Alan Warde with Jane Mark-Lawson, *Localities, Class and Gender*, London, Pion.

Marquand, Judith (1980), *The Role of the Tertiary Sector in Regional Policy: A Comparative Study*, Brussels, Regional Policy Series no. 19, Commission of the European Communities.

Marsh, A. I., Evans, E. O. and Garcia, P. (1971). *Workplace Industrial Relations in Engineering*, London, Kogan Page.

Martin, Del (1976), *Battered Wives*, San Francisco, New Glide.

Martindale, Hilda (1938), *Women Servants of the State 1870–1938: A History of Women in the Civil Service*, London, Allen and Unwin.

Marvel, Howard P. (1977), 'Factory Legislation: A Reinterpretation of Early English Experience', *Journal of Law and Economics*, October, 379–402.

Marwick, Arthur (1968), *Britain in the Century of Total War: War, Peace and Social Change 1900–1967*, London, MacMillan.

Marwick, Arthur (1977), *Women at War, 1914–1918*, London, Fontana.

Marx, Karl (1954), *Capital*, vol. 1, London, Lawrence and Wishart.

Marx, Karl (1969–72), *Theories of Surplus Value*, vol. 4 of *Capital*, London, Lawrence and Wishart.

Massey, Doreen (1978), 'Regionalism: Some Current Issues', *Capital and Class*, no. 6, 106–125.

Massey, Doreen (1979), 'In What Sense a Regional Problem?', Centre for Environmental Studies Paper, London, Centre for Environmental Studies.

Massey, Doreen and Meegan, Richard (1982), *The Anatomy of Job Loss: The how, why and where of employment decline*, London, Methuen.

Massey, Doreen (1984), *Spatial Divisions of Labour: Social Structures and the Geography of Production*, London, Macmillan.

Matthaei, Julie (1982), *An Economic History of Women in America: Women's Work, the Sexual Division of Labour, and the Development of Capitalism*, Brighton, Harvester.

Mcillassoux, Claude (1972), 'From reproduction to production: a Marxist approach to economic anthropology'. *Economy and Society*, vol. 1, no. 1, 93–105.

Merck, Mandy (1979), 'Sexism in the Media?' in Carl Gardner (ed.) *Media, Politics and Culture: A Socialist View*, London, MacMillan.

Middleton, Chris (1981), 'Peasants, Patriarchy and the Feudal Mode of Production in England', *Sociological Review*, vol. 29, no. 1, 105–54.

Middleton, Lucy (ed.) (1977), *Women in the Labour Movement: The British Experience*, London, Croom Helm.

Milkman, Ruth (1976), 'Women's Work and the Economic Crisis: Some Lessons of the Great Depression', *Review of Radical Political Economy*, vol. 8, no. 1, Spring.

Millett, Kate (1977), *Sexual Politics*, London, Virago.

Mincer, Jacob (1962), 'Labor Force Participation of Married Women: A Study of Labor Supply' in National Bureau of Economic Research, *Aspects of Labor Economics: A Conference of the Universities – National Bureau Committee for Economic Research*. Princeton, Princeton University Press.

Mincer, Jacob (1966), 'Labor-force Participation and Unemployment: A Review of Recent Evidence' in Robert A. Gordon and Margaret S. Gordon (eds) *Prosperity and Unemployment*, New York, John Wiley & Sons.

Mitchell, Juliet (1975), *Psychoanalysis and Feminism*, Harmondsworth, Penguin.

Molyneux, Maxine (1979), 'Beyond the Domestic Labour Debate', *New Left Review*, 116, 3–27.

Moore, D. C. (1973), 'The Corn Laws and High Farming' in Peter Stansky (ed.) *The Victorian Revolution: Government and Society in Victoria's Britain*, New York, New Viewpoints, Franklin Watts.

Moorhouse, H. F. (1978), 'The Marxist Theory of the Labour Aristocracy', *Social History*, vol. 3, no. 1, 61–82.

Moraga, Cherrie and Anzaldua Gloria (eds) (1981), *This Bridge Called My Back: Writings by Radical Women of Color*, Watertown, Mass., Persephone Press.

More, Charles (1980), *Skill and the English Working Class 1870–1914*, London, Croom Helm.

Morrell, Caroline (1981), *'Black Friday': Violence Against Women in the Suffrage Movement*, London, Women's Research and Resource Centre.

Müller, Wolfgang and Neusüss, Christel (1975), 'The Illusion of State Socialism and the Contradiction between Wage Labor and Capital', *Telos*, no. 25, 13–90.

Murgatroyd, Linda (1982), *Gender and Occupational Stratification*, Lancaster Regionalism Group Working Paper no. 6, Lancaster, Lancaster Regionalism Group.

Musson, A. E. (1972), *British Trade Unions, 1800–1875*, London, MacMillan.

NALGO (1981), *Equality? Report of a Survey of NALGO Members*, National Association of Local Government Officers.

Neff, Wanda Fraiken (1929), *Victorian Working Women: An Historical and Literary Study of Women in British Industries and Professions 1832–1850*, London, George Allen and Unwin.

National Women's Aid Federation (1978), *Battered Women, Refuges and Women's Aid*, London, National Women's Aid Federation.

Oakley, Ann (1974), *The Sociology of Housework*, London, Martin Robertson.

Oakley, Ann (1976), 'Wise Woman and Medicine Man: Changes in the Management of Childbirth' in Juliet Mitchell and Ann Oakley (eds) *The Rights and Wrongs of Women*, Harmondsworth, Penguin.

Oakley, Ann (1982), *Subject Women*, London, Fontana.

O'Brien, John E. (1975), 'Violence in Divorce-Prone Families' in Suzanne K. Steinmetz and Murray A. Straus (eds), *Violence in the Family*, New York, Dodd, Mead & Co.

O'Brien, Mary (1981), *The Politics of Reproduction*, London, Routledge and Kegan Paul.

O'Connor, James (1973), *The Fiscal Crisis of the State*, New York, St. Martin's Press.

OECD (1976), *The 1974–5 Recession and the Employment of Women*, Paris, Organization for Economic Co-operation and Development.

O'Laughlin, Bridget (1977), 'Production and Reproduction: Meillasoux's Femmes, Greniers et Capitaux', *Critique of Anthropology*, no. 8, 3–32.

Oren, Laura (1973), 'The Welfare of Women in Labouring Families in England 1860–1950', *Feminist Studies*, Winter–Spring, vol. 1, nos. 3-4, 107–125.

Parkin, Frank (1972), *Class Inequality and Political Order: Social Stratification in Capitalist and Communist Countries*, New York, Holt, Reinhart and Winston.

Parkin, Frank (1979), *Marxism and Class Theory: a bourgeois critique*, London, Tavistock.

Parmar, Pratibha (1982), 'Gender, race and class: Asian women in resistance' in Centre for Contemporary Cultural Studies, *The Empire Strikes Back: Race and Racism in '70s Britain*, London, Hutchinson.

Penn, Roger (1982), 'Skilled manual workers in the labour process, 1856–1964' in Stephen Wood (ed.) *The Degradation of Work? Skill, Deskilling and the Labour Process*, London, Hutchinson

Perkins, Teresa (1983), 'A new form of employment: a case study of women's part-time work in Coventry' in Mary Evans and Clare Ungerson (eds) *Sexual Divisions, Patterns and Processes*, London, Tavistock.

Phillips, Anne and Taylor, Barbara (1980), 'Sex and Skill: Notes Towards a Feminist Economics', *Feminist Review*, no. 6, 79–83.

Phizacklea, Annie (ed.) (1983), *One Way Ticket: Migration and Female Labour*, London, RKP.

Phizacklea, Annie and Miles, Robert (1980), *Labour and Racism*, London, RKP.

Pinchbeck, Ivy (1981), *Women Workers and the Industrial Revolution, 1750–1850*, London, Virago (first published 1930).

Pizzey, Erin (1974), *Scream Quietly or the Neighbours Will Hear*, Harmondsworth, Penguin.

Pleck, Joseph Healey and Sawyer, Jack (eds) (1974), *Men and Masculinity*, Englewood Cliffs, Prentice-Hall.

Plummer, Kenneth (1975), *Sexual Stigma: an interactionist account*, London, Routledge and Kegan Paul.

Poulantzas, Nicos (1973), *Political Power and Social Class*, London, New Left Books.

Price, Richard N. (1977), 'Society, Status and Jingoism: The Social Roots of Lower Middle Class Patriotism, 1870–1900' in Geoffrey Crossick (ed.) *The Lower Middle Class in Britain 1870–1914*, London, Croom Helm.

Rathbone, Eleanor F. (1936), 'Changes in Public Life' in Ray Strachey (ed.) *Our Freedom and Its Results*, London, Hogarth.

Redstockings (1970), *Redstockings Manifesto*, in Leslie B. Tanner (ed.) *Voices from Women's Liberation*, New York, Signet.

Reid, A. (1978), 'Politics and Economics in the Formation of the British Working Class: A Response to H. F. Moorhouse', *Social History*, vol. 3, no. 3, 347–62.

Rex, John (1983), *Race Relations in Sociological Theory* (2nd edn), London, Routledge and Kegan Paul.

Rhee, H. A. (1968), *Office Automation in Social Perspective: The Progress and Social Implications of Electronic Data Processing*, Oxford, Basil Blackwell.

Richards, Eric (1982), 'Women in the British Economy since about 1700: an Interpretation' in Mary Evans (ed.) *The Woman Question: Readings on the Subordination of Women*, London, Fontana.

Roberts, David (1960), *Victorian Origins of the British Welfare State*, New Haven, Yale University.

Roberts, David (1973), 'Tory Paternalism and Social Reform in Early Victorian England' in Peter Stansky (ed.), *The Victorian Revolution: Government and Society in Victoria's Britain*, New York, New Viewpoints, Franklin Watts.

Robinson, Olive and Wallace J. (1984), *Part-time employment and Sex Discrimination legislation in Great Britain*, Department of Employment Research Paper no. 43, London, Department of Employment.

Rose, Hilary and Hanmer, Jalna (1976), 'Women's Liberation, Reproduction, and the Technological Fix' in Sheila Allen and Diana Leonard Barker (eds) *Sexual Divisions and Society: Process and Change*, London, Tavistock.

Routh, Guy (1980), *Occupation and Pay in Great Britain 1906–1979*, London, MacMillan.

Rowbotham, Sheila (1981), 'The trouble with "patriarchy"' in Feminist Anthology Collective (eds) *No Turning Back: Writings from the Women's Liberation Movement 1975–80*, London, The Women's Press.

Rubery, Jill (1978), 'Structured Labour Markets, Worker Organisation and Low Pay, *Cambridge Journal of Economics*, 2.

Rubery, Jill and Tarling, Roger (1982), 'Women in the Recession', *Socialist Economic Review*, London, Merlin Press.

Ruether, Rosemary Radford (ed.) (1974), *Religion and Sexism: Images of Women in the Jewish and Christian Traditions*, New York, Torchstone.

Russell, Diana E. (1975), *The Politics of Rape*, New York, Stein and Day.

Sandberg, Lars (1974), *Lancashire in Decline: A Study in Entrepreneurship*, Technology and International Trade, Columbus, Ohio State University Press.

Sarah, Elizabeth and Spender, Dale (eds) (1980), *Learning to Lose: Sexism and Education*, London, Women's Press.

Savage, Michael (1982), *Control At Work: North Lancashire Cotton Weaving 1890–1940*, Lancaster Regionalism Group Working Paper no. 7, Lancaster, Lancaster Regionalism Group.

Sayers, Janet (1982), *Biological Politics: feminist and anti-feminist perspectives*, London, Tavistock.

Scharf, Lois (1980), *To Work and To Wed: Female Employment, Feminism, and the Great Depression*, Contributions in Women's Studies no. 15, Westport, Connecticut, Greenwood Press.

Schreiner, Olive (1918), *Woman and Labour*, London, Fisher Unwin.

Sebastyan, Amanda (1979), 'Tendencies in the Movement: Then and Now', in *Feminist Practice*, London, In Theory Press.

Seccombe, Wally (1974), 'The housewife and her labour under capitalism', *New Left Review*, 83, 3–24.

Seccombe, Wally (1975), 'Domestic Labour – reply to critics', *New Left Review*, 94, 85–96.

Sear, Nancy (1968), 'The Position of Women in Industry' in Royal Commission on Trade Unions and Employers' Associations, *Two Studies in Industrial Relations*, Research Paper no. 11, London, HMSO.

Smart, Carol (1984), *The Ties That Bind: Law, marriage and the reproduction of patriarchal relations*, London, Routledge and Kegan Paul.

Smelser, Neil J. (1959), *Social Change in the Industrial Revolution: An Application of Theory to the Lancashire Cotton Industry, 1770–1840*, London, Routledge and Kegan Paul.

Smelser, Neil J. (1967), 'Sociological History: The Industrial Revolution and the British Working-Class Family', *Journal of Social History*, vol. 1, 17–35.

Smith, Anthony D. (1973), *The Concept of Social Change*, London, Routledge and Kegan Paul.

Smith, Harold (1981), 'The Problem of "Equal Pay for Equal Work" in Great Britain during World War II', *Journal of Modern History*, 53, 652–72.

Smith, Paul (1978), 'Domestic labour and Marx's theory of value' in Annette Kuhn and Ann Marie Wolpe (eds) *Feminism and Materialism: Women and Modes of Production*, London, Routledge and Kegan Paul.

Snell, Mandy, Glucklich P. and Povall, M. (1981), *Equal Pay and opportunities: A study of the implementation and effects of the Equal Pay and Sex Discrimination Acts in 26 organisations*, Dept. of Employment Research Paper no. 20, London, Dept. of Employment.

Snell, Mandy (1979), 'The Equal Pay and Sex Discrimination Acts: their impact in the workplace', *Feminist Review*, no. 1, 37–57.

Social Science Department, The London School of Economics (1960), *Woman Wife and Worker*, Department of Scientific and Industrial Research Problems in Industry no. 10, London, HMSO.

Soldon, Norbert C. (1978), *Women in British Trade Unions 1874–1976*, Dublin, Gill and Macmillan.

Spender, Dale (1980), *Man Made Language*, London, Routledge and Kegan Paul.

Spender, Dale (1983), *Women of Ideas (and what men have done to them) From Aphra Behn to Adrienne Rich*, London, Ark.

Spender, Dale (1984), *Time and Tide Wait for No Man*, London, Pandora.

Stanley, Liz and Wise, Sue (1983), *Breaking Out: Feminist Consciousness and Feminist Research*, London, Routledge and Kegan Paul.

Stanworth, Michelle (1984), 'Women and class analysis: a reply to John Goldthorpe', *Sociology*, 18, 2.

Strachey, Ray (1978), *The Cause: A Short History of the Women's Movement in Great Britain*, London, Virago (originally published 1928).

Steinmetz, Suzanne K. and Straus, Murray A. (1975), 'General Introduction: Social Myth and Social System in the Study of Intra-Family Violence' in Suzanne K. Steinmetz and Murray A. Straus (eds) *Violence in the Family*, New York, Dodd, Mead & Co.

Stewart, A., Prandy, K. and Blackburn, R. M. (1980), *Social Stratification and Occupations*, London, MacMillan.

Summerfield, Penny (1984), *Women Workers in the Second World War*, London, Croom Helm.

Tass (n.d. – estimated 1975), *Women's Rights and What We are Doing to Get Them*, Richmond, Technical Administrative and Supervisory Section of the Amalgamated Union of Engineering Workers.

Taylor, John G. (1979), *From Modernization to Modes of Production: A Critique of the Sociologies of Development and Underdevelopment*, London, MacMillan.

Tholfsen, Tryque R. (1973), 'The Transition to Democracy in Victorian England' in Peter Stansky (ed.) *The Victorian Revolution: Government and Society in Victoria's Britain*, New York, New Viewpoints, Franklin Watts.

Thomas, Maurice Walton (1970), *The Early Factory Legislation: A Study in Legislative and Administrative Evolution*, Westport, Connecticut, Greenwood Press.

Thompson, E. P. (1965), 'The Peculiarities of the English', *The Socialist Register*, 1965.

Thompson, E. P. (1968), *The Making of the English Working Class*, Harmondsworth, Penguin.

Tilly, Louise A. and Scott, Joan W. (1978), *Women, Work and Family*, New York, Holt, Reinhart and Winston.

Tolson, Andrew (1977), *The Limits of Masculinity*, London, Tavistock.

Toner, Barbara (1977), *The Facts of Rape*, London, Hutchinson.

Townsend, Peter (1979), *Poverty in the United Kingdom: A Survey of Household Resources and Standards of Living*, London, Allen Lane.

TUC (1955), *Women in the Trade Union Movement*, London, Trades Union Congress.

TUC (1970), *Special Report on Equal Pay to 40th Women's Conference*, London, Trades Union Congress.

Tuchman, Gaye, Daniels, Arlene Kaplan and Benet, James (eds) (1978), *Hearth and Home: Images of Women in the Mass Media*, New York, Oxford University Press.

Turner, Herbert Anthony (1962), *Trade Union Growth, Structure and Policy: a comparative study of the cotton unions in England*, Toronto, Toronto University Press.

Ure, Andrew (1935), *A Philosophy of Manufactures*, London, Charles Knight.

Urry, John (1981a), *The Anatomy of Capitalist Societies: The Economy, Civil Society and the State*, London, MacMillan.

Urry, John (1981b), 'Localities, regions and social class', *International Journal of Urban and Regional Research*, vol. 5, 455–74.

Urry, John (1982), 'Rurality, Restructuring and Recomposition', paper presented to SSRC/BSA Rural Economy and Society Study Group.

Vanek, Joann (1980), 'Time Spent in Housework' in Alice H. Amsden (ed.) *The Economics of Women and Work*, Harmondsworth, Penguin.

Vinnicombe, Susan (1980), *Secretaries, Management and Organization*, London, Heinemann.

Wadsworth, Alfred P. and de Lacymann, Julia (1931), *The Cotton Trade and Industrial Lancashire 1600–1780*, Manchester, Manchester University Press.

Walby, Sylvia, (1985a), *Gender Relations and Job Loss: A Study of 30 North-West Establishments*, Lancaster Regionalism Group Working Paper no. 11, Lancaster, Lancaster Regionalism Group.

Walby, Sylvia (1985b), 'Spatial and historical variations in women's unemployment' in Linda Murgatroyd, Mike Savage, Dan Shapiro, John Urry, Sylvia Walby and Alan Warde with Jane Mark-Lawson, *Localities, Class and Gender*, London, Pion.

Walby, Sylvia (1986a), 'Gender class and stratification: Towards a New Approach', in Rosemary Crompton and Michael Mann (eds) *Gender and Stratification*, Cambridge, Polity.

Walby, Sylvia (1986b), *Occupational Segregation by sex: Theoretical Issues and Comparative Analysis*, Institute of Industrial Relations Working Paper 107, University of California at Los Angeles, Institute of Industrial Relations.

Walby, Sylvia (1987) (forthcoming), *Gender and Inequality*, Oxford, Basil Blackwell.

Walby, Sylvia, Hay, Alex and Soothill, Keith (1983), 'The Social Construction of Rape', *Theory, Culture and Society*, no. 4.

Warde, Alan (1982), *Changes in the Occupational Structure of Lancaster 1901–1951*, Lancaster Regionalism Group Working Paper no. 8, Lancaster, Lancaster Regionalism Group.

Webb, Mrs Sydney (ed.) (1902), *The Case for the Factory Acts*, London, Grant Richards.

Webb, Sydney (1911), Preface to B. C. Hutchins and A. Harrison, *A History of Factory Legislation*, London, P. S. King & Son.

Webb, Sydney and Webb, Beatrice (1894), *A History of Trade Unionism*, London, Longmans, Green & Co.

Weber, Max (1947), *The Theory of Social and Economic Organization*, New York, Free Press.

Weekes, B. C. M. (1970), *The Amalgamated Society of Engineers 1880–1914: A Study of Trade Union Government, Politics and Industrial Policy*, Ph.D. thesis, University of Warwick.

Weeks, Jeffrey (1977), *Coming Out*, Quartet Books.

Werneke, Diane, (1985) 'Women: the vulnerable group' in Tom Forester (ed.) *The Information Technology Revolution*, Oxford, Basil Blackwell.

West, D. J., Roy, C. and Nichols, Florence L. (1978), *Understanding Sexual Attacks*, London, Heinemann.

West, Jackie (1978), 'Women, sex and class' in Annette Kuhn and Ann Marie Wolpe (eds) *Feminism and Materialism: Women and Modes of Production*, London, Routledge and Kegan Paul.

Westergaard, John and Resler, Henrietta (1975), *Class in a Capitalist Society: A Study of Contemporary Britain*, London, Heinemann.

Wilkinson, Frank (ed.) (1981), *The Dynamics of Labour Market Segmentation*, London, Academic Press.

Wilson, Elizabeth (1977), *Women and the Welfare State*, London, Tavistock.

Wood, Stephen (ed.) (1982), *The Degradation of Work Skill, Deskilling and the Labour Process*, London, Hutchinson.

Wright, Gordon (1968), *The Ordeal of Total War, 1939–1945*, New York, Harper Torch Books.

Young, Iris (1981), 'Beyond the unhappy marriage: a critique of the dual systems theory' in Linda Sargent (ed.) *Women and Revolution: The Unhappy Marriage of Marxism and Feminism*, London, Pluto Press.

Zaretsky, Eli (1976), *Capitalism, the Family and Personal Life*, London, Pluto Press.

Index